KAREN BROWN'S

Italian
Country Inns & Itineraries

KAREN BROWN TITLES

California Country Inns & Itineraries

English Country Bed & Breakfasts

English, Welsh & Scottish Country Hotels & Itineraries

French Country Bed & Breakfasts

French Country Inns & Itineraries

German Country Inns & Itineraries

Irish Country Inns & Itineraries

Italian Country Bed & Breakfasts

Italian Country Inns & Itineraries

Spanish Country Inns & Itineraries

Swiss Country Inns & Itineraries

KAREN BROWN'S

Italian Country Inns & Itineraries

Written by

CLARE BROWN

Sketches by Barbara Tapp

Cover Painting by Jann Pollard

Travel Press
Karen Brown's Country Inn Series

Travel Press editors: Karen Brown, June Brown, Clare Brown,
Nicole Franchini, Susanne Lau Alloway, Iris Sandilands
Technical support: William H. Brown III, Aide-de-camp: William H. Brown
Illustrations: Barbara Tapp; Cover painting: Jann Pollard.
Maps: Susanne Lau Alloway—Greenleaf Design & Graphics

Travel Press, P.O. Box 70, San Mateo, CA 94401, U.S.A. tel: 415-342-9117. fax: (415) 342-9153,

Book written in cooperation with Town & Country-Hillsdale Travel, San Mateo, CA 94401, U.S.A.

Distributed in U.S.A. & Canada by The Globe Pequot Press, tel: 203-395-0440, fax: (203) 395-0312
P.O. Box 833, Old Saybrook, CT 06475-0833, U.S.A-

Distributed in Europe by Springfield Books Ltd., tel: (01484) 864 955. fax: (01484) 865-443
Norman Rd., Denby Dale, Huddersfield HD8 8TH, West Yorkshire, England,

Distributed in Australia by Little Hills Press Pty. Ltd., tel: (02) 437-6995, fax: (02) 438-5762
1st Floor, Regent House, 37-43 Alexander St, Crows Nest NSW 2065, Australia

Distributed in New Zealand by Tandem Press Ltd., tel: (0064) 9 480-1452, fax: (0064) 9 480 1455
P.O. Box 34-272, Birkenhead, Auckland 10, New Zealand

A catalog record for this book is available from the British Library

Library of Congress Cataloging-in-Publication Data
Brown, Clare.
    Karen Brown's Italian country inns & itineraries / written by
Clare Brown ; sketches by Barbara Tapp.
       p. cm. -- (Karen Brown's country inn series)
    Includes index.
    ISBN 0-930328-28-0 : $16.95
    1. Hotels,--Italy--Guidebooks. 2. Italy-   -Guidebooks. I. Title.
 II. title: Italian country inns & itineraries. III. Series.
  TX907.5.I8B76 1994   92-16274
  647.944501--dc20   CIP

As Always
to
My Best Friend, Bill
With Love and Gratitude for
Many Miles of Memories

Contents

Introduction
to
Italy

Of all the countries in the world, there is none more magical than Italy: truly a tourist's paradise—a traveler's dream destination. No one could be so blasé, that within Italy's narrow boot there would not be something to tantalize their fancy. For the archaeologist, there are some of the most fascinating and perfectly preserved ancient monuments existing today—just begging to be explored. For the gourmet, there is the finest food in the world. For the outdoors person, there are towering mountains to conquer and magnificent ski slopes to sample. For the lover of art, the museums are bursting with the genius of Italy's sons such as Michelangelo, Leonardo da Vinci, and Raphael. For the architect, Italy is a school of design—you are surrounded by the ancient buildings whose perfection has inspired the styles of today. For the history buff, Italy is a joy of wonders—her cities are veritable living museums where you are surrounded by the ghosts of Julius Caesar. For the wine connoisseur, Italy produces an unbelievable selection of wine whose quality is unsurpassed. For the adventurer, Italy has intriguing medieval walled villages tucked away in every part of the country. For the beach buff, Italy's lakes and islands hold the promise of some of the most elegant resorts in the world. For the religious pilgrim, Italy is the cradle of the Christian faith and home of some to the world's most famous saints. The miracle of Italy is that all these treasures come packaged in a gorgeous country of majestic mountains, misty lakes, idyllic islands, wonderful walled villages and gorgeous cities. Plus, the climate is ideal and the people warm and gracious. Italy is truly a perfect destination.

ABOUT THIS GUIDE

This guide is written with two main objectives: to describe the most romantic small hotels throughout Italy and to tie these hotels together with itineraries that include enough details so that you can plan your own holiday.

This introduction explains how to use the guide and also touches upon what to expect while traveling. After the introduction comes the main part of the guide that is divided into three sections: the Itinerary Section, the Hotel Description Section, and the Map Section. The *Itinerary Section* outlines itineraries with sightseeing suggestions along the way. The *Hotel Description Section* includes a comprehensive list of hotels (appearing alphabetically by town). The *Map Section* has fourteen maps to help you pin point each town where we recommend a hotel.

We have personally inspected each place that we recommend and describe its ambiance and merits in our write up which is followed by an illustration and practical information such as address, telephone and fax numbers, rates, etc. **None of the places to stay ever pays to be included**—our choices are strictly based on hotels we think you would most enjoy. Frequently we hear, "I don't care where I stay—I'm rarely in my room except to sleep." If this is your true philosophy, then this book is *not* for you. To our way of thinking, where you stay weaves the very fabric of your trip and your choice of hotels is of absolute prime importance. Not that the hotel needs to be expensive. A moonlight dinner on the terrace of a simple inn can be as memorable as dining at a fancy hotel—sometimes even more so because the owner is there to pamper you.

The recommendations in our guide vary tremendously: some are grand hotels—fit for a king and priced accordingly; others are simple, inexpensively-priced cottages tucked away in remote hamlets. We include them if they have personality, romantic charm, and antique ambiance. In each region we choose the hotels that we consider the most outstanding. We are very selective. A few hotels are included that do not live up to our normal standards of old-world-charm. These have been included because in their particular area there just were no perfect choices. Since you might need a place to stay, we tried to find the very best hotel available. *NOTE:* The hotel descriptions are followed by fourteen maps that pinpoint the locations of featured places to stay.

CURRENT–ELECTRICITY

You need a transformer plus an adapter if you plan to use an American-made electrical appliance in Italy. The voltage is usually 220, but sometimes it is 115 or 125. Check with the manager before plugging anything into an outlet if you have any question. It is very embarrassing to have the electricity go out all over the hotel because you were drying your hair. *NOTE:* Many hotels have hair dryers in the room or else can loan you one.

DRIVING

DRIVER'S LICENSE: An American or British driver's license is valid if you are in Italy on a holiday. However, if you are renting a car, certain age limits apply. Please check on the age limit policy with the car rental company.

GASOLINE: Gasoline (petrol) is very expensive so plan ahead and budget this cost as part of your trip if you are driving. Most of the service stations located on the main expressways accept credit cards.

ROADS: The Italian roads are nothing short of spectacular. You discover some of the finest highways in the world. In fact, the Italians are absolute geniuses when it comes to their engineering feats (which actually is not such a surprising fact when you think what a fantastic road system the Romans built two thousand years ago). Nothing seems to daunt the Italian engineers. You would think the mountains are of clay instead of solid rock, the way the roads tunnel through them. Sometimes a roadway seems endlessly suspended in mid-air, as it bridges a mountain crevasse.

TOLL ROADS: Italy has a network of super expressways that draws the whole country into an easily manageable destination by car. Once you are on the toll roads, the kilometers slip by and you can go quickly from almost any area of Italy to another. However, be forewarned—these toll roads are very expensive. It seems that about every half hour a toll station appears and you must pay again. But, every cent is well spent when you consider the alternative of creeping along within a maze of trucks and buzzing motorcycles, taking forever to go only a few kilometers. Use the toll roads for the major distances you need to cover, and then choose the small roads when you wish to meander leisurely through the countryside. The toll roads are mystifying until you learn the system—even then it is confusing because just when you think you have the operation down pat you find it varies slightly. This is the most common routine: first follow the green expressway signs toward the toll road. Sometimes these signs begin many kilometers from the expressway so be patient and continue the game of follow-the-sign. Each entrance to the expressway handles traffic going in both directions. As you enter into the toll gate there is usually a red button you push and a card pops out of a slot. After going through the toll station you choose the direction you want to go. Leaving the expressway there is a toll station where your ticket is collected and you pay according to how many miles were traveled.

ROAD SIGNS: Before starting on the road prepare yourself by learning the international driving signs so that you can obey all the rules of the road and avoid the embarrassment of heading the wrong way down a small street or parking in a forbidden area. There are several basic sign shapes. The triangular signs warn that there is danger ahead. The circular signs indicate compulsory rules and information. The square signs give information concerning telephones, parking, camping, etc.

FOOD and DRINK

It is almost impossible to get a bad meal in Italy. Italians themselves love to eat. Dining is a social occasion to be with family and friends. Restaurants are bustling not only with tourists, but also with the Italians who dawdle at the tables long after the meal is over, chatting and laughing with perhaps a glass of wine or a last cup of coffee.

You soon get in the spirit of the game of deciding which kind of restaurant to choose for your next meal. The selection is immense, all the way from the simple family trattoria where mama is cooking in the kitchen to the most elegant of gourmet restaurants with world renowned chefs. Whichever you choose, you won't be disappointed. The Italians are artists when it comes to pasta, seen on every menu and prepared in endless, fascinating ways. Delicious green salads are always on the menu.

Wine of course is offered with every meal. You rarely see an Italian family eating without their bottle of wine on the table. Unless you are a true wine connoisseur we suggest the regional wines. If you ask your waiter to assist you with the choice, you flatter him and discover many superb wines.

Some of the most popular wines which you see on the Italian menus are: CHIANTI, a well-known wine produced in the Tuscany area south of Florence; MARSALA, a golden sweet wine from Sicily (a favorite of Lord Nelson); SOAVE, a superb light wine produced near Venice; ORVIETO, a semi-sweet wine from the Umbria region near Assisi, and EST EST EST, a beautiful semi-sweet wine produced near Rome. The story that we heard about the last wine, Est Est Est, is lots of fun and perhaps even true. It seems that many years ago a wealthy nobleman was traveling south. Being a true gourmet both of food and drink, he sent his servant before him to pick out all the best places to eat and drink along the way. When the servant neared Rome he discovered such a divine wine that all he could relay back to his master was *Est Est Est* which students of

Latin will remember means Yes Yes Yes. Today you will think the same about most of the wines you enjoy in Italy—the answer is still Yes Yes Yes.

HOLIDAYS

It is very important to know Italian holidays because most museums, shops, and offices are closed. National holidays are listed below:

New Years Day (January 1)
Epiphany (January 6)
Easter (and the following Monday)
Liberation Day (April 25)
Labor Day (May 1)

Assumption Day (August 15)
All Saints' Day (November 1)
Christmas (December 25)
Santo Stefano (December 26)

In addition to the national holidays, each town has its own special holiday to honor its patron Saint. Some of the major ones are listed below:

Bologna-St Petronio (Oct 4)
Florence-St John the Baptist (June 24)
Milan-St Ambrose (December 7)

Palermo-Santa Rosalia July 15
Rome-St Peter (June 29)
Venice-St Mark (April 25)

The Vatican in Rome has its own schedule. The museums are closed every Sunday, except the last Sunday of each month when the admission is free.

HOTELS—GENERAL INFORMATION

HOTELS—BASIS FOR SELECTION: This guide does not try to appeal to everyone. It is definitely prejudiced: each hotel included is one we have seen and liked. It might be a splendid villa elegantly positioned overlooking one of Italy's romantic lakes or a simple little chalet snuggled high in a mountain meadow. But there is a common denominator—they all have charm. Therefore, if you too prefer to travel spending your nights in romantic old villas, appealing chalets, dramatic medieval castles, ancient monasteries, converted peasants' cottages and gorgeous palaces, we are kindred souls. Follow the paths we have suggested and each night will be an adventure.

For some of you, cost will not be a factor if the hotel is outstanding. For others, budget guides your choices. The appeal of a simple little inn with rustic wooden furniture beckons some, while the glamour of ornate ballrooms dressed with crystal chandeliers and gilded mirrors appeals to others. What we have tried to do is to indicate what each hotel has to offer, and describe the setting, so that you can make the choice to suit your own preferences and holiday. We feel if you know what to expect, you won't be disappointed, so we have tried to be candid and honest in our appraisals. Also, some hotels are ideal for children while others are definitely adult oriented. We have indicated these special situations under the hotel descriptions.

HOTELS–COST The price for a room in Italy has soared. Even simple places to stay seem desperately over-priced. However, with the dollar growing stronger in relationship to the lire, the prices are not as outrageous as a few years ago. If you study carefully the rates given in the back of this guide, you can still find a few bargains available and can plan your trip using one of the less expensive hotels as your hub from which to venture out each day. We also publish *Karen Brown's Italian Country Bed & Breakfasts* which makes an ideal companion to this guide. The maps in both are similar, making it easy to choose a place to stay from either book. Not only can you save money by sometimes choosing a bed and breakfast for a night's accommodation, but also enjoy the experience of staying where you have the opportunity to know your host and fellow guests. We highly recommend choosing a combination of places to stay from both books.

HOTELS–CREDIT CARDS: Many small hotels do not accept credit cards. Those hotels that do accept plastic payment are indicated in the hotel description section using the following abbreviations: AX–American Express, DC–Diners Club, EC–Eurocard, MC–MasterCard, VS–Visa, or simply–All major. *NOTE:* When calculating how much cash you will need, be aware that some hotels will accept a credit card to guarantee the reservation, but will not let you pay your bill by credit card.

HOTELS–DECOR: It is difficult to find hotels in Italy furnished in a simple style. Italian hotels frequently reflect a rather formal opulence—tending toward a rather fussy decor. There are some exceptions. In a few instances (which we note in the hotel descriptions) the hotels are decorated in a more rustic ambiance using country antiques, but this is not the norm. When antiques are used, they are very often the fancy, gilded variety.

HOTELS–GROUPS & AFFILIATIONS: There are two well-known groups of hotels to which many of the hotels in this guide belong. The *Romantik Hotel* group is an affiliation of charming small hotels that are managed by the owner and are usually located in an historic building. You can recognize the hotels that belong to this group because they have the word *Romantik* connected to their name. The *Relais & Chateaux* group is an affiliation of luxurious small hotels that are very expensive, with extremely high standards of excellence. You can tell which of the hotels in our guide belong to this group because we have indicated "Relais & Chateaux member" in the hotel's description.

HOTELS–HOW TO INTERPRET THE RATES: In the hotel reference section in the back of the book each hotel shows a rate that reflects the approximate nightly cost for two persons including tax, service and continental breakfast. There are a few hotels where breakfast and one other meal (either lunch or dinner) are included in the rate and, if so, this too is noted. Please use the rates given only as a general guides because each hotel has such a wide range of price possibilities that it is impossible to project with complete accuracy. Also, each year there is some inflation. However, the lire price quoted helps you anticipate the approximate cost. When you plan your holiday, check the current exchange rate with your bank.

HOTELS–HOW TO ECONOMIZE: For those of you who want to squeeze the most value out of each night's stay, we have several suggestions:

1) Travel off season—spring and fall are usually lovely in Italy and the hotels often have less expensive rates.

2) Ask for a room without a private bathroom—some hotels have very nice rooms, usually with a washbasin in the room, but with the bathroom down the hall.

3) Ask if there is a weekly rate—frequently hotels offer a price break for guests staying a week or more. If traveling with children, ask if there is a special family suite at a lesser price than separate rooms.

4) Supplement your hotel accommodations with a few nights in a bed and breakfast chosen from *Karen Brown's Italian Country Bed & Breakfasts*. This companion guide features places to stay throughout Italy in private homes, villas and farmhouses that open their doors to paying guests. This book is available in book stores or can be purchased directly from the publisher, the order form is at the back of this guide.

5) Ask about rates with meals included. If staying for three days or longer, many hotels offer a special rate including meals: MAP (Modified American Plan) means two meals a day are included, AP (American Plan) means three meals a day are included.

6) Last, but not least, is the most important way to save money. Stay in the countryside instead of in the cities. We cannot stress enough how much more value you receive when you avoid the cities—especially the tourist centers such as Rome, Florence, Milan and Venice. Of course stay right in the heart of town if you are not watching your budget, but if you are trying to squeeze the greatest value from your lire, choose hotels in the countryside and take side trips to visit the pricey tourist centers.

HOTEL RESERVATIONS–HOW TO MAKE THEM

People frequently ask, "Do I need a hotel reservation?" The answer really depends on how flexible you want to be, how tight your time schedule is, in which season you are traveling, and how disappointed you would be if your first choice is unavailable.

It is not unusual for the major tourist cities to be completely sold out during the peak season of June through September. Be forewarned: hotel space in Rome, Florence, Milan and Venice is really at a premium and unless you don't mind taking your chances on a last-minute cancellation or staying on the outskirts of town, make a reservation as far in advance as possible. Space in the countryside is a little easier. However, if you have your heart set on some special little inn, you certainly should reserve as soon as your travel dates are firm. Reservations are confining. Most hotels want a deposit to hold your room and frequently refunds are difficult should you change your plans. So it is a double bind: making reservations locks you into a solid framework, but without reservations you might be stuck with accommodations you do not like. During the height of the tourist season, some small hotels only accept reservations for a minimum of three or more nights. However, do not give up because almost all of the hotels that have this policy take a last-minute booking for a shorter period of time if you call along the way and there is space available. For those who like the security blanket of having each night pre-planned so that once you leave home you do not have to worry about where to rest your head. Several options for making reservations are listed on the following pages.

TRAVEL AGENT: A travel agent can be of great assistance—particularly if your own time is limited. A proficient agent can expertly handle all the details of your holiday and tie them together for you in a neat package—including hotel reservations, airline tickets, boat tickets, train reservations, ferry schedules, theater tickets, etc. For your airline tickets there usually is no service fee (unless you using some kind of a discount coupon), but the majority of travel agencies do charge for their other services such as theater tickets, etc.). The best advice is to talk with your agent. Be frank about how much you want to spend and ask exactly what he or she can do for you and what the charges are. If your travel agent is not familiar with all the small places in this guide (many are so tiny that they appear in no other major publications), you can loan him or her your book—it is written as a guide for travel agents as well as for individual travelers.

LETTER: If you start early, you can write directly to the hotels and request exactly what you need. Clearly state the following: number of people in your party; how many rooms you desire; whether you want a private bathroom; date of arrival and date of departure; ask the rate per night and if a deposit is needed. When you receive a reply, send the deposit requested and ask for a receipt and a map. *NOTE:* When corresponding with Italy, be sure to spell out the month. Do not use numbers since in Europe they reverse the American system—such as 6/9 means September 6, not June 9. Allow six weeks for an answer—mail to Italy is *very* slow. Although most hotels can understand a letter written in English, on page 264 there is a letter written in Italian with an English translation. Photocopy it and use it for your reservation request letters.

TELEPHONE: Our preference in making reservations is to telephone. The cost is minimal if you direct dial. You can have your answer immediately, and if space is not available, you can then decide on an alternate. Ask your local operator when to call for the lowest rates. Also consider what time it is in Italy when you call (even the most gracious of owners are sometimes a bit grouchy when awakened at 3 am). If you are dialing from the United States, the system is to dial 011 (the international code) 39 (Italy code). Compose these five numbers then dial the city code (dropping the 0) and the hotel telephone number that appears under the hotel listings. Almost all of the hotels have someone who speaks English. There are a few exceptions and when very little English is spoken, we have tried to indicate this under the hotel's description. The best chance for finding the owner or manager who speaks English is to call when it is late afternoon in Italy (Italy is six hours ahead of New York). Be aware that Italy's telephone numbers are constantly changing, so if you cannot reach a hotel, ask for operator assistance.

FAX: If you have access to a fax machine, this is a super-efficient way to reach a hotel. The majority of hotels in Italy have fax numbers which we have listed in the back of the book under each hotel listing. Again, be sure to be specific as to your arrival and departure dates, number in your party, and what type of room you want. And, of course, be sure to include your fax number for their response. You can photocopy and use the request letter written in Italian and English (see page 264).

UNITED STATES REPRESENTATIVE: Some hotels have a United States representative through whom reservations can be made. Many of these representatives have a toll free telephone number. This is an extremely convenient and efficient way to secure a reservation. However you might find it less expensive to make the reservation yourself since sometimes a representative makes a charge for his service, reserves only the more expensive rooms, or quotes a higher price to protect himself against currency fluctuations and administrative costs. Furthermore, usually only the larger or more expensive hotels can afford the luxury of a representative in the United States. Nevertheless, if you understand that it might cost you more, contacting the hotel representative is an easy way to make a reservation. If a hotel has a representative, the name and telephone number for the representative are listed under the specific hotel's description. In the back of the book there is information on Hidden Treasures of Italy (HTI), a company specializing in travel arrangements in Italy that for a fee, makes hotel reservations. These various hotel booking services are given solely as a source of information for you. We are in no way affiliated with any of the hotel representatives and cannot be responsible for reservations made through them or money sent as deposits or prepayments.

INFORMATION SOURCES

If you have questions not answered in this guide or need special guidance for a particular destination, the Italian Government Travel Offices can assist you. These offices are usually open from 9 am–1 pm, Monday through Friday.

Australia and New Zealand: Covered by the Tokyo office: Italian Government Travel Office, Itaria Seifu Kanko Kyoku (ENIT) Lion's Building-1-1-2, Moto Akasaka Minato-Ku, Tokyo 107, Japan; telephone (00813) 347-82051, fax: (00813) 347-99356

Canada: Italian Government Travel Office, 1 Place Ville Marie, Suite 1914, Montreal, Quebec H3B 3M9, Canada; telephone: (514) 866-7667, fax: (514) 392-1429

England: Italian State Tourist Office, Princes Street 1, London WIR 8AY, England; telephone: (0171) 408 12 54, fax: (0171) 493 66 95

Italy: Italian Government Travel Office, Via Parigli, 11, Rome 00185, Italy, telephone: (06) 48.81.851, fax: (06) 48.19.316.

U.S.A., Chicago: Italian Government Travel Office, 401 North Michigan Avenue, Suite 3030, Chicago, IL 60611, U.S.A.; telephone: (312) 644-0990, fax: (312) 644-3019

U.S.A., Los Angeles: Italian Government Travel Office, 12400 Wilshire Blvd. Suite 550, Los Angeles, CA 90025, U.S.A.; telephone: (310) 820-0098, fax: (310) 820-6357

U.S.A., New York: Italian Government Travel Office, 630 Fifth Avenue, Suite 1565, New York, NY 10111, U.S.A.; telephone:(212) 245-4822, fax: (212) 586-9249

ITINERARIES–GENERAL INFORMATION

In the itinerary section of this guide you'll be able to find an itinerary, or portion of an itinerary, that can be easily tailored to fit your exact time frame and suit your own particular interests. If your time is limited, you could certainly follow just a segment of an itinerary. In the itineraries we have not specified the number of nights at each destination, since to do so seemed much too confining. Some travelers like to see as much as possible in a short period of time. For others, just the thought of packing and unpacking each night makes them shudder in horror and they would never stop for less than three or four nights at any destination. A third type of tourist doesn't like to travel at all. The destination is the focus and he uses this guide to find the perfect resort from which he never wanders except for daytime excursions. So, use this guide as a reference to plan your personalized trip.

Our advice is, if possible, do not rush. Part of the joy of traveling is to settle in at a hotel that you like and use it as a hub from which to take side trips to explore the countryside. When you dash too quickly from place to place you never have the opportunity to get to know the owners of the hotels and to become friends with other guests. Look at the maps in the back of this guide to find the hotels in the areas where you want to travel. Read about each hotel in the hotel description section of this book and decide which places to stay sound most suited to your taste and budget. Then choose a base for each area you want to visit.

MAPS

With each itinerary there is a map showing the routing and suggesting places of interest along the way. These are artist's renderings and are not intended to replace a good commercial map. To supplement our generalized routings, you definitely need a set of detailed maps that indicate all of the highway numbers, expressways, alternate little roads, expressway access points, and exact distances. Our suggestion is to purchase a comprehensive set of city maps and regional maps before your departure, and with a highlight pen mark your own personalized itinerary and pinpoint your city hotels. If you live in a metropolitan area you should have no problem buying maps in a travel bookstore or else your local bookstore should be able to place a special order. Our personal preference for Italy are the Rand McNally HALLWAG maps (there are Rand

McNally stores in many major cities so Hallwag maps are readily available). Depending upon your itinerary, you need either the Hallwag map *Southern Italy* or their map *Northern Italy*—or both (don't purchase the Hallwag map that covers the whole of Italy—it is too general). Each map comes with a small index booklet to help you find the towns you are seeking. Almost every town in our guide can be found on the Hallwag maps. A superb complement to the Hallwag maps are a series of three atlases published by the *Touring Club Italiano*. These cannot be purchased in the United States, but can be found in the shops located in the service stations along the main expressways. The atlases are divided into three volumes, which can be purchased individually: North, Central and South. They are expensive, but highly recommended. They are so detailed and well-indexed that it makes finding your way much easier.

PROVINCES

Italy is divided into Provinces. These provinces appear in abbreviated form in addresses. They also are shown on license plates—it is fun to watch the cars to see where they are from. Some of the provinces you are likely to see and their abbreviated codes are:

AL	*Alessandria*	AN	*Ancona*	AO	*Aosta*	AR	*Arezzo*
AP	*Ascoli Picino*	AT	*Asti*	BA	*Bari*	BL	*Belluno*
BG	*Bergamo*	BO	*Bologna*	BZ	*Bolzano*	BS	*Brescia*
BR	*Brindisi*	CZ	*Catanzaro*	CO	*Como*	FI	*Firenze*
FO	*Forli*	GE	*Genova*	GO	*Gorizia*	GR	*Grosseto*
LU	*Lucca*	MN	*Mantova*	MI	*Milano*	MO	*Modena*
NA	*Napoli*	NO	*Novara*	PD	*Padova*	PR	*Parma*
PV	*Pavia*	PG	*Perugia*	PS	*Pesaro*	PI	*Pisa*
PT	*Pistoia*	PZ	*Potenza*	RA	*Ravenna*	SA	*Salerno*
SV	*Savona*	SI	*Siena*	TA	*Taranto*	TR	*Terni*
TO	*Torino*	TN	*Trento*	TV	*Treviso*	VE	*Venezia*
VC	*Vercelli*	VR	*Verona*	VI	*Vicenza*	VT	*Viterbo*

REGIONS

In addition to provinces, Italy is divided into twenty regions. Some, such as Tuscany and Umbria, are well-known to the tourist. Others, such as Abruzzo and Puglia, are not as familiar. A map showing the location of each region is found in the back of the book on page 266. Below is a list of the regions and their capital city.

REGION	CAPITAL CITY	REGION	CAPITAL CITY
Abruzzo	*L'Aquila*	Molise	*Campobasso*
Basilicata	*Potenza*	Piedmonte	*Torino*
Calabria	*Catanzaro*	Puglia	*Bari*
Campania	*Naples*	Sardenia	*Cagliari*
Emila Romagna	*Bologna*	Sicily	*Palermo*
Fiuli-Venezia Giulia	*Trieste*	Tuscany	*Florence*
Lazio	*Rome*	Trentino-Alto Adige	*Trento & Bolzano*
Liguria	*Genova*	Umbria	*Perugia*
Lombardia	*Milan*	Valle d'Aosta,	*Aosta*
Marche	*Ancona*	Veneto	*Venice*

SECURITY WHILE TRAVELING

The Italians are wonderful hosts. They are friendly, outgoing, gregarious and merry—no one is a stranger. In fact, it seems every Italian has a brother or cousin in the United States, and so the warmth of camaraderie is further enhanced. In spite of the overall graciousness of the Italians, there are instances where cars are pilfered or purses snatched, but this happens all over the world. Just be cautious. Watch your purse. Don't let your wallet stand out like a red light in your back pocket. Lock your valuables in the hotel safe. Use travelers' checks. Don't leave valuables temptingly exposed in your car. In other words, use common sense. Unfortunately, we have heard of incidents of groups of gypsy children who flock to you, usually in congested, tourist areas, and attempt to steal your wallet or purse. If this should happen to you, shoo them away and call for the police. *NOTE:* Whenever you travel to any country, it is wise to make a photocopy of the pages of your passport showing your picture, passport number, date and where issued. With this photocopy in hand it is much easier to get a replacement passport.

SHOPPING

Italy is definitely a shopper's paradise. Not only are the stores brimming with tempting merchandise, but their displays are beautiful, from the tiniest fruit market to the most chic boutique. Each area has its specialty. In Venice items made from blown glass and handmade laces are very popular. Milan is famous for its clothing and silk-wear (gorgeous scarves, ties and blouses). Florence is a paradise for leather goods (purses, shoes, wallets, gloves, suitcases) and also for gold jewelry (you can buy gold jewelry by weight). Rome is a fashion center. You can stroll the pedestrian shopping streets browsing in some of the world's most elegant, sophisticated shops. You can buy the latest designer creations and, of course, religious items are available, especially near St Peter's. Naples and the surrounding regions (Capri, Ravello, Positano) offer delightful coral jewelry and also a wonderful selection of ceramics.

SIGHTSEEING

Ideas on what to see and do are suggested throughout the six itineraries. However, we just touch upon some of the sightseeing highlights. There is a wealth of wonders to see in Italy, plus of course many local festivals and events. Before you leave, check with the tourist office for further information targeted at exactly where you plan to travel. And, once on the road, make it a habit to always make your first stop the local tourist office to pick up maps, schedules of special events, and sightseeing. Even more important, before you drive out of your way to see a particular museum or place of interest, check when it is open. As a general guideline—most museums are closed on Mondays and for a couple of hours in the middle of the day. Small museums are usually open only in the morning. Outdoor museums usually open at 9 am and close about an hour before sunset. Most national monuments and museums close on holidays (see HOLIDAYS on page 6).

TELEPHONES–HOW TO MAKE CALLS

CALLING HOME: Calling overseas is very expensive from Italy. In addition, hotels usually add a hefty surcharge to telephone calls charged to your room. The best bet is to use one of the many available international telephone cards. With these you can make a local call within Italy and be connected with your at home operator. When you arrive home, the cost appears on your telephone bill. Ask your local telephone company what access number to use. In the United States all of the long distance phone companies including AT&T, MCI and Sprint offer this option.

CALLING WITHIN ITALY: Most telephones in Italy take either 100 or 200 lire coins. Becoming more common are the telephones that take a telephone credit card called a *Scheda.* These credit cards can be purchased at tobacco stores or telephone offices and are extremely handy. You choose a card costing 5,000 or 10,000 lire and use the card until the credit is used up by the calls you made. It is very simple. The instructions are on the telephone demonstrating how to use them. There are a few telephones still remaining that only take special tokens. These can usually be purchased at a vending machine near the telephone.

TRANSPORTATION

TRAINS: Italy has an excellent network of trains. The major express trains are usually a quick, reliable way to whip between the major cities. In contrast, the local trains stop at every little town, take much longer, and are frequently delayed. Each train station is well organized. There is almost always an information desk where someone speaks English who will answer any questions and advise you as to the best schedule. There is another counter where you purchase your tickets. Still a third counter is where seat reservations are made. We strongly recommend purchasing your train tickets in advance. It is quite time consuming to stand in two lines at each train station, only to find—particularly in summer—that the train you want is already sold out. You can purchase open tickets in the United States. However, it is almost impossible to purchase seat reservations in advance (except for major European routes). Therefore, go ahead and buy the open tickets, and then you can either purchase your seat reservations locally, or else pay the concierge at your hotel to handle this transaction for you. *NOTE:* Seat reservations cannot be made just before getting on the train—it is best to make them as far in advance as possible.

The very popular Eurailpass is valid in Italy. This pass allows travel for varying periods of time on most trains throughout Europe. However, if you are going to travel exclusively in Italy, buy instead an Italian Rail Pass. These bargain passes must be purchased outside of Italy. There is the *TOURIST PASS*—available for unlimited travel for a period of 8, 15, 21, or 30 days. Another option is the *FLEXI RAILCARD* where you can arrange your own travel time as follows: the *9 Day Pass* is valid for travel for any 4 days during a 9 day period, the *21 Day Pass* is valid for travel for any 8 days of a 21 day period, the *30 Day Pass* is valid for travel on any 12 days of a 30 day period. All of the Italian passes can be bought for either first or second class travel. You can purchase these passes through your local travel agent or, in the United States, from the Italian State Railways, 342 Madison Avenue, Suite 207, New York, NY 10173, telephone (212)

697-2100, fax: (212) 697-1394; or the Italian State Railways, 6033 West Century Boulevard, Los Angeles, CA 90045, telephone (310) 338-8616, fax: (310) 670-4269. *NOTE:* in the summer when rail traffic is very heavy, unless you make dining car reservations in advance you might not be able to have the fun of eating your meal enroute. If you have not made these reservations, as soon as you board the train, stroll down to the dining car and ask to reserve a table.

BOATS: Italy has gorgeous islands dotting her shorelines, a glorious string of lakes gracing her mountains to the north, and romantic canals in Venice. Luckily for the tourist, the boat system is excellent—providing convenient access to Italy's stunning lakes.

All of Italy's islands are linked to the mainland and serviced frequently by a wonderful maritime network. The many outlying islands sometimes have overnight ferries that offer sleeping accommodations and facilities for cars. The closer islands usually offer a choice—the hydrofoil that zips quickly across the water or the regular ferry that is slower.

One of the highlights of traveling in Italy is to explore her wondrous lakes by hopping on one of the ferry boats that glide romantically between the little villages clustered along the shoreline. Again, there is usually a choice of either the hydrofoil that darts between the hamlets, or the ferry that glides leisurely across the water and usually offers beverage and food service on board. The boat schedules are posted at each pier, or you can request a timetable from the Italian tourist office. *NOTE:* these little boats are punctual, to the minute. Be right at the pier with your ticket in hand so you can jump on board during the brief interlude that the boat stops at the shore. If at all possible, try to squeeze in at least one boat excursion. It is a treat you will long remember.

WEATHER

Italy is blessed with lovely weather. However, unless you are a ski enthusiast following the promise of what the majestic mountains have to offer in the winter, or must travel in summer due to school holidays, we highly recommend traveling in spring or fall. Travel at either of these times has two dramatic advantages: you miss the rush of the summer tourist season when all of Italy is packed and you are more likely to have beautiful weather. In spring the meadows are painted with wildflowers. In fall the forests are a riot of color and the vineyards are mellow in shades of red and gold. Although the mountains of Italy are delightfully cool in summer, the rest of the country can be very hot, especially in the cities. *NOTE:* many hotels are not air conditioned, and when they are, an additional charge is frequently included on the bill.

WHAT TO WEAR

During the day informal wear is most appropriate including comfortable slacks for women. In the evening, if you are at a sidewalk cafe or a simple pizzeria, women do not need to dress up nor men to wear coats and ties. However, Italy does have some elegant restaurants, where a dress and coat and tie are definitely the proper attire. A basic principle is to dress as you would in any city at home. There are perhaps a few special situations: the churches are still very conservative, shorts are definitely inappropriate as are low cut dresses. Some of the cathedrals still insist that women have their arms covered. It is rare that a scarf on the head is required, but to wear one is a respectful gesture. If you have an audience with the Pope, then the dress code is even more conservative.

The layered effect is ideal. Italy's climate runs the gamut from usually cool in the mountains to frequently very hot in the south. The most efficient wardrobe is one where light blouses and shirts can be reinforced by layers of sweaters that can be added or peeled off as the day demands.

Florence

ITINERARY SECTION

Highlights by Boat & Train-or Car

Romantic Hilltowns of Tuscany & Umbria

Mountain & Lake Adventures

Rome to Milan via the Italian Riviera

Highlights of Southern Italy

Exploring the Wonders of Sicily

Colosseum, Rome

Italian Highlights
by Train & Boat-or Car

Riva

Lake Garda

Verona

Milan

Desenzano

Sirmione

Padua

Venice

Florence

● Overnight stops
○ Sightseeing
▬ Itinerary route

Rome

ROME

Naples

Pompeii

Sorrento

Capri

Italian Highlights by Train & Boat—or Car

Island of Burano, near Venice

If you delight in the freedom of following a whim to explore a back road, this itinerary can easily be duplicated by car. However, the thought of Italian expressways sometimes intimidates even the bravest breed of tourist. Therefore we have given you the formula to see the highlights either way—by public transportation or by car. It is true that the Italians love driving fast: it would seem that many are practicing for the Grand Prix. But, an aversion to driving does not mean that your *only* alternative is the confining structure of a package tour. Italy can be seen splendidly by train and boat. This is a glorious way to travel and has many advantages: everyone can watch the scenery instead of the road, a glass of wine can be enjoyed with lunch, and you arrive rested and ready to enjoy the sights. Perhaps the best advantage of all is that while using public transportation you make friends. Perhaps there is just a smile at first, then maybe the sharing of a piece of fruit, and, later comes the admiration of each other's family photographs. Somehow barriers break down on a long journey and the universal warmth of friendliness—at this the Italians are masters—spans any language barriers.

This itinerary covers some of the most famous destinations within Italy. For a short holiday it is impossible to include all the places of interest. However, following this pathway easily provides you with a glimpse of some of the highlights of Italy and will tempt you to return quickly to delve more deeply into the wonders that Italy has to offer. This itinerary is woven around towns that are conveniently linked by public transportation. Of course, if your time is extremely limited, this itinerary lends itself well to segmentation. If you cannot travel with us all the way, then choose what fits into your schedule and what most appeals to you. No matter what portion you include, a delightful holiday awaits.

In the following itinerary approximate train and boat times have been included. Please note that these are given only as a reference to show you how the pieces of this itinerary tie together. Schedules are constantly changing, so these must be verified. Also, many boats and some trains are seasonal, so be very meticulous in making your plans.

ORIGINATING CITY   MILAN

This highlight tour begins in Milan, a most convenient city since it is the hub of airline flights from Europe, plus it is blessed with non-stop air service from the United States. Also, Milan is strategically located for trains arriving from all over Europe. Trains rush into its busy station via the Gotthard, Simplon and Bernina passes. However, it is not location alone which makes Milan an ideal starting point. Although frequently bypassed as an enormous industrial city of little tourist interest, Milan has, at its core, a truly charming old section. Be forewarned. Not only is this a major city, but it also hosts many merchandise fairs. Consequently, hotel space is limited and rates very expensive.

While in **Milan** you must not miss visiting the **Duomo**. Facing a massive square, the Duomo is a gingerbread fantasy adorned with 135 spires. This third largest cathedral in the world also has over 2,000 statues.

Duomo, Milan

Milan's other great claim to fame is **La Scala**, one of the world's most famous opera houses. In addition to the opera, other performances are given here. Tickets are sold in the ticket office located around the left-hand side of the theater. If Opera Season, try your best to go to a performance. If not Opera Season, try to get tickets for whatever is playing. It is such fun to watch the lights go down and the curtains go up in this fairy-tale-like theater with row upon row of balconies rising like layers on a wedding cake.

Between the Duomo and La Scala is one of the world's most beautiful arcades, the forerunner of the modern shopping mall, but with much more style. Even if you are not a shopper, stop to browse and have a cup of tea in the **Galleria Vittorio Emanuele.** In this Victorian-era fantasy, there are two main, intersecting wings, both completely domed with intricately patterned glass. Along the pedestrian-only arcades are boutiques and beautiful little restaurants with outside tables for people watching. Milan also has its share of museums would save the museums and churches for Venice, Florence and Rome.

The train for Desenzano (the station you want for your destination of **Sirmione**) usually departs from Milan's Central Station. However, sometimes the trains leave instead from the Porto Garibaldi station, so it is vital that schedules be checked very carefully.

  12:10 pm depart Milan Central Station by train
    1:24 pm arrive Desenzano

When the train arrives in the ancient port of **Desenzano**, you can take a taxi to the pier where hydrofoils, steamers and buses leave regularly for Sirmione. However, although more expensive, we suggest you splurge and take a taxi directly to Sirmione (only about 10 kilometers away). This is definitely the most convenient means of transportation since you are taken directly to your hotel.

Sirmione is a walled medieval village fabulously located on a tiny peninsula jutting out on Lake Garda. The peninsula where Sirmione is located seems like an island because it is connected to the mainland by just a thread of land. To enter the ancient town, you first cross over a moat, and then enter through medieval gates. If traveling by car (unless you are one of the lucky ones with a hotel confirmed for the night) you are not be permitted to pass within the town walls, since only pedestrians are allowed through the entrance. But if you have hotel reservations, stop near the entrance at the information office where you are given a pass to enter with your automobile or by taxi.

There are several hotels in the heart of Sirmione, but the most glamorous choice, the **Villa Cortine Palace Hotel,** is located in a park-like estate on the outskirts of town. The entrance is absolutely Hollywood. You must ring a bell at the impressive gates that then slowly swing open, allowing you to wind your way up through the truly beautiful park to the hotel that crowns the small hill. Previously, this was a sumptuous private villa. Now a new wing has been built which doubles the original size. Although the newer wing looks a bit sterile from the outside, the rooms are delightful and most have better views than those in the old section. Demi-pension (breakfast and dinner) are required if you are staying at the Villa Cortine Palace. In addition, reservations are usually taken only for stays of at least three nights. Neither should prove a problem—you will never want to leave such a romantic setting.

From the Villa Cortine Palace Hotel it is an easy walk to the wharf in the middle of town. There study the posted schedule in order to decide which boat you want to take for your day's excursion. You can glide around the lake all day and have a snack on board, or get off in some small jewel of a town and enjoy lunch at a lakefront cafe. There is a choice of transportation: either the romantic ferry boats or the faster hydrofoils.

There are also some **Roman Ruins** on the Sirmione peninsula. These are located on the very tip of the peninsula and can be reached either on foot, or if you prefer, by a miniature motorized train that shuttles back and forth from the village to the ruins.

NOTE FOR TRAVELERS BY CAR: The Villa Cortine Palace Hotel is an excellent hotel choice if you are traveling by public transportation. However, if you are traveling by car, consider staying in **Gargnano, Gardone,** or **San Vigilio**—these towns are also located on Lake Garda and offer wonderful places to stay.

DESTINATION II   VERONA

There are trains almost every hour that cover the half-hour journey between Desenzano and Verona. But if it is a beautiful day, it is much more romantic to incorporate sightseeing into your transportation and take a boat and bus instead of the train. If this appeals to you, the following gives an idea of how this can be done.

9:50 am depart Sirmione by ferry
1:25 pm arrive Riva

You can have lunch on board the ferry or else you can wait until you reach the medieval town of **Riva**, located on the northern shore of Lake Garda. The outdoor terrace overlooking the lake at the **Hotel Sole** (located just across from where the ferry docks) provides a serene luncheon setting. The interesting ancient core of Riva is small, so it doesn't take long to stroll through the old city.

After lunch and a walk through the old part of town, depart Riva by bus for Verona (buses run every 15 minutes in summer). The scenic route follows the eastern shore of Lake Garda and then on to Verona.

When you arrive in **Verona,** you are in for a treat. This is a town that is all too frequently bypassed by the tourist, but what a prize it is. Buy a detailed map and be on your way. This medieval gem is the perfect city to explore on foot.

Definitely not to be missed is the **Roman Amphitheater,** one of the largest in Italy. This dramatic arena, dating from the 1st Century, has perfect acoustics and hosts operatic performances in summer. As you continue to wander through Verona's enchanting streets you discover many delights, including the **Piazza delle Erbe** (Square of Herbs), which is the old Roman forum where chariot races used to take place. Follow your map to nearby 23 Via Cappello to find the 13th-century **Capulets' Palace** and the balcony where Juliet met Romeo. Another colorful square, the **Piazza dei Signori,** has a stature of Dante in its center and 12th and 13th-century buildings. The **Castelvecchio** (Old Castle), built by Congrande I Scaligerbuthe in the 14th Century, houses an art museum with paintings and sculptures plus jewelry and armaments. The 14th-century **Ponte Scaligero** (Scaliger Bridge) links the Castelvecchio with the opposite side of the river. The **Cathedral,** dating from the 12th Century, is well worth a visit to see its fine red marble columns and richly adorned interior. Just across the river from the heart of the old city, visit the old **Roman Theater** where performances are still held in summer.

Verona has several good hotels to complement her marvelous sights. A favorite in the heart of the city is the **Hotel Gabbia d'Oro**, which is brimming with charm and conveniently located near all the places of interest. If you are traveling by car, you have the option of choosing a hotel in the countryside outside of Verona where you get more value for your money. Hotels we suggest in the area are: in **Pedemonte** and **Gargagnago**.

Amphitheater, Verona

DESTINATION III   VENICE

When you are ready to leave Verona, there is frequent train service to Venice so the following departure time is just a suggestion. *NOTE:* As you approach **Venice**, be sure not to get off the train at the Venice Mestre station, but instead wait for the next stop, the Santa Lucia station (about ten minutes further).

2:27 pm depart Verona Porto Nuova station by train
3:52 pm arrive Venice, Santa Lucia station

St Mark's Square, Venice

As you come out of the front door of the train station you find that the station is directly on the Grand Canal. It is a few short steps down to where you can board a boat to take you to your hotel. The **Vaporetti** are the most popular means of transportation and are a very inexpensive means of getting about the city. They are like boat buses that constantly shuttle back and forth from the train station to **St Mark's Square**. The Number Two ferry makes only major stops while the Number One ferry pauses at every stop to exchange passengers. Much more expensive, but a little faster, are the **Motoscafi** (water-taxis) that deliver you right to the door of your hotel, provided there is a motor boat dock. The third choice is a **gondola**, but these are much slower and very expensive, so save your gondola ride for a romantic interlude rather than a train connection.

Venice has many fine hotels in every price range. Look in the back of this guide for various suggestions of places that we recommend. If you want to splurge, consider the very expensive, very sumptuous, **Gritti Palace**, a former home of the immensely wealthy Doge Andrea Gritti. If you are on a more limited budget, the intimate, family-operated **Hotel Flora** is a gem in its category. Note the closest boat stop so that you know where to disembark if you take the Vaporetti from the train station.

Venice has so many sights: marvelous restaurants, beautiful boutiques, and fascinating little alleyways to explore, that you could happily stay for weeks.

Of course, you must savor the incomparable ambiance of **Piazza San Marco** (St Mark's Square). Late afternoon is especially romantic as music wafts across the enormous square, courtesy of the tiny orchestras entertaining guests as they enjoy an aperitif. A colonnaded walkway encloses the square on three sides, forming a protected walkway while window shopping at the beautiful boutiques and fancy cafés. The fourth side of the square is dominated by the **Basilica di San Marco** (St Mark's Cathedral) richly endowed with gold and mosaics. The church dates back to the 12th Century when it was built to house the remains of St Mark. Next to the church, rises the 99 meter-tall **Campanile** (bell tower) where in the 15th Century priests were suspended in a cage to repent their sins. If in the plaza on the hour, watch the two Moors strike the hour with their huge bronze hammers as they have done for 500 years. To the right of the basilica is the **Palazzo Ducale** (Doge's Palace), a sumptuous fantasy of pink and white marble—open now as a museum. The Palazzo Ducale faces on to the **Piazzetta,** a wide square opening onto the **Grand Canal.** The nick name used to be the *Piazzetta Il Broglio* (Intrigue) because in days of yore, only nobles were allowed in the square between 10 am and noon, at which time the area buzzed with plots of intrigue. Adorning the center of the square are two granite columns, one topped by the **Lion of St Mark** and the other by a statue of **St Theodore.**

Most of the boats that ply the Grand Canal stop at the St Mark's dock. There is no better way to get the mood of Venice than to join crowd as they

Glass Blowing, Island of Murano

climb aboard one of the ferries that ply the waterways. It is a real bargain to board the Vaporetto and enjoy the many wonderful palaces bordering the **Grand Canal**. In addition to exploring the canals that lace Venice, you can take ferries to the outlying islands. Go either on your own or on a tour to the three islands: **Murano** (famous for its hand-blown glass), **Burano** (famous for its colorfully painted fishermen's cottages and lace making), and **Torcello** (once an important city but now just a small village with only its lovely large church to remind you of its past glories).

Another all-day outing by boat is to take the **Il Burchiello**, named for a famous 17th-century Venetian boat. From April to November, this boat departs Tuesdays, Thursdays and Saturdays at 8:45 am from the Pontile Giardinetti pier near St Mark's Square and travels the network of rivers and canals linking Venice and Padua. (The schedule might change, so verify dates and times.) This little boat, with an English speaking guide on board, stops at several of the exquisite palaces enroute. Lunch is served and there is time for sightseeing in **Padua** before returning to Venice by bus. Reservation Office: Siamic Express, Via Trieste 42, Padua, Italy, telephone: (049) 66 09 44, fax: (049) 66 28 30.

A favorite pastime in Venice is wandering—just anywhere—exploring the maze of twisting canals and criss-crossing back and forth over some of the 400 whimsical bridges. One of the most famous, the **Rialto Bridge** (arching high over the canal), is especially colorful because it is lined by shops. Also much-photographed is the **Bridge of Sighs**, so named because this was the bridge prisoners passed over before their execution.

Although all of Venice is virtually an open-air museum, it has many inside museums. Two excellent ones are both easy to find near the Accademia boat stop. The **Galleria dell'Accademia** abounds with 14th to 18th-century Venetian paintings. Within walking distance of the Galleria dell'Accademia, is the **Peggy Guggenheim Museum**, featuring 20th-century art. The paintings and statures were the gift of the now-deceased wealthy American heiress, Peggy Guggenheim. The lovely museum was her canal-front home.

When leaving Venice, there are several direct trains each day from Venice to Florence: however, in summer, space is at a real premium, so be sure to reserve a seat in advance. Some of the express trains must have prior seat reservations and require a supplemental fee. *NOTE:* During the busy season, if you want to dine on the train it is necessary to make advance reservations when you buy your ticket.

    2:42 pm depart Venice, Santa Lucia station (reservations obligatory)
    5:27 pm arrive Florence

When you arrive in **Florence**, take a taxi to your hotel unless you have chosen **Mario's** (a moderately-priced hotel close enough to the train station to walk). There are outstanding places to stay in Florence in every price range. If you want to be right on the Arno with a balcony overlooking the Ponte Vecchio, the **Lungarno Hotel** is fabulous.

Ponte Vecchio, Florence

For tasteful luxury, the **Hotel Helvetia and Bristol** is a small jewel. For old world ambiance, the **Monna Lisa** stars. For price and location, the **Loggiato dei Serviti** is excellent. We recommend these and many other hotels in and around Florence—study the descriptions in the back of the guide and you are sure to find one that is perfect for your taste.

Be generous with your time and do not rush Florence—there is too much to see. You must, of course, pay a visit to **Michelangelo's David** in the **Galleria dell'Accademia** (located just off the **Piazza San Marco**).

Palazzo Vecchio in Piazza della Signoria

During your explorations of Florence, you will cross many times through the **Piazza della Signoria**, located in the heart of the old city. Facing this characterful medieval square is the 13th-century **Palazzo Vecchio**, a stern stone structure topped by a crenellated gallery and dominated by a tall bell tower. It was here that the *Signoria* (Florence's ruling administrators) met for two months each year while attending to government business. During this period they were forbidden to leave the palace (except for funerals) so that there could not be a hint of suspicion of intrigue or bribery. Of course you cannot miss one of Florence's landmarks, the **Ponte Vecchio.** Spanning the Arno in the heart of Florence, this colorful bridge is lined with quaint shops just as it has been since the 14th Century.

Also, don't miss the fantastic museums and cathedrals—the world will probably never again see a city that has produced such artistic genius. Florence's **Duomo** is one of the largest in the world. Its incredible dome (over 100 meters high) was designed by Brunelleschi. The **Battistero** (the Baptistry) has a beautiful mosaic dome, but is even more famous for its incredible bronze doors. The main door shows scenes from the life of John the Baptist, the north door shows the life of Jesus, and the east door shows stories from the prophets of the Old Testament. The **Uffizi Museum** (housed in a 16th century palace) is undoubted one of the finest museums in the world. Also, do not miss the **Pitti Palace** with its fabulous art collection, including paintings by Titian and Raphael.

Be sure to buy a guidebook and city map at one of the many magazine stalls and study what you want to see. We just touch on the many highlights. However Florence is best appreciated by wandering the historic ancient streets. Poke into small boutiques. Stop in churches that catch your eye—they all abound with masterpieces. Sit and enjoy a cappuccino in one of the little sidewalk cafes and people watch. Stroll through the piazzas and watch the artists at their craft—many of them incredibly clever—as they paint portraits and do sculptures for a small fee. End your day by finding the perfect small restaurant for delicious pasta made by mama in the back kitchen.

DESTINATION V   ROME

There is excellent train service from Florence to Rome. It is probably best to take one of the midday trains—a choice that allows you to enjoy lunch as you soak in the beauty of the Tuscany hills flowing by your window. Remember that you need both seat and dining reservations.

   12:02 pm depart Florence via train
    1:55 pm arrive Rome, Termini station

As the train pulls into Rome, you feel overwhelmed by its size and confusion of traffic, but once you settle into your hotel, you realize that **Rome** is really not as cumbersome as

"She Wolf" with Rommulus and Remus

it looks. The ancient part of the city is manageable on foot—a fabulous city for walking with its maze of streets and captivating boutiques just begging to be explored. We recommend many places to stay in this expensive city. If you are looking for a well-located small deluxe hotel, the **Hotel d'Inghilterra** is a superb choice near the bottom of the Spanish steps. The super-deluxe **Hotel Hassler,** located just at the top of the Spanish steps, is also a very popular choice. But you do not need to splurge. There are many less-expensive places to stay recommended in the Hotel Description Section that are excellent and equally well-located (such as **La Residenza** and the **Hotel Gregoriana**).

According to legend, Rome was founded in 753 BC by Rommulus, who along with his twin brother, Remus (whom he later conveniently "did in") was suckled by a *She Wolf.* As you might guess, the story goes Rome was named for this infamous forefather. Although far less colorful, historians concur that it was the Etruscans who first settled here and gave the city its name. By the time Christ was born, Rome controlled the entire Italian boot plus many areas around the Mediterranean.

Rome is bursting with a wealth of fantastic museums, ancient monuments, spectacular cathedrals, gourmet restaurants, beautiful boutiques, colorful piazzas, whimsical fountains, inspiring statues, theater and opera—the city itself is virtually a museum. You cannot possibly savor it all. Either before you leave home or once you arrive in Italy, purchase a comprehensive guidebook and decide what is top priority for your special interests. There are many stalls along the streets as well as bookstores throughout Rome where guidebooks are available. Also, every hotel has brochures available that tell about sightseeing tours. If there are several in your party, then a private guide might be money well spent since he will custom tailor your sightseeing. With a private guide you squeeze much more sightseeing into a short period of time.

To even begin to do justice to Rome's many wonders, this entire book would need to be devoted to its sightseeing possibilities. However, we cannot resist mentioning a few places you must see.

Vatican-Swiss Guard

Of course you cannot go to Rome and miss seeing the **Vatican City** with **St Peter's Basilica,** whose original construction was begun in the 4th Century by Emperor Constantine over the site of the St Peter's tomb. In 1506 Pope Julius II began plans for the new cathedral, which took over 100 years to build. It is no wonder the complex is so breathtaking—all of Italy's greatest Renaissance artists were called upon to add their talents (Bramante, Raphael, Sangallo, and Michelangelo to name just a few).

The Vatican is a miniature nation tucked within the city of Rome. It is ruled by the Pope, has its own flags, issues its own postage stamps, has its own anthem, mints its own coins, and even has its own police force—the Swiss Guard that still wears the costume designed by Michelangelo.

Fronting the cathedral is the **Piazza San Pietro,** a breathtaking square designed by Bernini. It is so large it can hold 400,000 people (making the square a favorite place for the Pope to address large audiences). A double semicircle of columns encloses the square, so perfectly designed that the columns fade into each other, giving the illusion that there is a single row. In the center of the square is a towering ancient Egyptian obelisk—adorned of course by a Christian cross. As you stand from a distance, the Piazza San Pietro forms a visual frame for the cathedral.

St Peter's Basilica, Rome

To fully appreciate all the Vatican city has to offer, you could easily spend two days—one day in **St Peter's Basilica** (the largest church in the world) and one day in the **Vatican Museums**. The Basilica is a virtual museum. Not only is the structure magnificent, but the works of art inside, are almost unbelievable. Imagine gazing at such masterpieces as the **Pietà** (the ethereal sculpture of Mary holding Jesus in her arms after the crucifixion, carved by Michelangelo when he was only 25) and the **Baldaccchino**, the bronze canopy over the papal altar designed by Bernini. Also, be aware when you gaze up at the double columned dome, that this too was designed by Michelangelo.

The Vatican has many museums. The best known, the **Sistine Chapel**, is well-worth a trip to Rome just to savor the breathtaking beauty of its ceiling painted by Michelangelo. In addition to the St Peter's Basilica and the Vatican museums, the gardens and the rest of the Vatican can be visited, but only on guided tours. If you are interested, inquire at the *Ufficio Informazioni Pellegrini et Turisti* in St Peter's Square. *NOTE:* The Vatican museums are closed on Sundays, except for the last Sunday of the month when they are open free of charge.

The Vatican City, as spectacular as it is, is just one small part of what Rome has to offer. You cannot miss seeing the gigantic **Colosseum**, the entertainment center for the ancient citizens of Rome. Here 50,000 people gathered to be entertained by flamboyant spectacles, which included gladiatorial events, races, games, and contests where Christian martyrs fought against wild beasts.

Another landmark is the **Forum**. It is difficult to make out much of this site because it is mostly in ruins, but at one time this was the heart of Rome. Once filled with elegant palaces, government buildings and shops, it once teemed with people from throughout the known world. My favorite building in Rome is the **Pantheon.** It is almost difficult to imagine that this perfectly preserved jewel of a temple dates back to 27 BC. Step beyond the heavy bronze doors that open into a relatively small, beautifully proportioned room—lit only by light streaming in from an opening in the top of the dome.

No trip to Rome would be complete without a stroll down the **Via Veneto**, lined by fancy hotels, and luxury boutiques. There are also many outdoor restaurants where a cup of coffee costs almost as much as a meal in a simple *trattoria*. However, along with your coffee, you are paying the price for the fun of people watching along one of Rome's most elite avenues.

While walking the back streets of Rome, you find many picturesque squares, usually enhanced by a fountain adorned with magnificent sculptures. Especially popular is the **Trevi Fountain** where tourists go to throw a coin—assuring that they will return to Rome.

Spanish Steps, Rome

The **Spanish Steps** are definitely a landmark of Rome. Topped by the twin spires of the Church of the Trinity of the Mountains, the wide avenue of steps leads down to the **Piazza di Spagna** (Spanish Square). This large square is highlighted by the **Fountain of Baraccia** (Fountain of the Boat), a masterpiece by Bernini. The steps are usually crowded both with tourists who come to capture the moment on film and vendors who lay out their wares to sell.

From the Piazza di Spagna, the **Via Condotti** is an avenue lined by shops selling the finest of merchandise. Leading off the Via Condotti are the narrow lanes of **Old Rome**, again featuring exquisite small boutiques.

When ready to relax, walk to the **Villa Borghese**, a splendid large park in the center of Rome that originated in the 17th-century as the private gardens of the Borghese family. Stroll through the park watching the children at play. If you are not saturated with sightseeing, there are many museums to see in the park. One of the loveliest is the **Museo di Villa Giulia** a museum in a pretty villa that features artifacts from the Etruscan era.

You could spend weeks discovering the museum that is Rome, but if you have time to add a few more highlights, include Sorrento and Capri. There is frequent train service from Rome to Naples and from there it is a short Aliscafi (hydrofoil) ride to Capri. However, for the adventurous it is fun to include Pompeii and Sorrento en route to Capri. Please be advised that this makes a long day of travel and takes some manipulating of schedules, but the rewards are great.

You need an early start to accomplish a tour of Pompeii on your way to Sorrento, but this is a must. How could you be so close without visiting this intriguing city of the Romans that was destroyed, yet preserved forever by the ashes of Vesuvius.

   9:15 am depart Rome, Termini station
  11:58 am arrive Pompeii, Main station

You arrive in **Pompeii** at the Main station, but you depart from Pompeii at the Villa d'Misteri station, located just across from the main entrance to the archaeological site. Since it's no fun to lug your suitcases around while you do your sight-seeing, take a cab from the Main station to the Villa d'Misteri station where there is a place to check luggage. Then just walk across the street to the main gate of Pompeii. There is a nice terrace restaurant by the entrance and also a cafe inside. If you want to do your own touring, you can buy a guidebook in English from a stall, or else you can negotiate with one of the licensed guides for a personal tour. You may have heard that the earthquake of 1980 destroyed much of Pompeii. It is true that many of the sites were damaged, but now almost everything has been reconstructed.

An aura of mystery lingers in the air as you wander the streets of Pompeii. All visitors are touched by this ancient city of an estimated 25,000 inhabitants, that in one day, became frozen for all time. Probably there is no where else in the world where you can so vividly step back in time. Much of what you see today has been reproduced, but the reality is pure. Plaster was poured into molds formed by the lava that demolished the buildings and buried so many families that fateful day. Thus it became possible for later day archaeologists to reconstruct houses and make reproductions of people and pets. Walk through the town along the sunken streets with crossed by high stepping stones, strategically placed so that the pedestrians did not get their feet wet on rainy days. Be sure not to miss some of the reconstructed villas that allow you a glimpse into the daily life of long ago. The **Casa del Fauna,** a fine example of how the wealthy lived, has two inner courtyards and several dining rooms. The **Casa del Poeta Tragico,** a more modest home, has a sign in mosaic *Cave Canem* (beware of the dog). At the **Villa di Giulia Felice** you see the example of an entrepreneur—in addition to being a private villa, the owner rented out rooms, had shops on the ground floor and operated an adjacent bathhouse. If traveling with children, you might want to go alone into the **Lupanare** (Pompeii's brothel) where there are erotic paintings on the walls. At the **Terme Stabiane** you see a sophisticated underground system where water was heated for the baths.

There are many more places to visit than those listed above. As you explore Pompeii, there is no need to watch the time. There is a narrow gauge train departing from the Pompeii Villa d' Misteri station about every twenty minutes for the half-hour scenic journey to Sorrento.

When you arrive in **Sorrento,** stay at the **Grand Hotel Excelsior Vittoria,** a romantic old villa at the center of town in a prime cliff location overlooking the harbor. The hotel's once perfect grandeur is perhaps a bit faded, but as you sit on the terrace in the evening and watch the sun turning the bay to shades of red and gold, the atmosphere is perfection. There is also a pool for relaxing and sunning. If within your budget, splurge and ask for a deluxe room with a view.

When it is time to leave Sorrento there is excellent service by either hydrofoil or ferry to Capri. The following schedule is a suggestion:

3:45 pm depart Sorrento by hydrofoil
4:10 pm arrive Capri

Your hydrofoil arrives at the **Marina Grande,** a small harbor filled with colorful boats and edged by brightly painted shops. When the boat docks, you find hotel porters on the pier along with carrier services that go to all of the hotels. They relieve you of your luggage and take it directly to the hotel of your choice, freeing you to take either a minibus or the funicular to the main town of Capri that is located on a flat saddle of land high above the sea.

There are many charming places to stay on **Capri.** Since this is a very popular tourist destination, the hotels are generally speaking expensive, but the ones we recommend are all special. Some are located in the heart of town, others a short stroll away—read our descriptions and choose one that suits you.

Capri has many wonders. The most famous is its submerged cave, the **Blue Grotto,** which can be reached by boat when the seas are calm. Large boats begin leaving the harbor every morning at 9:00 am for the short ride to the entrance to the Blue Grotto, where you are transferred into tiny rowboats. The excursion is an adventure in itself. As your little boat approaches the tiny cave opening it seems impossible that there is adequate room, but suddenly the sea surges forward and in you squeeze. Like magic you see it—the mysterious stunning blue light reflecting from some hidden source that illuminates the grotto.

Capri is a superb island for walking. As you stroll the trails, all your senses are treated by the fragrant flowers, the gorgeous vistas of the brilliant blue waters and the sound of birds luring you ever onward. There are many spectacular walks. Follow the trail winding down the cliffs to the small harbor **Marina Piccola**, located on the opposite side

Marina Grande, Capri

of the island from where the ferries dock. There are lovely views of the shimmering aqua waters as you make your way to the small beach where you can enjoy a swim before your return. Instead of walking back up the hill, take the little bus that delivers you quickly back to the main square. *NOTE:* On our last visit to Capri, the romantic walking path to Marina Piccolo was closed for repairs, but hopefully it will be back in operation by the time you arrive. If not, you can take the bus in both directions.

Another absolutely spectacular walk—although a long one of at least 45 minutes each way—is to Emperor Tiberius' Palace, **Villa Jovis**, perched high among the trees on the cliffs on the western tip of the island. This is the grandest of the palaces left by Tiberius. Although mostly in ruins, you can easily appreciate its former magnificence as you climb about exploring the ruins of the terraced rooms. From the palace there are stunning panoramic vistas. You have an overview of the whole island and can watch the ferries shuttling back and forth to the mainland. A much shorter walk, but one equally as beautiful, is to the **Cannone Belvedere**. This path guides you near delightful private villas hidden behind high walls (you get glimpses through the gates) and on to a promontory overlooking the sea.

Another excursion is to **Anacapri** (the only other town on the island) to visit the **Villa San Michel**, a lovely villa overlooking the sea that was the home of the Swedish scientist Axel Munthe. His residence is now open as a museum. Anacapri is bit too far to easily walk, buses leave regularly from the main square in town.

During the day, Capri is swarming with tourists who descend like a hoard of locusts from the constant stream of hydrofoils and ferries on package tours. You might surmise that in the evening the activity subsides, but it isn't so. The tour groups leave at dusk but then a new group of people emerges from the secreted villas and fancy hotels. Guests in chic clothes and fancy jewelry strolling the streets—both to see and be seen. The joy of over-nighting in Capri is that you can relax during the heat of the day when the tourist scene is at its height, then enjoy the magic of the balmy evenings.

When the real world calls and you must leave Capri, there is frequent ferry or hydrofoil service back to Naples. From Naples, you can take a train to Rome or a plane to your next destination.

Romantic Hilltowns
of Tuscany and Umbria

FLORENCE

Greve

Reggello

San Gimignano

Panzano

A₁

Castellina

Radda

San Sano

San Leonino

San Gusime

O
Arezzo

SIENA

Sovicille
Pretale

Sinalunga

Montefellonico

A₁

Lake
Trasimeno

Perugia

Assisi

Cetona

Montefalco

O *Orientation*
* *Alternate hotel suggestions*
● *Overnight stops*
══ *Itinerary route*

Rome

Bashi

O
Todi

Spoleto

Orvieto

Monteluco

O
Terni

A₁

49

to Rome

Romantic Hilltowns of Tuscany & Umbria

Assisi

Nothing can surpass the exquisite beauty of the countryside near Florence in the spring. It is breathtaking. It is not only in the spring that this region is beautiful. If you meander into the hilltowns of Tuscany and Umbria any time of the year, all your senses are rewarded with the splendors that this enchanting area of Italy has to offer. Almost every hillock is crowned with a picture-perfect walled village. The fields are brilliant with vibrant red poppies. The vineyards lace the fields in all their glory and promise. The olive trees dress the hillsides in a frock of dusky gray-green. Pine forests unexpectedly appear to highlight the landscape. As if these attributes were not enough, tucked into the colorful villages are a treasure trove of some of the finest small hotels in all the world. If this is still not sufficient to tempt you away from the normal tourist route, be reminded that the food and wines of Tuscany and Umbria are unsurpassed.

When planning your trip to Italy, allow time to treat yourself to a unique adventure. Save at least a few days to slip away from the cities and into the country. Perhaps you won't have time to follow this entire itinerary, but at least sneak in a few days in Umbria and Tuscany. You will be well-rewarded with a wealth of memories that will linger long after you return home. The following itinerary makes a southern loop from Florence. Along the way are three suggested stops—one in Umbria, one in the southern region of Tuscany, and one in the northern region of Tuscany. If possible, stay several days in each of these hubs and make excursions into the countryside.

ORIGINATING CITY   FLORENCE

Your journey begins in **Florence**. Allow enough time to savor this marvelous city but, if you are reluctant to leave, be consoled. There are many treats in store for you in the delightful hilltowns that surround Florence. Magnificent art is not confined to the city limits of Florence and you will see impressive cathedrals and beautiful works of art throughout the neighboring areas. On pages 36-38 we offer a few sightseeing suggestions for Florence.

DESTINATION I   ASSISI

The traffic around Florence is congested. Follow signs in town that lead to the expressway A1 to Rome. Follow the A1 until you come to the turnoff for **Arezzo**, which is located about 10 kilometers east of the highway. You might want to bypass Arezzo. Although it has a rich, medieval history dating back to the Etruscan Era, it is a large city and it is not as quaint as some of its smaller neighbors.

Following the main road 71 south from Arezzo, you soon arrive at **Cortona**. This is a beautifully situated walled town climbing up a steep hillside covered with olive trees. Stop to enjoy the atmosphere of this medieval town. Its crazy narrow twisting streets,

St Francis of Assisi

jumble of small squares and colorful buildings are delightful. A mighty castle dramatically stands guard over the town.

Leaving Cortona, continue south toward **Lake Trasimeno**. Just before you reach the lake, take the four lane expressway that skirts the northern shore of the lake heading east to **Perugia**, a large medieval city surrounded by ramparts. An important Umbrian city since Etruscan days, the heart of the old city is the **Piazza IV Novembre**, a beautiful square with an appealing fountain, the **Fontana Maggiore**, built in the late 13th Century.

It is only a short drive farther east from Perugia to **Assisi**. Built up the steep slopes of Mount Subasio, this magical city is a tribute to St Francis. Although he was born into a family of wealth, after several visions in which Christ appeared to him, St Francis left his privileged life. Obviously a person with a deep poetic soul, his tender teachings of reverence for the beauties of nature and kindness to all animals and birds still appeal to us today.

Even if it were not for the lingering memory of the gentle St Francis, Assisi would be a *must see* for it is one of the most spectacular hilltowns in Umbria. Perhaps there are a few too many souvenir shops, but this is a small price to pay for such a very special place. The town walls begin on the valley floor and completely enclose the city as climbs the steep hillside, climaxing in an enormous castle. Assisi is a marvelous town for walking: you need sturdy shoes to wind your way up and down the maze of tiny streets. It is great fun. You come across intriguing little lanes that open into small squares. When you stop to rest, there are marvelous vistas of the breathtaking Umbrian fields stretching out below.

To truly appreciate the beauty of Umbria, it is best to spend several nights in the area. Luckily, there are several good hotel choices—not only in Assisi, but also in nearby towns (see Map 9 for alternate towns with recommended hotels). If you prefer to stay right in Assisi, consider the **Hotel Umbra**. Superbly located in the heart of town, it is a most appealing small, family-run hotel that is highly recommended for those who don't expect the height of luxury. The **Hotel Subasio**, a larger hotel that tends more tour groups, is also recommended. It is beautifully situated with one of its walls forming a section of the Piazza of the St Francis' Basilica. The Subasio is not a deluxe hotel, but has much to entice the tourist. Perhaps its most impressive attribute is the view from the vine covered dining terrace over the undulating Umbrian fields that glow with a special mellow golden radiance.

In Assisi you must see **St Francis' Basilica**. You cannot miss this enormous structure whose massive supporting arches soar from the valley floor. The Basilica, which also houses a monastery, faces onto a large square bound by columns forming vaulted covered walkways. In addition to the monastery, there are two Basilicas—the upper and lower ones. Both are adorned with excellent frescoes. Be sure not to miss in the Upper Basilica the twenty-eight scenes depicting the life of St Francis. Also while in Assisi, be sure to visit **Santa Chiara** (St Clara's Church). Clara, a close friend of St Francis, founded the Order of St Clares. In the church view the lovely frescoes of St Clara and her sisters. Hike up to the **Rocca Medioevale**, an enormous 14th-century fortress, perched on the hillside above the city. From here you have a magnificent bird's eye view of the city.

While staying at Assisi, take a side-trip to nearby **Torgiano** where there is a splendid wine museum. You would never dream that such a tiny town could boast such a stunning museum, but it is not a coincidence. The Lungarotti family owns the vineyards for miles in every direction. Indeed, they must be a very clever and dedicated family for they also own a delightful hotel in the center of town, Le Tre Vaselle. A charming spot for lunch or overnight, **Le Tre Vaselle** has the ambiance of a lovely country manor house. In addition to overseeing the decoration of this exquisite hotel, Signore Lungarotti also furnished the museum with artifacts pertaining to every aspect of the production of wine from the earliest days. The collection is interesting and beautifully displayed, worthy of a detour by anyone interested in wines.

DESTINATION II   CETONA

Get an early start this morning because it is going to be difficult to squeeze in all of the enchanting hilltop towns enroute. Driving south on 3 from Assisi you soon come to **Spoleto,** an intriguing town. Not only is medieval Spoleto dramatically perched atop a hill, but it also has an almost unbelievable bridge dating from Roman times. This **Ponte delle Torri,** spanning the deep ravine between Spoleto and the adjoining mountain, was built over an aqueduct existing in the 14th Century. This incredible engineering wonder is 230 meters long and 81 meters high. It is supported by a series of ten Gothic arches and has a fort at the far end as well as a balcony in the center. The 12-century **Cathedral** in Spoleto is also so lovely that it alone would make a stop in this charming town worth a detour. The exterior of this very old cathedral, with its beautiful rose window and intricate mosaics, is truly charming.

Before leaving the vicinity of Spoleto, if you are a St Francis enthusiast, make the short detour to visit **Monteluco,** where St Francis lived as a hermit. You'll appreciate why he chose Monteluco for his meditations after you twist to the top of the mountain and enjoy the glorious view of the surrounding hillsides covered with olive trees. *NOTE:* On the road that twists to the top of Monteluco, you can spot on your left the **Eremo delle Grazie,** a charming hotel, almost hidden in the dense woods. In the town of Spoleto, we recommend the **Hotel Gattapone**, strategically perched on the side of the cliff overlooking the Ponte delle Torri.

From Spoleto you can either take the 418, a short cut that twists west over the hills to the BIS 3, or the longer route that loops south toward **Terni**. About 4 km pass Terni, watch for and take the BIS 3 north. Watch carefully for the turn off to the west to **Todi**, located just off the main road. Take time to park and explore this truly picture-perfect hilltop walled village. Stop for a cappuccino in one of the sidewalk cafes. However, do not linger too long in Todi because the next town, Orvieto, is the real prize.

Whereas Todi is a small, easily managed village, **Orvieto** is a city spread across the top of a hill that drops down on every side in steep volcanic cliffs. You wonder how the town could ever have been built. Drive as far as you can up to the city, park your car and proceed on by foot. Have a good map handy because you pass so many churches and squares that it is difficult to orient yourself. Continue on the Orvieto's center where a glorious **Duomo** dominates the immense piazza.

Duomo, Orvieto

You may think you have seen sufficient stunning cathedrals to last a lifetime, but Orvieto's Duomo is truly special—brilliantly embellished with mosaic designs and accentuated by lacy slender spires that stretch gracefully into the sky. Also of interest in Orvieto is **St Patrick's Well**. This well is hewn out of solid volcanic rock to collect and store water in case of a siege. Pope Clement VII took refuge in Orvieto in 1527. To ensure the town's water supply in case of siege, he ordered the digging of a 62 meter deep well. What makes it unusual are the 70 windows which illuminate it and the two spiral staircases that wind up and down without meeting.

After seeing Orvieto, head directly north on the A1 for about 40 km to the turnoff for your night's destination, **Cetona**. As you exit the freeway, follow the signs that wind circuitously into Cetona. Go through the village and follow signs for Convento San Francesco, the convent where your suggested hotel, **La Frateria di Padre Eligio**, is located in a 16 hectare forest. After spending time in Assisi, it is most appropriate to stay in a 13th-century convent founded by St Francis. This idyllic hideaway is well-suited for a base from which to explore the wealth of places to see in this lower region of Tuscany.

From Cetona make daily forays into the beautiful countryside. One day visit **Pienza**—a jewel of a tiny walled village crowning a hilltop. Stop for lunch here and then continue taking the back roads for about 35 km to **Abbazia di Monte Oliveto Maggiore**, serenely situated among the cypress forest. Of special interest in this abbey are the beautiful terra cottas adorning the entrance (created by the famous artist, Luca della Robbia), and the charming frescoes in the cloisters portraying the life of St Benedict.

Another day take an all-day excursion from Cetona to **Siena**, another of the strategically built walled hilltowns. This is an entrancing city and deserves many hours to savor all its attributes. The ramparts are perfectly preserved with a series of massive gates guarding a meticulously maintained medieval stronghold. Drive as close as you can to the main square, park your car, and set out to explore on foot. The giant plaza is a sight in itself: it is immense and, instead of being square, is fan shaped. Eleven streets surrounding the square converge like spokes of a giant wheel into the **Piazza del Campo**. It is in this gigantic piazza that the colorful *Palio delle Contrade* takes place in July and August every year. The horse race is only a part of a colorful spectacle of medieval costumes, wonderful banners and parades. You can check for the exact dates, but the festivities extend beyond the actual date of the races. Monopolizing one side of the Piazza del

Camp is the 13th-century Gothic **Palazzo Pubblico** (Town Hall) whose graceful arches are embellished with the coat of arms of Siena. The Palazzo Pubblico is open as a museum where you can stroll through the governor's living quarters. Also, visit Siena's 12th-century **Cathedral,** facing the Piazza del Duomo, just a short walk from the Piazza del Campo. Save time to visit the interior of this fabulous cathedral with its bold patterns of black and white marble because within is an excellent museum of antique religious art and sculptures.

NOTE: While Cetona is suggested as the hub from which to explore this southern portion of Tuscany, look at Map 9 in the back of this guide to see other choices nearby. There is a marvelous selection of places to stay in this region—any one of which would make an excellent base for your explorations.

DESTINATION III   PANZANO IN CHIANTI

Your next destination is **Castellina,** deep in the heart of Chianti country. Here you find the **Tenuta di Ricavo,** a cluster of charming stone cottages deep in the pine forest. The entire village has been converted into a romantic small hotel with tastefully decorated rooms. For a choice of other towns in Chianti region where we recommend places to stay, study Map 8. Any one of the recommended hotels would make an ideal hub for exploring this part of Tuscany.

Of all the beautiful areas of Tuscany, the picture perfect Chianti region is the most special. It lives up to every dream—hills crowned by walled villages, straight rows of towering cypress, romantic villas, ancient stone farmhouses, vast fields of brilliant poppies, forests of pine trees, vineyards stretching to the horizon. In Chianti the sightseeing is mostly just meandering through the countryside, stopping at quaint hamlets, wandering through perched villages. Do not be too structured. Take a detailed map so that if you get lost you can find your way home, but otherwise, just explore. Enjoy the freedom to discover your own *perfect village,* your own favorite restaurant.

During your adventures, the one town you must not miss is San Gimignano. What is so dramatic about **San Gimignano** is that at one time this walled town was surrounded by 72 towers. During the Middle Ages it was a status symbol for noble families to build personal towers for protection—the higher the tower, the greater the image of wealth and importance. It is amazing that fourteen of the original towers are still standing. They make a striking silhouette, soaring like skyscrapers. On a clear day you can seem them on the horizon from far away. San Gimignano is truly a jewel. *NOTE:* if you want to spend the night, we highly recommended the **L'Antico Pozzo**, a charming hotel in the center of the village. Even if you do not overnight, plan to spend the day in San Gimignano. There are many shops and marvelous restaurants tucked along the maze of streets. Hotel La Cisterna on the main square and La Mangiatoia near L'Antico Pozzo, both serve excellent food. When it is time to complete your loop, Florence is about an hour's drive away.

San Gimignano

Mountain & Lake Adventures

Chiavenna

Merano · Bressanone

Aosta

Tiers-St- Zyprian · Cortina

Pescatori · Bellagio · Trent · Belluno

Champoluc · Riva · Maser

Stresa · Bergamo · Asolo

Sirmione · S. Viglio

Milan

Venice

Genoa · Bologna

Florence

Rome

● Overnight stops
○ Sightseeing/orientation
▬ Itinerary route

*Suggested alternate hotels
see Maps 1–4*

Mountain & Lake Adventures

Santa Maria Rezzónico, Lake Como

For the traveler who wants to combine the magic of seeing some of the world's most splendid mountains with the joy of visiting Italy's scenic northern lakes, this itinerary is ideal. Contrasts will heighten the impact of visual delights as you meander through lovely mountain passes. Along the way you pass lush green meadows laced with wildflowers, giant mountains piercing the sky with their jagged granite peaks. Further on you come to lazy blue lakes whose steep shorelines are decorated with villages wrapped in misty cloaks of siennas and ochre's. What a glorious holiday to wind across northern Italy enjoying some of its most beautiful landscapes. This itinerary can stand alone. However, it is also perfect for the traveler arriving or departing from neighboring

Mountain & Lake Adventures

countries. We show detours for the tourist who will be leaving or entering from Austria, Switzerland, or France. All too often the tourist thinks he has finished Italy when his tour ends in Venice, and he rushes north into Austria or Switzerland. What a waste. A very picturesque region still remains. Please linger to enjoy the mountains and lakes that truly are some of Italy's greatest natural treasures.

ORIGINATING CITY   VENICE

This itinerary begins in **Venice**, one of the most romantic cities in the world. Her many narrow waterways are criss-crossed by storybook bridges and shadowed by majestic palaces whose soft hues reflect warmly in the shimmering water. Black gondolas quietly glide through the narrow canals as the gondolier in his red and white striped shirt softly serenades his passengers with an operatic selection.

Venice is not a traditional city with streets and automobile traffic, rather an archipelago of 117 islands glued together by 400 bridges. There is a wealth of things to do while in Venice. Pick up a guide book at one of the tourist stalls to give you an idea of what you want to see. On pages 33-36 we give brief sightseeing suggestions.

DESTINATION I   ASOLO

You need not rush your departure this morning. Venice is a city that should be enjoyed slowly and since your journey today is short, you can certainly have the luxury of a last leisurely breakfast before embarking on your countryside adventure.

Since all the "streets" in Venice are canals, you will need to take a boat to your car. It will probably be at the **Piazzale Roma** where most of the car rental companies are located. Also in the Piazzale Roman there are overnight car parks for storing your car if you drive into Venice. The choice of conveyance will depend upon your budget and your inclination. The **Vaporetti** are the most reasonable. Similar to river buses, the Vaporetti leave regularly from **St Mark's Square** for the approximately half-hour ride to the Piazzale Roma. The Vaporetto Number One stops at most of the little docks along the route whereas Vaporetto Number Two is an express boat that stops at only a few major points. The **Motoscafi** are motorboats that duck through the back canals and usually take about fifteen minutes to the **Piazzale Roma**. The Motoscafi are like private cabs and are much more expensive than the "bus," but can be very convenient, especially if your hotel has a private motor boat landing. The most deluxe mode of transportation is by private **Gondola**: however, these are very expensive and usually take about an hour to reach the Piazzale Roma.

Once you have retrieved your car from the parking garage, head north from Venice toward **Treviso**, which requires about an hour's drive. If time allows, stop here. Stroll through this picturesque city spider-webbed with canals and surrounded by 15th-century ramparts. Perhaps have a cup of coffee or a bite of lunch before heading north toward Asolo. Treviso is famous for its arcaded streets, churches lavishly decorated with frescos, and painted houses. You might want to climb the ramparts for a view of the Alps beckoning you on. From Treviso it is approximately another hour to Asolo. However, just a few miles before you reach Asolo you see signs for the town of **Maser** where the **Villa di Maser** (some of your books might use the name of **Villa Bararo**) is located. This is a splendid villa designed by Palladio and fabulously decorated with frescos by **Paolo Veronese**. This elegant villa has erratic days and hours when it is open to the public—usually in late afternoons on Tuesdays, Saturdays and Sundays. However, it is only about one mile out of your way, so well worth a detour to investigate. There is also a very interesting museum of old carriages and antique cars at Villa di Maser.

Your prize tonight is **Asolo**, a gem of a medieval village snuggled on the side of a hill with exquisite views of the countryside. As you drive toward Asolo, the terrain does not seem to hold much promise—just modern towns and industry. Then a side road winds up a lovely hillside and into the intimate town of Asolo. Although definitely a tourist destination, Asolo maintains the atmosphere of a *real* town with colorful fruit stands, candy shops, and the neighborhood grocer for those lucky few who live here. Plus, there are boutiques with exquisite merchandise for the tourist. Of course a castle adorns the hill above the village—mostly in ruins but setting the proper stage. Naturally, there is a wonderful cathedral dominating the square, just as it should. You will find all this plus vineyards and olive trees on the hillsides and the scent of roses in the air.

Villa Cipriani, Asolo

No wonder Robert Browning fell in love with Asolo and chose it as his home. It might not be possible for all to live here, but at least you have the marvelous option of staying at the **Villa Cipriani**, an enchanting, villa that was once Robert Browning's home. Here you can dream on the peaceful terrace in the evening and watch the soft lights paint the distant villa-dotted hills in mellow shades of gold. *NOTE:* For those on a budget, **Hotel Duse** is an alternate choice.

DESTINATION II   CORTINA D'AMPEZZO

There are a couple of towns that are worth seeing before leaving the Asolo area. If brandy holds a special interest for you, visit **Bassano del Grappa**, an old town famous for its production of grappa (or brandy). The town is also a pottery center. However, it is rather large, and, in our estimation, much less interesting than **Marostica**, a tiny town just a few miles farther. If you are in this area in September, check your calendar and consider a stop in Marostica. Here, during the first part of September (in alternate years) the central square is transformed into a giant chess board and local citizens become the human chess pieces. Even if it isn't the year of the chess game, Marostica is a picturesque little medieval town encircled by ramparts. Its pretty central square is enclosed by colorful buildings and castle walls. There is also a second castle guarding the town from the top of the hill.

The Dolomites

As you head north into the **Dolomites** there are various routes from which to choose. The major highway heads north through **Feltre** and **Belluno** and then on to Cortina d'Ampezzo.

If the day is nice and your spirit of adventure is high, there is really nothing more fun than the back roads through the mountains. Journey through tiny hamlets and gorgeous mountain valleys far from the normal tourist path; always keeping a map accessible so that you don't wind up hopelessly lost.

You might want to travel casually and stop in a village that captures your heart as you drive through the picturesque valleys of the Dolomites. But if you are making reservations (and in the summer season this is highly recommended), a good choice for an overnight stop is **Cortina** d'Ampezzo. This is not a small town. It has grown into a large tourist center due to its excellent skiing facilities. However, its location is truly breathtaking—the town spreads across a sunny meadow ringed by gigantic granite peaks. Our choice for where to stay on the outskirts of town, is the **Hotel Menardi**, with a history that dates back far before the skiing craze. It used to be a simple farmhouse, but today it is a proper hotel where the guests sleep in comfortable beds with fine linens and down comforters.

Although the true allure of Cortina d'Ampezzo is its beauty, there are a few places you can go if you want to do some sightseeing—see the beautiful frescoes in the Romanesque **Church of SS Filippo e Giacomo,** visit the stadium where the Olympic ice competition was held in 1956, go to see the geological display and the contemporary art exhibition, both housed in the **Museo Ciasa de Ra Regoles.**

DESTINATION III   TIERS–ST ZYPRIAN (*Tires–San Cipriano*)

When it is time to leave Cortina, take the Old Dolomite Road heading west from Cortina toward Bolzano. Quite frankly, we think this is one of the most stunning regions of Italy—the mountains are truly breathtaking. Our favorite adventure is exploring the tiny back roads in the Dolomites in an effort to add a wider choice of places for you to stay. Look on map 2 in the back of this guide to find our selection of hamlets where we have discovered small inns. Read about each of them and decide where you want to spend the night—anyone of them would make a good base for walking and soaking in the beauty of these soaring, saw-tooth mountain peaks. Before leaving Cortina, buy a very detailed map of the region because this is a confusing area for driving. Added to the confusion of finding your way is the fact that most of the towns have two names: one Italian and one Austrian. Before the first World War this section of Italy belonged to the Austrian Empire, and most of the towns have retained their original name along with their new one.

We suggest an overnight sojourn in the especially scenic village of **St Zyprian** (*San Cipriano*), tucked into the mountains just a few kilometers from Tires (*Tiers*). However, no matter which town you decide to choose for your mountain interlude, you will leave Cortina via the historic Dolomite Road originally used by the merchants of Venice on their way to Germany.

From Cortina follow the highway S 48 as it leaves the valley floor and climbs over a windswept barren pass surrounded by towering granite peaks. The road then drops into a valley before climbing again to conquer the **Pordoi Pass** and then down into the Fassa Valley. About 12 kilometers beyond **Canazei**, highway S 48 splits off to the south. At this point, keep to your right and continue west on S 241 that goes through Vigo di Fassa. From the turnoff onto S 241, it is about 10 kilometers further to where you turn right on the road leading to Bolzano by way of Tiers (*Tires*). This road loops over the mountains and then drops down to an idyllic meadow where **St Zyprian** (*San Cipriano*) located. As you drive into town, you will see a signpost on your right indicating the **Pensione Stefaner**, a simple chalet-style inn that is run by the gracious young Villgrattner family.

If you enjoy the out of doors, plan to spend at least several days in the Dolomites so that you can enjoy the splendor of the mountains. Join other travelers from throughout Europe who come to trek the well-marked trails that feather out into the hills. (At gift shops or tourist offices, you can purchase detailed hiking maps that show every little path.)

DESTINATION IV   MERANO

When you depart St Zyprian, follow the road signposted to Bolzano. Before you reach Bolzano, watch for signs to the E6. Get on the expressway heading north in the direction of the **Brenner Pass**. Soon after getting on the expressway, there is an exit for **Bressanone**. Try to allow time to stop in Bressanone. This medieval walled town ringed by mountains has much to offer including a charming village square and a river (lined on both banks by promenades) meandering through its center. Bressanone hides another treasure, the **Hotel Elefant**. This inn is famous for its exquisite cuisine. In its beautiful dining rooms only the freshest foods and wines are served—usually from the hotel's own farms and vineyards. But the hotel also has an intriguing history. In 1550, King John III of Portugal sent, as a special gift, an elephant to Emperor Ferdinand of Austria. It seems this *gift* grew weary of walking by the time it arrived in Bressanone and so was housed at the local inn—you guessed it, the Elefant. The story alone merits a stop, but the joy is that the Elefant also retains so much character and serves such excellent food.

From Bressanone continue north for a short distance on the expressway toward the Brenner Pass. Then near Vipiteno, exit and head southwest along a twisting road that maneuvers along the **Monte Giovo Pass** as it twists its way through the mountains. It then drops down into the valley to follow the Passiria River as it winds a path into Merano. *NOTE:* If your destination is Austria, then at Vipiteno continue north on the expressway for the short drive to the Brenner Pass leading into Austria.

Hotel Castel Freiberg, Merano

In **Merano** the **Castel Freiberg** is an enchanting fairytale castle that majestically dominates the surrounding countryside from its romantic hillside perch. This fabulous castle truly has everything: setting, view, marvelous architecture, gourmet food, beautiful rooms, priceless antiques, pool, tennis, and an efficient, friendly management. Since this is a luxury hotel, you might want to consider the **Hotel Castel Labers** (located just below the Castel Freiberg) or the mountain top **Hotel Vigiljoch** in nearby **Lana**. You will find a write-up of both of these less expensive hotels in the Hotel Description Section at the back of this guide.

It is a short drive south from **Merano** to **Bolzano.** Here you again join the expressway (E7), but this time heading south toward Trent. **Trent** is best known as the town where the Catholic Council met in the 16th Century to establish important articles of faith that emphasized the authority of the Catholic church.

Northern Italian Lake District

Leave the freeway at Trent and head west on 45 toward the small, but lovely, green **Lake Toblino** that is enhanced by a superb castle on its north shore where you can stop for lunch. From Toblino head south on the pretty country road, lined with fruit trees and vineyards, heading directly south toward Lake Garda, Italy's largest lake. When you come to Arco, the road splits. Take the road to the left and continue south to Lake Garda and then follow 249 as it curves along the eastern shore of the lake.

Allow several nights in the **Lake Garda** area so that you can leisurely enjoy several excursions on the lake and a side trip to nearby **Verona**. On Map 3 you can find many towns where we recommend places to stay in every price range that are on or close to the lake. However, we cannot resist sharing with you one or our favorites, **Locanda San Vigilio**.

San Vigilio

As you follow 249 that traces the eastern shore of Lake Garda, continue about 4 kilometers beyond the town of Torri d'Benaco. Then turn right when you see San Vigilio sign posted. There is a gate where you will be stopped by an attendant who will want you to pay for parking **(San Vigilio** is also a park). Say you are a guest at the hotel and you will be allowed to pass. Drive as far as you can and then park your car. Walk down the path. Turn left at the stately villa (glimpsed through tall gates). Follow the lane until it dead-ends at the Locanda San Vigilio, a 16th-century stone building, so close to the water's edge that waves lap beneath the windows. With such a setting, it is not surprising that Winston Churchill used to come here to paint. Inside, you will not be disappointed. The rooms are tastefully decorated with country antiques complemented by color coordinated fabrics. If you want to splurge, ask for a suite overlooking the lake, but no matter which room you choose, they are all most appealing. There is a romantic dining room where you can eat in your own little niche by a window overlooking the lake.

When you are ready to sightsee, drive a few kilometers further south along the lake to **Garda**. Park your car and take one of the ferries or hydrofoils that ply the lake. If you have the time, choose a different destination each day—perhaps planning to have a bite of lunch at an enticing little lakeside cafe. If have time for only one adventure, visit **Sirmione.** This is a wonderful walled village at the south end of Lake Garda positioned at the end of a miniature peninsula that proudly pokes its head into the lake. During the summer this town is absolutely bursting with tourists, but you can easily understand why: this is another one of Italy's *stage setting* villages, almost too perfect to be true. If you take the ferry or hydrofoil to Sirmione, your boat will dock in the center of the town. From here you can stroll through the little boutiques, perhaps have lunch at one of the beautiful terrace cafes overlooking the lake, and explore the tiny island-like village. If you want to go to the tip of the peninsula, there are small motorized trams that take you there.

If time permits, take the ferry to **Riva** on the northern shore of the lake. Although, much of the town is of new construction, it has at its medieval core the **Piazza III Novembre** and 13th-century Tower of Apponale. A good place to eat lunch is on the terrace of the **Hotel Sole,** located directly across from the boat dock.

Another excursion is by car to **Gardone Riviera** (on the western shore of the lake) to see a nearby museum, the **Vittoriale,** once the home of Gabriele D'Annunzio, the celebrated Italian poet. (For those of us who love stories of romance, **D'Annunzio** is also famous for his love affair with Eleanora Duse.) While there, if you enjoy gourmet food, the pink and white **Villa Fiordaliso,** located right on the lake, is a well-known restaurant. The

Villa Fiordaliso also has a tidbit of historical romance—this was once the hide-away of Mussolini and his mistress, Claretta. For a simpler meal, just a few kilometers further north along the lake at **Gargnano-Villa,** you can enjoy a wonderful seafood lunch on the sun-drenched deck of the **Baia d'Oro.**

It might be easier to leave the Lake Garda knowing that beautiful **Lake Como,** awaits your arrival.

Bergamo

On your way from Lake Garda to Lake Como, stop at **Bergamo,** about an hour's drive west on the A4. As you approach Bergamo, the congested city doesn't appear to be worth a stop. But it is. The shell of the city is deceiving because it hides a lovely kernel, the **Cita Alta,** or high city. The lower part of **Bergamo** is modern and a bit dreary, but the old medieval city snuggled on the top of the hill holds such treasures as the **Piazza Vecchia,** the **Colleoni Chapel,** and the **Church of St Mary Major.** Should you want to time your stop in Bergamo with lunch, there are several excellent restaurants. A suggestion would be at the **Agnello d'Oro,** a cozy, charming 17th-century inn in the Cita Alta.

From Bergamo it is a short drive on to **Bellagio,** a medieval fishing village located at the tip of a peninsula. This peninsula divides the lower section of Lake Como into two lakes, Lake Como on the west and Lake Lecco on the east. Bellagio makes an excellent base for exploring beautiful Lake Como. In the Hotel Description Section we list three hotel suggestions in various price ranges. The **Grand Hotel Villa Serbelloni,** found behind gates opening onto the main square of Bellagio, is a large imposing old world palace. It offers everything you could wish for in a lakeside interlude—tennis, swimming pool, boat excursions, private beach, and more. It is very ornate, still retaining its glory of bygone days with soaring, intricately painted ceilings, heavy chandeliers, and fabulous sweeping staircase. The setting of the Villa Serbelloni is superb and overshadows what might be perceived as the slightly faded elegance of the hotel's decor. Just outside the gates of the Villa Serbelloni, with a prime location across from the lake, the **Hotel Florence** is also very highly recommended. This moderately priced small hotel is more intimate than the Villa Serbelloni and offers the warmth of welcome only found at family-run hotels. If you are on a really tight budget, consider **Il Perlo Panorama**, a simple hotel on the knoll of the hill overlooking Bellagio.

Bellagio, Lake Como

Bellagio is a delightful town. Not only can you meander through the quaint medieval village, but you can walk to the pier for one of the boats that will take you to all corners of the lake. **Lake Como** is absolutely beautiful—especially the lower eastern branch of the lake called **Lake Lecco** where cliffs enclose the shorelines like gorgeous walls and give a fjord-like beauty to the area. There are numerous romantic steamers that glide in and out of the picturesque, softly hued little hamlets dotting the lake shore. You can settle onto a steamer equipped with bar and restaurant. From your armchair lazily enjoy the constantly changing, but always intriguing shoreline as the boat maneuvers in and out of the colorful little harbors, past elegant private villas, by postcard-pretty villages. From Bellagio you can also step on board one of the swift hydrofoils that will whisk you about the lake. Or, you can put your car right on the ferry to either **Cadenabbia** on the western shore of Lake Como or **Varenna** on the eastern shore. With Bellagio as a base there are several sightseeing possibilities. An excursion to visit the **Villa Carlotta**, a fairytale-like 18th-century palace—worthy of the Prussian Princess Carlotta for whom it was named—is enjoyable. You can take the car ferry from Bellagio to Cadenabbia on the western shore. From there it is just a short drive along the beautiful tree lined Via del Paradiso to the Villa Carlotta that is encircled by its own gorgeous park of terraced gardens.

DESTINATION VII   ISOLA DEI PESCATORI

NOTE: If you plan to leave Italy and head into Switzerland, this would be an excellent point to begin your journey. Head north along Lake Como and on to Chiavenna where you then turn east for the short drive (only about 10 kilometers) to the Swiss border. From there it is a lovely drive through the Engadine Valley to St Moritz.

Continuing on toward **Lake Maggiore**, take advantage of the expressways to make your drive as easy as possible because there is usually heavy traffic in this part of Italy. It is best to head directly south from Bellagio to pick up the freeway in the direction of Milan. Keep on the bypass that skirts to the north of Milan and follow the freeway northwest to Lake Maggiore. When you reach the lake continue along the western shore to **Stresa**. It seems only suitable that for a *Mountain and Lake Adventure* one of your hotels should be located on an island in a lake—so we have chosen for you one of the **Borromean Islands, Isola dei Pescatori** (Fisherman's Island), located in Lake

Maggiore. This is an enchanting little island with twisting, narrow alley-like streets and colorful fishermen's cottages. As the name implies, this is still an active fishing village. During the tourist season the island teems with people and the streets are lined with

Isola Bella, Lake Maggiore

rather tacky souvenir shops, but it is hard to dull the charm of this quaint town.

Isola dei Pescatori can be reached by ferry from **Stresa, Baveno,** or **Pallanza,** but the most convenient of these is Stresa from where there are frequent scheduled departures to the island. Take one of the public ferries from Stresa to Isola dei Pescatori. Be sure to take one of the scheduled ferries—these are very reasonable in contrast to the very expensive private speed boats that will attempt to take you to the island. Your best choice for a place to stay here is the **Hotel Verbano.** This is not a deluxe hotel, but its setting is superb, and over the years (since our first visit) the decor of this most romantic hotel has improved enormously. The bedrooms are pleasantly decorated, but lovely vistas are their most enchanting feature. The view from the terrace is also outstanding. It is here that guests enjoy dining while overlooking the lake. The food is delicious, and the service of the Zacchera family, who own and manage the Verbano, is warm and gracious. This tiny archipelago consisting of **Isola Bella** (Beautiful Island), **Isola dei Pescatori** (Fisherman's Island), and **Isola Madre** (Mother Island) are world-famous for their dramatic palaces and spectacular, fragrant gardens. How smug you will feel to settle into your room. Enjoy a drink on the lovely terrace while watching the last of the tourists hustle onto the boat for shore, leaving you to enjoy the sunset. *NOTE:* The closest island is Isola Bella—be sure to allow enough time to visit its sumptuous palace and glorious terraced gardens before returning to the mainland.

DESTINATION VIII   CHAMPOLUC

NOTE: If your next destination is Switzerland, then it is time to leave Italy by heading north in the direction of Domodossolo. About 16 kilometers beyond Domodossolo you arrive at Iselle. Here you drive your car piggyback style onto the train and ride in your car as you zigzag through the fabulous Simplon Tunnel and emerge about 20 minutes later in Brig.

From Verbano drive south to the main freeway and head west toward **Turin**. Before reaching Turin watch for the signs and take the branch of the expressway heading toward Aosta. When you come to Verres, leave the highway and take the small road north to Champoluc, an hour's drive. The road follows the Evancon River as it cuts its path through the mountains. At first the valley is quite steep and narrow and then opens up into wide meadows lazily stretching out on both sides of the river. In early summer the meadows are truly lovely, blanketed in brilliantly colored wildflowers.

Just before the road leaves **Champoluc** you see a marker for the Anna Maria. At this sign turn to the right and follow the road for a very short drive up the hill until you see the hotel. It is beautifully located amid the pine trees and has views in every direction of the spectacular mountains. The **Villa Anna Maria** is a small chalet-style inn. The dining room is cozy and inviting with gay red checked curtains at the windows and rustic Alpine-style carved wooden chairs. The bedrooms, although small, all have private bathrooms and are very appealing with paneled walls and a country flavor.

When it is time to leave Champoluc you have two options if you want to travel into Switzerland. First you must drive back to the main expressway and head west. In about a half hour you will come to Aosta at which point you can leave the expressway for the road leading north to the San Bernardino tunnel and into Switzerland's Rhone Valley. Or, by continuing on the expressway west through the village of Courmayeur, you arrive at the Mont Blanc tunnel. This delivers you briefly into France, and then on to Geneva via the main highway. Of course, by taking the short drive to Milan you can easily tie in with another Italian holiday suggested in this guide.

Villa Anna Maria, Champoluc

Rome to Milan via the Italian Riviera

- ● **MILAN**
- ○ **Pavia Carthusian Monastery**
- A7
- **Genoa** ○ A12
- **Camogli** — ✳
- **Finale Liguri** ✳
- **Portofino** ●
- **Cinque Terre** — ○
- **La Spezia** —
- **Chiavari a Leivi** ✳
- **Levanto** ●
- **Carrara** ○
- **Lucca** ○
- **Pisa** ○
- ✳ **FLORENCE**
- **Grosetto** ○
- **Orbetello Peninsula** —
- ✳ **Scansano**
- **Porto Ercole** ●
- **Tarquina** ○
- **Civitavecchia** ○
- ● **ROME**
- Rome

Legend:
- ● Overnight stops
- ✳ Suggested alternate hotels
- ○ Sightseeing
- ▬ Itinerary route

Rome to Milan via the Italian Riviera

Vernazza, Cinque Terre

This itinerary traces the western coast of Italy as far as Genoa before heading north for the final stretch to Milan. To break the journey, stop first in Orbetello, a picturesque peninsula-like island joined to the coast by three spits of land. Next destination is Cinque Terre—a string of five tiny peninsulas along the coast that have not yet fallen prey to a great influx of tourists. As you follow the highway up the coast, it becomes a masterpiece of engineering—bridging deep ravines and tunneling in and out of the cliffs that rise steeply from the sea. Along the way you pass picturesque small towns snuggled into small coves. Then it's on to Portofino—one of the Italy's most treasured jewels— before the final destination of Milan.

ORIGINATING CITY   ROME

This itinerary begins in **Rome**, a perfect introduction to Italy. The joy of Rome is that every place you walk you are immersed history. The whole of the city is a virtual museum—buildings over 2,000 years old, ancient fountains designed by the world's greatest masters, the Vatican, Rennaissance paintings that have never been surpassed in beauty. On pages 39-44 we give just a few suggestions of places you must not miss, but we just touch on the wealth of sightseeing possibilities. Buy a guidebook at one of the many bookstores or magazine stands to plan what you most want to see and do. Also buy a detailed city map and mark each day's excursion. Most places are within walking distance—if not, consider taking the subway that stretches to most of the major points of interest.

Rome has a rich selection of places to stay. We suggest that you browse through the hotel section in the back of this guide where we describe hotels we think are especially appealing. Make a reservation in advance because space is very tight—particularly during the busy tourist season. Plan to stay in Rome for several days. When you are saturated with the overwhelming number of sights and are ready to continue your journey, ask at the hotel desk for help in marking your map for the best route out of town.

DESTINATION I   ORBETELLO–PORTO ERCOLE

From Rome follow the well-marked signs for the expressway heading west toward the Leonard di Vinci airport. About five kilometers before you arrive at the airport, head north on A12 in the direction of Civitavecchia.

About 20 kilometers beyond Civitavecchia, turn off at **Tarquinia,** the Etruscan city that supposedly dates back to the 12 Century BC. Even if not quite that old, archaeologists have established that people were living here as early as 600 years before Christ. There are virtually thousands of tombs scattered on the wind-swept hill where the ancient city once stood. To understand the Roman civilization better, it is important to delve back even further to their predecessors, the Etruscans. The paintings in the tombs show their daily life. There is no way you can visit all the burial chambers, but one of the most popular is the **Tomb of the Leopards** where there is a well-preserved banquet scene. If time allows, visit the **Museo Nazionale Tarquiniese** (housed in the 15th-century Vitelleschi Palace). This contains many Tuscan artifacts along with several tombs that have been reconstructed.

After your touch of Etruscan civilization, continue north for approximately 50 kilometers to Scalo/Orbetello where you turn west. The road crosses 6 kilometers of lagoons on a narrow spit of land (going through the town of Orbetello) before reaching the large, bulbous peninsula dominated by Monte Argentario. Turn left when you reach the island and continue through the town of **Porto Ercole** following signs to the exquisite resort of **Il Pelicano,** romantically perched on the cliffs overlooking the sea. If time and pocketbook allow, settle in to relax for a few days in this hideaway of the rich and famous before heading north. Enjoy the romantic setting, the swimming pool, tennis courts, and excellent food. Also explore the small peninsula, admire the many splendid yachts in the harbor at Porto Ercole, then continue on to the picturesque old fishing village, **Porto San Stefano.**

NOTE: If Il Pelicano exceeds your budget, or catching a glimpse of the rural area of the southern-most part of Tuscany tempts you, the following is an alternate stop-over suggestion. Instead of taking the exit for Orbetello, continue north on 1 for about 7 kilometers to Albinia. There turn left and follow signs to Scansano on the 323. The narrow road weaves up into the mountains. Two kilometers west of **Scansano** is the **Attico Casale di Scansano,** a simple 200-year old farmhouse that has been converted into a small inn. Horse back riding is a specialty here, along with exploring the many walled towns in the area.

When it is time to continue, return to highway 1 and head north. The A12 is scheduled to be completed all the way up the coast. However, as we go to press the expressway ends near Civitavecchia. It doesn't pick up again until near **Livorno** (except for short stretches of four-lane that are finished). So be patient and allow more time than usual because there are many trucks and slow-moving traffic on the road. Get an early start if you want to stop in Pisa, Lucca and Carrara along the way.

Leaning Tower of Pisa

The next large town after Livorno is **Pisa.** Exit here and follow signs into the congested center of the old town. There is such a solid mass of tourists and souvenir shops during the summer season that you can hardly find a place to park before trying to squirm your way to the central piazza. Admittedly, Pisa's gleaming white **Duomo** with its companion **Leaning Tower** are impressive, and such a symbol of Italy that you should stop once to see it if you have never done so before.

Even more interesting and not nearly so touristy as Pisa is the extremely picturesque city of **Lucca,** located only a few kilometers to the north. Lucca too is an ancient city, even more perfectly preserved than its neighbor, Pisa. Completely surrounding the city is enormous wall—a wall so wide that it even shelters pretty small parks and a road that runs along the top. Lucca is truly a jewel. Take time to wander through her maze of narrow streets, admiring characterful mansions and colorful squares

Leaving Lucca, return to the expressway A12 and head north to **Genoa**. Along the way you see what appears to be a glacier shimmering white in the mountains that rise to the right of the highway. This is not snow at all, but rather your introduction to the renowned white Italian marble. It might be too late in the day, but if time allows, detour to visit some of the marble quarries. Exit the highway at **Carrara** and take the winding drive up into the hills to the ancient village of **Colonnata**—famous through the ages for its marvelous white marble. As you wander this tiny town you're following the footsteps of **Michelangelo,** who used to come to Carrara to choose huge blocks of marble from which to carve his masterpieces.

Leaving Carrara return to the A12 and continue north for an entirely different kind of experience—exploring the five little isolated towns on the coast called **Cinque Terre**. This area is quickly becoming linked with civilization so do not tarry if you love the thrill of discovering old fishing villages still untouched by time. To begin this portion of your journey take the small road from Carrara west returning to the main highway and continuing on to the port of **La Spezia,** a large seaport and navy town. From here you might want to take the short drive to the tip of the peninsula south of La Spezia to visit the old fishing village of **Portoverere** that clings to the steep rocks rising from the sea. This was one of Lord Byron's haunts when he lived across the bay at **San Terenzo.** Return to La Spezia and continue north on S1 to Levanto.

We could not find any suitable places to stay in any of the villages dotting along the Cinque Terre so have chosen **Levanto,** as a hub for your explorations. Levanto, at one time a prosperous fishing port, lacks the luster of chic resorts, yet a faded, somewhat bedraggled charm remains. There are no luxury resorts here, just a smattering of simple places to stay. Our recommendation, **Hotel Stella Maris,** is a basic two star hotel, which like the town, harks back to past grandeur. The small hotel is found up a narrow staircase that leads to the second floor of a 17th-century palace, which in its hey day was a real show place with manicured gardens stretching to the sea. Remnants of the past can be seen in frescoed ceilings, paneled walls, and antique furnishings. Although this is not a hotel

Cinque Terre

for those who expect a decorator perfect ambiance, the genuine hospitality really grows on you. The charming Alexandro Italiani gladly helps you plan each day's excursion. His gracious, cheerful wife, Renza, has a hearty meal waiting at the end of each day's adventures.

Along the Cinque Terre there used to be five completely isolated fishing villages dotted along the coast between La Spezia to the south and Levanto to the north. First only a footpath connected these hamlets, then a train was installed, and now civilization is encroaching with a road under construction that will open them to greater commercialism. Three of these small villages, **Riomaggiore, Monterosso** and **Manorola,** are already accessible by road. Still completely cut off from car traffic are the fishing hamlets of **Vernazza** and **Corniglia.**

In Levanto you do not need to use your car. Instead, take a boat that connects the towns during the summer season. Or, you can walk to the station and hop aboard one of the many trains in the direction of La Spezia. Most of these make stops at the Cinque Terre villages enroute.

Let your mood, the time, and the weather dictate your explorations. You can hop on and off trains to investigate each town, take the small ferry between them, or hike the spectacular trails that thread the rocky coast connecting the villages. Best yet, combine all these options.

If you have time to see only one of the scenic towns, **Vernazza**, which clings perilously to a rocky promontory that steps down to a tiny harbor, is the most picturesque. This colorful jewel has brightly painted fishermen's houses, quaint restaurants, a harbor with small boats bobbing in the clear water, and a maze of twisting narrow steps that lead up to a promontory overlooking the village.

DESTINATION III   PORTOFINO

After Cinque Terre, continue north along the coast. Stop for lunch along the along the way in **Sestri Levante**, one of the most picturesque coastal villages enroute. Continue along the small coastal road that goes through **Chiàvari** and on to **San Margherita** where you take the small road south for the short drive to the picture book village of **Portofino**. This last section of the road, especially in summer, is jammed with traffic, but the plum at the end is worth the trials endured to reach it. Portofino is by no means undiscovered, but it is well-deserving of its accolades. Without a doubt it is one of the most colorful old fishing harbors in the world.

Before you reach Portofino, watch on your right for the sign for the **Hotel Splendido**. From the main road, a small lane winds up the wooded hillside to the magnificent villa-style hotel. Be prepared: the deluxe Splendido is a super expensive hotel whose prices include breakfast and dinner. But what a gorgeous setting. The hotel is perched in the hills above Portofino with breathtaking views of the sea and the harbor. A swimming pool and tennis courts nestle below the hotel and enchanting little paths thread their way through the gardens, offering strategically placed benches for quiet moments to savor the stunning view. It is an easy walk into Portofino if you can bear to leave this haven.

NOTE: If you are on a tight budget, the **Hotel Eden,** located in the heart of town, is recommended. This basic, twelve-room hotel is at the opposite end of the measure for ambiance and luxury, but has a great location and the warmth and caring of a family-owned small hotel.

Portofino

Portofino is a national treasure—it truly is a jewel. Her tiny harbor is filled with glamorous yachts, small ferries, and colorful fishing boats. In the center of town is a small square. Enveloping the harbor are narrow fishermen's cottages, poetically painted in warm tones of sienna, ochre, and pink and all sporting green shutters. Bright flower boxes accent the windows and the laundry flaps gaily in the breeze. Vivid reflections of these quaint little houses shimmer in the emerald water. Beyond the town the heavily forested, beautiful green hills rise steeply to complete this idyllic scene.

NOTE: While staying in Portofino, if you appreciate gourmet dining, drive south to one of Italy's finest restaurants, the **Ca'Peo**, located in **Chiavari a Leivi**. You must make prior reservations because Franco and his wife, Melly, only take guests who call ahead since the food is specially prepared depending upon how many will be dining: telephone (0185) 319090. The Ca'Peo, whose origins date back to a very old farmhouse, is located high in the hills overlooking the coast. Be forewarned, the meals are VERY expensive (although if you want to spend the night, there are moderately-priced suites available).

DESTINATION IV   MILAN

NOTE: For those of you traveling to the French Riviera, we wish you farewell in Portofino. From Portofino continue to follow the coastal highway west to Genoa along the Italian Riviera into the principality of Monaco and then across the border to France.

For the rest of *our group,* after leaving Portofino return to the A12 highway and continue west for about 30 kilometers to Genoa. As you circle the city, watch for the freeway A7 going north to Milan.

An interesting detour on the last leg of your journey is the **Pavia Carthusian Monastery** (*Certosa di Pavia*). Probably the simplest way to find it is to watch for the turnoff to **Pavia** (96 kilometers north of Genoa). At this point take the road east to Pavia and from there go north about 10 kilometers to the Pavia Carthusian Monastery. Lavishly built in the 15th Century, this splendid monastery is claimed by some to be one of the finest buildings in Italy. (Check carefully the days and hours open—the monastery is usually closed on Mondays and for several hours midday.) The outside of the monastery is lavishly designed with colorful marble and intricate designs. Inside, the small cloisters are especially charming with 122 arches framed by beautiful terra cotta moldings. There is also a baroque fountain within, plus several small gardens. Next to the monastery you find the **Palace of the Dukes of Milan** that is now a museum. After your tour of the monastery it is approximately 26 kilometers farther north to **Milan**.

The outskirts of Milan is not very inviting—frustrating traffic and modern commercial buildings. However, the heart of Milan has much to offer. If you enjoy shopping (and Milan has some of the finest in Italy), the splendid **Galleria Vittorio Emanuele**, is one of the prettiest shopping arcades in the world. Located between Milan's other two sightseeing stars, the Duomo and La Scala, the Galleria Vittoriio Emanuele is the forerunner of the modern shopping mall, but with much more pizzazz. Even if you are not a shopper, you must take time to browse. In this Victorian-era fantasy, there are two main, intersecting wings, both completely domed with intricately patterned glass. Along the pedestrian-only arcades, you find many boutiques and colorful restaurants with outside tables where everyone seems to stop for a cup of tea or an aperitif.

After a stroll through the arcade, you emerge into an imposing square dominated by the truly spectacular **Duomo**, the third largest cathedral in the world. Not only is the size impressive, but this sensational cathedral has a multi-colored marble facade enhanced by over 100 slender spires piercing the sky. This spectacular cathedral faces onto an enormous square that is lined with cafes, office buildings, and shops. Stop to have a snack at one of the outdoor restaurants—you could sit for hours just watching the people go by.

Also, a must to see is Milan's opera house. Every opera buff knows about **La Scala**. Even if you have not been an opera enthusiast in the past, if you are in Milan during the opera season (which usually runs from December to May) write ahead and try to get tickets. The theater is stunning and an experience not to be missed. When it is not opera season, there is usually some other performance or concert featured. If you haven't purchased seats in advance, you can try to buy them the day of the performance (the ticket office is located down a flight of stairs to the left of the opera house).

Milan does not offer a wealth of charming places to stay: most are modern, commercial hotels, seemingly way over-priced, with minimal old world appeal. Happily (if your budget can handle a deluxe hotel) there is an exception, the intimate, expertly managed, **Hotel Pierre Milan**, which abounds in antiques and charm.

La Scala, Milan

Rome to Milan via the Italian Riviera

Highlights of
Southern Italy

ROME

Anzio
Nettuno

Abbey of
Monte Cassino

Trani

Castel del Monte

Bari

Monopoli

Alberobello

to Corfu·Greece

Naples

Salerno

Pompei

Matera

Sorrento

Capri

Positano

Ravello

Paestum

Acquafredda

Potenza

Brindisi

Taranto

Maratea

Sibari

● Overnight stops
∗ Suggested alternate hotels
○ Sightseeing
━━━ Itinerary route
······ Suggested sidetrips

Tropea

Messina

PALERMO

Erice

Trapani

Marsala

Cefalu

Gangvecchio

Villa San Giovanni

Taormina

Enna

Catania

Selinunte

Agrigento

Piazza
Armerina

Syracuse

Rome

Highlights of Southern Italy

Amalfi Coast

Having visited the famous trio of Rome, Florence, and Venice, most tourists think that they have *seen* Italy. Childhood geography lessons call forth such names as Pompeii, Herculaneum and Paestum. Yet, all too frequently the urge to visit these jewels of archaeological wonders is lost in the misconception that southern Italy is an uninteresting destination. What a mistake. Southern Italy has fascinating ruins, gorgeous coastlines, beautiful medieval walled villages, lovely beaches, marvelous hilltowns, and some of the most unusual sights in Italy. So see the south of Italy. Return home and casually mention to your dinner partner that you think the Emerald Grotto on the Amalfi Coast rivals the Blue Grotto of Capri, or that the Greek ruins of Paestum outshine many found in Greece, or that you are still haunted by the mysterious town of Alberobello.

Therefore, for those of you who have already seen the fantastic highlights of Northern Italy, we take pleasure in presenting to you the best of Southern Italy. This itinerary makes a circle of Southern Italy in order to suit the travel needs of a wide selection of tourists. Follow the entire route or select the portion best for you since this itinerary lends itself especially well for the traveler who wants to take only a segment. As an example, the journey from Rome to Brindisi is a popular one for the lucky tourist on their way to Greece. Or the west coast is a popular drive for the tourist who wants to visit Sicily and then return to Rome by air or ferry. Most popular of all is the segment from Rome to the Amalfi Drive. This itinerary allows you to custom tailor your journey and gives you tantalizing sightseeing along the way.

ORIGINATING CITY   ROME

Rome is a most convenient starting point to begin a tour of southern Italy. Rome Airport is the destination of planes from all over the world and here passengers begin their *Roman Holiday*. In Rome you can immerse yourself in a wealth of history, art, architecture, museums, and monuments—and build a foundation for the sights that will be encountered on your journey southward. See pages 39-44 for suggestions of what to see and do in Rome.

There is a wide selection of accommodations in Rome in various price categories and locations. Choose the hotel that best suits your personality and budget from the Hotel Description Section in the back of this guide. You will find that Rome has many excellent hotels and, even though the city is large, most of the hotels are still within walking distance of both shopping and sightseeing highlights. If you do not like to walk, ask the concierge at your desk to call you a taxi or direct you to the nearest subway station. (Rome's main subway line stretches across the city—conveniently connecting most of the places of interest for the tourist.)

When leaving the city by car, bear in mind that Rome always has a monumental traffic problem. Within the city look for strategically placed signs that indicate that there is an expressway ahead. It might be quite a distance, but be patient as these signs lead you to the outskirts of Rome to the highway that makes a ring around the city with various spokes going off to different destinations. Follow the ring and take the exit for the A2, the expressway heading south toward Naples. Continue south for approximately 128 kilometers to the exit for **Cassino**. Actually you can spot your destination from several kilometers away. The **Abbey of Monte Cassino** crowns the top of a large mountain to the left of the highway as you drive south. When you reach Cassino, turn off the expressway. The road that winds up to the summit of the mountain to the Abbey of Monte Cassino is clearly marked about midway through Cassino. This abbey, founded by St Benedict in 529 AD, is extremely interesting both religiously and historically. For war historians the abbey brings back many battle memories—this is where the Germans staunchly held out against the Allied forces for almost a year in World War II. When the mountain was finally conquered in May 1944, it opened the way for Allied forces to finally move into Rome. As you read your history books it seems strange that one fort could hold out for so long, but when you see the abbey you understand. It is an enormous building on the crest of a precipitous mountain. In the siege the abbey was almost destroyed but it has been rebuilt according to the original plans.

NOTE: For those of you who for sentimental or historical reasons are especially interested in World War II, there is another destination you might well want to visit in this day's journey. **Anzio** is a town on the coast about 56 kilometers south of Rome and could easily be included as a stop before Cassino. It was at Anzio that the British and the Americans landed in January 1944. The emotional reminder of this terrible battle is a few kilometers south at **Nettuno** where 8,000 white crosses and stars of David range— row after row across the green lawn. There is a circular drive around the beautifully manicured, park-like grounds where you also find a memorial chapel and small war museum. For those who lost family or friends during the invasion, there is an information office to the right as you drive in. You can stop here to find out exactly where your loved ones are buried—you will need help because the park is huge.

From Cassino return to the expressway and continue south for about 60 kilometers until you see the sign for Pompeii. Unless you have absolutely NO interest in archaeology you must see the city of your childhood geography books. This is where time was frozen in the year 79 AD for the 25,000 people who were smothered by ashes from the eruption of **Vesuvius**. If you are a dedicated student of archaeology you must also visit the **National Archaeological Museum** in **Naples** where many of the artifacts from Pompeii are housed.

Time slips eerily back 2,000 years as you wander the streets of **Pompeii** and visit the temples, lovely homes, wine shops, bakery, and public baths. There is probably no other place on earth where you can feel so strongly the pulse of ancient days. Many of the private homes have been reconstructed so you can marvel at the lovely inner courtyards, beautiful dining rooms in Pompeii-red with intricate paintings on the walls, fountains, servants' quarters, bath rooms, and gardens. At the entrance to Pompeii there are souvenir stands where you can purchase a guide book to the city, or, if you prefer, you can hire a private guide at the entrance. Pompeii is so fascinating that you might well want to come back to spend a complete day visiting the city and the nearby ruins of **Herculaneum** that are also very interesting.

Leaving Pompeii, head to the coast in the direction of Sorrento where the **Amalfi Drive**, tracing one of the most beautiful stretches of coast in the world, begins. Be sure to time your journey when there is sufficient daylight because you want to be sure to glimpse every magnificent vista as well as safely negotiate this extremely twisty and precipitous road.

There are many excellent choices for hotels along the Amalfi Drive. Concentrated in just a few kilometers are some of the most splendid hotels in all of Italy.

It is hard to recommend our favorite place along the Amalfi Coast since each is has its own personality: **Sorrento** is convenient for side trips to Capri, Ischia and Naples. **Ravello** is a tiny village perched in the clouds with absolutely dazzling views. **Positano** is a village with white-washed houses terraced down a steep enbankment to an ancient fishing cove. Study the various hotel choices in Sorrento, Positano, and Ravello in the Hotel Description Section to see what most appeals to you.

From whatever hub you choose as your hotel base, venture out to do some exploring. The traffic during the tourist season is staggering with buses and trucks and cars all jockeying for position on the narrow twisting roads. Prepare for much shouting, waving of hands, honking, and general bedlam as long buses inch around the hairpin curves. The best advice is to relax and consider the colorful scene as part of the sightseeing. Also, begin your excursions as early in the day as possible to try to avoid the major traffic jams.

If you are not overnighting in **Ravello**, you must plan to take the narrow winding road up to this romantic cliff-top town. When you arrive, leave your car in one of the designated parking areas and stroll through the village. Pick up a map at the tourist office. Then walk along the well-marked path to the **Villa Rufolo** and/or the **Villa Cimbrone**—both have enchanting views of the Bay of Salerno.

If you are not over-nighting in **Positano**, by all means make this a day's excursion. The town is a photographer's dream—houses painted a dazzling white step down the impossibly steep hillside to a pebble beach, lapped by brilliant blue water.

Positano

Positano is laced by staircases, the only way to reach the small plaza dominated by a church with a colorful mosaic tiled dome. Today Positano attracts artists and tourists from around the world, but in the 16th and 17th Centuries it was an important sea port with tall-masted ships bringing in wares from around the world. When steamships came into vogue in the 19th Century, Positano's prosperity declined and three-fourths of its population emigrated to the United States.

If you have not been able to include an interlude on **Capri** during your Italian holiday it is easy to arrange an excursion to this enchanted island as a side-trip from the Amalfi Coast. Steamers and hydrofoils depart regularly from Sorrento, Amalfi, and Positano. Ask at the tourist bureau or at your hotel for the schedule. (When the seas are rough it is more difficult to leave from Positano since there is no pier, making it necessary to take a small boat from the shore to the ferry.) *NOTE:* If you have the leisure of time, you could leave your car in Sorrento and spend several nights on Capri. See pages 46-48 for further information on what to see and do on Capri.

While exploring the Amalfi Coast, visit the **Emerald Grotto**, located between the towns of Amalfi and Positano. After parking, buy a ticket and descend by elevator down the steep cliff to a small rocky terrace. Upon entering the water-filled cave, you're rowed about the grotto in a small boat. Your guide explains how the effect of shimmering green water is created by a secret tunnel allowing sunlight to filter from deep below the surface. The cave is filled with colorful stalactites and stalagmites that further enhance the mysterious mood. There is also a nativity scene below the water that magically appears and then drifts again from view.

DESTINATION II — GULF OF POLICASTRO–MARATEA

When it is time to leave the Amalfi area, take the coastal road south as it twists and turns along the dramatic cliffs toward Salerno. At Salerno, join the expressway A3 for about 19 kilometers until the turnoff for **Paestum** that is located on a side road about a half-hour drive from the freeway. Magically, when you enter the gates of the ancient city you enter a peaceful environment of a lovely country meadow dotted with some of the world's best preserved Greek temples. As you walk the remains of the streets criss-crossing the city, your senses are thrilled by the sound of birds singing and the scent of roses. (Before leaving Paestum, stop for a snack at the **Marini Sea Garden**, a former villa set in a garden whose gates open onto the west side of the excavation.)

From Paestum return to the A3 and continue south until you come to the Lagonegro Nord-Maratea exit. Do not be tempted by some of the short cuts you see on the map that lead to the coast, but stay on the main road 585. In about 25 kilometers the road comes to the sea where you turn north at Castrocucco, following signs to **Maratea**.

We have three hotel choices in this area, each lovely, each with its special merits. **La Locanda delle Donne Monache,** housed in an 18th-century convent, is snuggled in the hills above the quaint town of Maratea. The **Hotel Santavenere** has a prime location hugging high cliffs that drop down to the sea. The **Villa Cheta Elite**, located a short drive north of Maratea in **Acquafredda**, is a moderately-priced hotel whose gracious owners welcome guest as friends.

Maratea, Gulf of Policastro

If possible, spend several days in Maratea. Not well know to tourists, this lovely section of coast (called the **Gulf of Policastro**) is a popular resort area for Italians. The loveliest section of the road is between Maratea and Sapri where the road traces the sea along a high corniche, providing lovely vistas of small coves and rocky promontories. This is not an area for intensive sightseeing, rather a quiet interlude for several days to relax.

From the Gulf of Policastro, take road 585 back to the A3 and continue south for about 75 kilometers and turn east at Frascineto/Castrovillari toward the instep of Italy's boot. After about 25 kilometers you near the coast. Here you turn left on 106 to Taranto. Stop to see the ancient port of **Taranto** that is connected by a bridge to the modern city of Taranto. Even if you are not interested in ancient history it is fun to see the Italian naval ships—giant gray monsters sitting in the protected harbor. From Taranto, take 172 north and continue on for about 45 kilometers following signs to Alberobello. If you are staying in **Alberobello**, follow signs to the **Hotel dei Trulli** in the trulli district of town. If your chosen destination is **Monopoli**, do not go into town. Instead, turn right and follow the ring road around Alberobello watching for the road signs to Monopoli, which is 23 kilometers further. You arrive at **Il Melograno** before reaching Monopoli. Coming from Alberobello, turn left on a small road just before the four-lane road that by-passes Monopoli. The hotel is a bit tricky to find. When making your reservation, ask for detailed directions.

You are now in the province of **Apulia**. Not a well-known destination, but all the more fun to visit because it is off the beaten path. With either Monopoli or Alberobello as your hub, venture out to explore the fascinating sights in the area. Some suggestions are listed below.

Trulli District: Trulli houses (whose origins date back to at least the 13th Century) are some of the strangest structures in Italy—circular stone buildings, usually built in small clusters, standing crisply white with conical slate roofs and whimsical twisted chimneys. Outside ladders frequently lead to upper stories. Often several of these houses are joined together to form a larger complex. The houses are intertwined with cobbled streets. What a strange and fascinating sight. These bee-hive-like little houses form a jumble of a small village that looks as though it should be inhabited by elves instead of *real* people. The heart of the trulli region is **Alberobello** where there are so many trulli houses (more than 1,000 along the narrow streets) that the trulli district of town has been named a national monument.

Trulli Houses, Alberobello

The trulli houses are not confined to the town of Alberobello although this is where you find them composing an entire village. In fact, the trulli houses you see in the vicinity of Alberobello are sometimes more interesting than those in the town itself. As you drive along the small roads, you spot gorgeous villas cleverly converted from trulli houses that are now obviously the homes of wealthy Italians. Others are now farmhouses with goats munching their lunch in the front yard. Occasionally you spot a charming old trulli home cozily nestled in the center of a vineyard. But most fun of all are the trulli homes of the free spirits. Their homes, instead of displaying the typical white exteriors, have been painted a brilliant yellow or pink or bright green with contrasting shutters.

Grotte di Castellana: As you are exploring the countryside near Alberobello, take the short drive north to see Castellana Caves—the largest in Italy. In a two-hour tour you see many rooms of richly colored stalagmites and stalactites.

Coastal Villages: Be sure to include in your sightseeing some of the characterful towns along the coast. They look entirely different than the colorful fishing villages in the north of Italy. These are Moorish-looking with stark white houses lining narrow, alley-like streets. The Adriatic looks even deeper blue as laps against the white buildings, many of which rise from the sea with small windows perched over the water. Some of the coastal towns to see are **Monopoli, Polignano a Mare,** and **Trani**.

Castel del Monte

Castel del Monte: On a the same day that you explore the coastal villages, include a visit to the 13th-century Castel del Monte. Built by Emperor Frederick II of Swab, it is somewhat of a mystery, having none of the fortifications usually associated with a medieval castle. Nevertheless, it is dramatic—a huge pastel stone structure crowning the top of a hill with eight circular towers that stretch 24 meters into the sky. There are stunning views in every direction. (Check with the tourist office before you go, the castle is not open every day of the week.)

When it is time to leave Apulia, you can breeze back to Rome by an expressway. Or, if your next destination is **Greece**, it is just a short drive to **Brindisi** where you can board the ferry for Corfu, Igoumenitsa or Patras. Best of all, if you can extend your holiday in Italy, join the following itinerary *Exploring the Wonders of Sicily.*

Exploring the
Wonders of Sicily

Overnight stops
Suggested alternate hotels
Sightseeing
Itinerary route
Suggested sidetrips
Archaeological sites

Exploring the Wonders of Sicily

Greek Theater, Taormina

Sicily, the largest island in the Mediterranean, is a wondrous destination. This triangular hunk of land jutting out from the tip of Italy's toe became the cross roads of the ancient world. Nowhere in your travels can you discover a more diverse archaeological treasure trove. Stone Age tools and figures carved in the rocks in the Grotta di Addaura at Monte Pellegrino indicate people were living in Sicily during the Palaeolithic Age. About 1270 BC the island was invaded by a Mediterranean tribe called Siculians. But they were not alone. Excavations show that tribes from Asia also settled here. Beginning in the 10th Century BC, pioneering Phoenicians took a fancy to this fertile land, followed later by their descendants, the Carthaginians. However, the true dawn of Sicily's reign of glory began with the colonization by the Greeks. Their enormous influence permeates Sicily today. The rich fabric of Sicily's heritage though does not end with the Greek influence. Later the Romans invaded. Then the Normans. Then the Spanish. And on and on. The result of this melting pot of cultures, makes Sicily an absolute MUST for those who delight in the romance of archaeology. The true magic of Sicily is that most of the ruins are so natural in their setting. Frequently you discover you are alone—the only tourist walking through a field of wildflowers to gaze in awe at an exquisite temple.

As mentioned, the greatest age of glory for Sicily began when the Greeks founded their first colony here about 770 BC. Apparently these early Greeks left their native country for economic and political reasons. Also, many were undoubtedly motivated by pure curiosity—the desire to discover what awaited across the sea. Like the immigrants who came to America, the early settlers wanted a fresh start in a new land and an opportunity to establish a better life for themselves. And they did. Prospering enormously from the richness of the fertile soil, the early Greeks became extremely wealthy. As the *nouveau riche* tend to do, they flaunted their success, building great cities, elaborate houses, theaters, spas, and stadiums—all *bigger and better* than those they left at home. Syracuse, the mightiest city in Sicily, eventually became more powerful than Athens. The temples they built surpassed in size and splendor those left in their native land. Not losing their passion for sports, every four years the new colonies sent their finest athletes back to Greece where they dominated the Olympic games.

ORIGINATING CITY TAORMINA

Exploring the Wonders of Sicily makes a natural extension from the previous driving tour, *Highlights of Southern Italy*. After ending that itinerary, drive to the tip of Italy's toe and take one of the ferries that cross the narrow channel twice an hour from **Villa San Giovanni** to **Messina**, Sicily. After buying your ticket, go to the indicated lane and wait with all the trucks, campers and other cars for the signal to drive onto the boat.

When on board, you may leave your car and go upstairs to the lounge area where snacks can be purchased while traversing the short channel. In thirty-five minutes, the large ferry draws up to the pier in Messina and you drive off to begin your adventures.

If you prefer to fly to Sicily, just reverse this itinerary. Start in Palermo and finish in Taormina. Alternately, you can take a ferry from Naples to Palermo (a ten-hour journey).

Taormina makes an ideal starting point for your introduction to Sicily. Whereas good hotels are scarce in most of Sicily, there are many to choose from in Taormina. Three that we especially recommend are: the luxury-category **San Domenico Palace** (a museum-quality 15th-century monastery that has been converted into a stunning hotel), the moderately-priced **Hotel Belvedere** (combining the charm of a family-run hotel with a stunning location overlooking the sea), and the budget-category **Villa Fiorita** (once a private villa, now a small hotel with rooms terraced up the steep hillside). Read about each in the Hotel Description Section to make your choice.

Picture-perfect **Taormina**, with the dramatic peak of **Mont Etna** as a backdrop, hugs the crest of a small peninsula that juts out to the sea. Steep cliffs drop to the coast below, washed by the unbelievably blue sea. Quaint streets wind through the colorful town where you can browse in the many smart boutiques, sip a cappuccino at a small cafe, or simply enjoy the incredible view. The scent of oranges is in the air and brilliantly-colored bougainvillea laces the medieval buildings.

But it is not just the natural beauty of its spectacular setting that makes Taormina so popular. Like all of Sicily, your leisure pleasure is enhanced with fabulous sights to see. The prime archaeological target for your sightseeing is the **Greek Theater**. From the center of town an easy walk up Via Teatro Greco takes you to a magnificent theater dug into the sloping hillside above the town. Built by the Greeks in the 3rd Century BC, the open-air amphitheater has only a token few of its original columns remaining, making the effect even more romantic. As you gaze beyond the rows of seats to the stage below and out to the vivid blue sea beyond, you will think there is no prettier picture in all of Italy.

After visiting the Greek Theater, most of the remainder of your sightseeing can be done informally while strolling through town. First pick up a map and general information at the tourist office located in the **Palazzo Corvaia,** a 15th-century palace located on the Piazza Vitt. Emanuele. From the Palazzo Crovaia, continue through town and stop the 17th-century **St Giuseppe Church** in Piazza Nove Aprile. As you walk on, be sure to step inside the 13th-century **Cathedral** in the Piazza del Duomo to enjoy the paintings. Further into the village you come to the 12th-century **Torre dell'Orologio,** the portal that leads into the oldest and most colorful part of Taormina, **Borgo Medieval.**

DESTINATION I   AGRIGENTO

When it is time to leave Taormina, follow the A18 south toward Catania. When you reach Catania, take the A19 west in the direction of Palermo. When the highway splits (not long after passing Enna), instead of continuing north to Palermo, head southwest in the direction of Caltanissetta and Agrigento. After Caltanissetta, the expressway ends and you are on a two-lane road for the final leg of your journey to Agrigento.

Along the route from Palermo to Agrigento, we recommend two side excursions. It would make your day too long to include them both. However, if you get an early start, you can squeeze in enough time for one of the following suggestions.

Suggested Side Excursion: If you are a Greek history buff, take this 128 kilometer detour to see one of the wealthiest, most powerful cities of the ancient Greek Empire (rivaling only Athens in importance). When you reach Catania, don't turn west toward Palermo, but continue south, following signs to **Syracuse,** founded in 734 BC by the Corinthians. In the **Archaeological Park** at the edge of town are two theaters—a 6th-century BC **Greek Theater** (one of the most magnificently preserved in the world) and the ruins of a

2nd-century AD **Roman Amphitheater** (one of the largest arenas the Romans ever built). From the Archaeological Park, skip the sprawling modern city and cross the Ponte Nuovo that spans Syracuse's harbor to **Ortygia,** the island where the Greeks first founded Syracuse. Visit the two main squares, the beautiful **Piazza del Duomo** where the Cathedral (built upon the ancient temple of Minerva) is located and the **Piazza Archimede** enhanced by a Baroque fountain. After sightseeing in Syracuse, return to Catania and take A19 west in the direction of Palermo.

Suggested Side Excursion: If you are a Roman history buff, take this 74 kilometer round trip excursion to visit the **Villa of Casale.** Enroute from Taormina to Agrigento on the A19, turn south at Enna to Piazza Armerina. Continue southwest beyond Piazza Armerina for 5 kilometers to your sightseeing target, Villa of Casale, rivaling in splendor the home built by Tiberius on the island of Capri. The foundations of this sumptuous Roman villa that were hidden under a blanket of mud for 700 years—not discovered by archaeologists until 1950. The fact that this ostentatious villa was built when the Roman Empire was on the verge of financial ruin is all the more fascinating. You cannot help but wonder if the obviously vast expense of its construction was indicative of the flamboyant spending style that led to the collapse of the Roman Empire. Built in the 3rd Century AD, this mansion surely must have belonged to someone of great importance— perhaps Emperor Maximilian. What remains is the outline of an enormous, summer home complex, with various buildings cut into the levels of the hillside, joined by passageways and courtyards. In all, the home covers an area almost three times the size of a football field. The outstanding feature are the 3,500 square meters of mosaics that decorated the floors of this sumptuous villa. Following the home's foundations are forty mosaic floors of extraordinary quality, sheltered by a clear protective cover. These beautifully-preserved ancient Roman mosaics are considered the finest in the world. Slip back almost 1,700 years and imagine what life must have been like. The scenes show hunting expeditions, wild animals, mythical sea creatures, chariot races, cupids fishing, slaves working, girls cavorting. Once you have visited this Roman show place, return north to Enna. Then turn west following the route to Agrigento.

Thankfully your hotel is not in the center of Agrigento, which is a congested, not very pretty city. Instead, follow the signs for the Valle dei Templi. This is the archaeological zone where both your sightseeing and hotel are located. The name is misleading. The site is actually on a plateau to the west of town—not in a valley at all. Go directly to your hotel, the **Villa Athena,** and get settled. The Villa Athena has a somewhat commercial ambiance. Buses will probably be parked outside since (due to its convenient location in

the heart of the archaeological zone) this is a favorite luncheon stop for small tour groups. But, although not an intimate hotel, the management is friendly and the setting incomparable. In Agrigento, the Villa Athena is definitely THE place to stay. Ask for a room with a view of the archeological zone. These cost a bit more, but are worth it. To wake up in the morning and look across at the sun rising on the Temple of Concordia is certainly the way to begin your day of sightseeing.

Plan to spend two nights in Agrigento so that you can spend one entire day leisurely seeing the ruins. From the gardens of the Villa Athena, walk down a foot path directly to the area where the

temples are located. A wide pedestrian road connects the temples. Start at one end and see them all. Most of these Doric temples are in ruins with only enough columns remaining to give you an idea of what they used to be in their glory. The best preserved is the Temple of Concordia that dates back to 440 BC. See them all: the **Temple of Juno,** the **Temple of Concordia,** the **Temple of Hercules,** the **Temple of Dioscuri,** the

Temple of Jupiter, and the Temple of Castor and Pollux. The setting is beautiful with the sea in the distance and wild flowers in the surrounding fields. It is a thrill to stroll from one temple to the other, marveling at their grandeur and trying to envision what these incredible structures dedicated to Greek gods looked like two thousand years ago.

To compliment your sightseeing at the temples, walk to the **Archaeological Museum** (take the same path as to the temples, but go in the opposite direction). The museum has a mock up of the Temple of Jupiter, plus many vases and artifacts from the site.

DESTINATION II   ERICE

From Agrigento, continue west on 115 toward Castelvetrano. About 10 kilometers before you arrive in Castelvetrano, turn left on the 115 dir toward the coast, signposted to Selinunte. For such major ruins, there is little commercialism. You might well miss the main east entrance that is on the 115 dir. As you drive toward the coast, look for a parking area to the right of the road (if you go under the railroad tracks, you have gone too far).

Park your car in the designated area, buy your ticket and walk through the tunnel into the enormous field where the remains of the temples of Selinunte lie scattered amongst the wildflowers. In its prime, **Selinunte** was one of the finest cities in Sicily. It met disaster in 407 BC when the Carthaginians (it is thought the siege took place under the command of Hannibal) razed the city, slaughtered 16,000 people, and took thousands into slavery. The giant temples, however, were probably destroyed by earthquake—not by the sword. Here, spread along a huge plateau overlooking the ocean, are the impressive remains of some of the most gigantic temples built by the Greeks. It is staggering to imagine how more than 2,500 years ago, they had the skill and technology to lift and piece together these huge blocks of stone weighing over 100 tons each (slaves undoubtedly helped). Of the original seven temples, only one has had been reconstructed, but the massive columns lying on the ground indicate the scope and grandeur of what used to be.

From Selinunte, return to the A 115, taking the coastal route to Erice. Stop for lunch at one of the restaurants along the sea-front promenade in **Mazara del Vallo**, an ancient city that was at one time a colony of Selinunte. Browse through the historical center to see the beautiful **Piazza della Repubblica** and the **Cathedral**.

The next large town after Mazara del Vallo is **Marsala**, a large city well-known throughout the world over for its excellent wine. Ironically, it was not an Italian, but an Englishman named John Woodhouse who experimented by lacing the native wine with a bit of alcohol.

Based on Woodhouse's formula, *Marsala* quickly became one of the staples of the British Navy and a special favorite of Lord Nelson. Along the road between **Selinunte** and **Marsala** are various wineries that are open to the public. One, of the most popular is the **Florio Winery**—one of the three original companies to produce *Marsala*.

From Marsala, the road heads north to Trapani. Bypass Trapani and head northeast to **Erice**. Positioned over 750 meters above the coast (about 10 kilometers from Trapani), Erice is a delightful medieval walled town, cooled by breezes from the sea. Park your car and walk through the **Porta Trapani** and up the cobbled street. A few blocks on your right is the **Moderno**, a friendly, well-run small hotel. There are no deluxe hotels in Erice. The Moderno is simple, but very pleasant, and well-located in the heart of town, close to restaurants and shopping.

Erice is best discovered by exploring on foot. Narrow cobbled streets and steep stairways form a maze throughout the town. The town is so small that you cannot get lost for long. Just wander, discovering tiny churches, picturesque squares, characterful houses stone houses, arcaded passageways, and shops selling the locally-produced hand-made carpets with colorful geometric designs. Walk to the **Castello Normanno**, built upon the ruins of the Temple of Venus. From the tower you have a splendid view over Trapani and out to the sea.

Erice, Sicily

If you like to get off-the-beaten path, from Erice drive down to Trapani and take a hydrofoil to the **Egadi Isles**, all within an hour by boat from Trapani. Just a short distance off-shore, the largest of the three islands, **Favignana**, was once a great center for tuna. The major cannery was owned by Ignazio Florio (the same Florio who founded the Florio Winery). **Levanzo**, the smallest of the islands, has a very small population due to its lack of fresh water. The furthest island from Trapani, **Maréttimo**, is basically a fisherman's island.

Erice also makes a convenient base for an excursion to visit **Segesta**. Wind down the hill from Erice and

Exploring the Wonders of Sicily

turn left on the A29 going east in the direction of Palermo. Thirty kilometers after getting on the freeway, take the Segesta Exit and follow signs for the Segesta archaeological site, located close the highway. Although you have seen many ruins by this stage of your holiday in Sicily, don't miss this one. It is special. First drive to the designated parking area and walk up the hillside to visit what most experts believe to be the world's finest example of a Doric Greek temple. The temple with 36 columns looks much as it must have in 400 BC. There is no roof—there never was because this isolated temple to some unknown God was never completed. One of the most superb aspects of this temple is its setting—there is nothing to jar the senses. The temple stands alone in a field of wildflowers with great natural beauty all around. Leisurely enjoy the romance of this gem, then drive down the hill and park your car by the information center where there is a nice restaurant. Eat lunch here and then walk the marked path to see the **Greek Theater**. It is about a kilometer away, but a lovely walk through untouched fields. There are so few signs you'll wonder if you are going the right way and be tempted to verify your destination with a fellow tourist you pass enroute. Again, the location is what makes this theater so special. What an eye the Greeks had for beauty. The stage is set in such a way that the spectators look out across the mountains to the sea. The theater is mostly in ruins, but sit in one of the ancient benches and enjoy the beautiful surroundings and imagine dramas that took place over two thousand years ago.

DESTINATION III   PALERMO

Palermo is a large, rather dismal, traffic-congested city. However, there are several places of interest to see in the area. Happily, as a saving grace, Palermo has an excellent place to stay, the deluxe **Villa Igiea Grand Hotel**. Located on the edge of the sea, on the west edge of town, the Villa Igiea Grand Hotel is expensive, but a welcome oasis of peace and quiet. It has a swimming pool on the bluffs above the sea and even has its own small ancient temple in the garden. *NOTE:* If you want to skip over-nighting in Palermo, the following sightseeing suggestions could also be accomplished from Erice.

The most dramatic sightseeing excursion (just 8 kilometers south of Palermo) is to visit **Monreale,** an awesome cathedral built by William II in 1174. It seems that William II was visited in a dream by an angel who told him of a secret treasure. How convenient. With his new found wealth, he built Monreale, one of the world's greatest medieval monuments. From the outside, the cathedral doesn't look special. But just wait. The interior is stunning. When you step inside, there are 130 panels of shimmering mosaic, illustrating stories from both the Old and the New Testaments. The bronze doors of the cathedral are spectacular, designed by Bonanno Pisano in the 12th Century.

Another sight near Palermo is **Monte Pellegrino**, a 600 meter mountain rising on the west edge side of the city. There are several caves in the mountain. The **Grotta di Addaura** is a three-chamber cave with carvings dating to the Palaeolithic Age. (You need to obtain permission from the National Archaeological Museum in Palermo if you want to visit these caves.) Another cave in the mountain has been transformed into a chapel, The **Sanctuary of Santa Rosalia** commemorating Santa Rosalia, the niece of King William II, who became a hermit—living and dying in this cave.

Another recommended side trip from Palermo is to visit the ancient fishing village of **Cefalù** built on a rocky peninsula about an hour's drive east from Palermo. Not only is this a very colorful fishing village, complete with brightly hued boats and twisting narrow streets, but there is also a splendid Norman **Cathedral** built by King Roger II in the 12th Century in fulfillment of a promise he made to God for sparing his life during a storm at sea.

When you are ready to leave Palermo there are several choices. You can take one of the many flights from Palermo to Rome, board a ferry to Naples, or complete your circle of Sicily by driving to Messina for the short ferry ride back to the mainland.

HOTEL DESCRIPTION SECTION

There is a fascinating section in southeastern Italy with a collection of strange round white buildings with gray stone conical shaped roofs. These ancient houses seem to be left over from some Moorish tribe that must have inhabited this part of Italy long ago. These houses are called *trulli* and are usually seen in groups of two or three. In the town of Alberobello there is actually a whole village of the conical little houses whose jumble of domed roofs, whitewashed walls, and crooked little chimneys create a most unusual sight. Fortunately there is a good hotel in the area that is located within walking distance of the *trulli* village. Not only is its location excellent, but the hotel captures the mood of the area since it is constructed within some of the *trulli* houses. Small bungalows are scattered around a large park-like area connected by winding pathways under the pine trees. Each bungalow is actually a suite with a living room with fireplace, one or more bedrooms, and a private patio. The recently renovated suites are spacious with attractively tiled bathrooms. The dining rooms and the reception area each occupy their own *trulli*. Within the grounds are a pool and children's play yard. If you are on your way to Greece, you will find the Hotel dei Trulli a convenient choice: very close to Brindisi and Bari, the two major ferry ports.

HOTEL DEI TRULLI
Manager: Luigi Farace
Via Cadore, 28
70011 Alberobello (BA), Italy
tel: (080) 93 23 555, fax: (080) 93 23 560
28 rooms: Double Lire 340,000*
*Rate includes breakfast and dinner
Open all year
Credit cards: all major
Restaurant open daily
68 km NW of Brindisi, 55 km SW of Bari

If you've ever dreamed of waking up in an Italian villa where you could open your bedroom windows to one of the world's most romantic views, then the Albergo Belvedere will surely capture your heart. This lovely 18th-century villa (with its mustard-yellow façade, crisp-white trim, and dove gray shutters) has a superb setting. Only a private terrace separates it from Lake Como. And amazingly, this intimate inn is an incredible value. But, do not expect a luxury hotel. The dated furnishings are simple. The guest rooms have no satellite TVs, direct dial phones, hair dryers or mini-bars. What you get is much more: an incomparable setting, genuine warmth of hospitality, and old-fashioned comfort enhanced by immaculate house-keeping. An added bonus is the outstanding food. Giorgio Cappelletti oversees the kitchen. Again, not fancy gourmet dishes, just simple, home cooking in the best Italian tradition. There is no menu. Your selection each evening is based upon what is the catch of the day and what produce is in season. Jane Cappelletti (born in Scotland) met and fell in love with Giorgio when visiting in Italy. Her friendliness and Scottish eye for a tidy house, are great assets. Steamers and hydrofoils depart from the dock just steps from the hotel, but you just might never want to leave the terrace with its view of the ever-so-blue lake, backdropped by magical green mountains that shelter clusters of romantic villages. Splurge and ask for a view of the lake. Rooms 7 and 15 are especially inviting.

ALBERGO BELVEDERE
Owners: Jane and Giorgio Cappelletti
Via Milano 8
22010 Argegno, Lake Como (CO), Italy
tel: (031) 82 11 16, fax: (031) 82 15 71
18 rooms: Double Lire 100,000-120,00O
Open mid-March to mid-November
Credit cards: EC, MC, VS
Restaurant open daily
On E shore of Lake Como
70 km N of Milan

As the road twists and turns ever further into the wooded hills above Assisi, one can't help wondering what treasure could await at the trail's end, or, if anyone could possibly have found it before you. What a surprise then to finally turn off the graveled road and discover the parking lot filled with luxury cars. In this secluded hillside setting with a sweeping panorama of wooded hills, worldly cares quickly slip away. Although the hotel is built into a cluster of ancient stone houses (dating back to the 10th Century), all the modern day luxuries are present including a beautiful swimming pool on the right as you enter and, on a lower terrace, tennis courts. Behind the main building is a separate stone house where you find a most appealing lounge with deep green sofas and chairs grouped around a giant fireplace. Doors from the lounge lead into an intimate little bar and beyond to a dining room with honey-colored stone walls, beamed ceiling, and terra cotta floors with tables dressed in the finest of linens. The individually decorated bedrooms sport a rustic, yet elegant, ambiance. The well-equipped bathrooms offer enormous towels, fragrant soaps, hair dryers, and bathrobes. *NOTE:* Le Silve di Armenzano is not in the town of Assisi. To find the hotel, follow the signs from Assisi toward Gualdo-Tadino and immediately as you leave the town-walls of Assisi, watch for and take the road to the right sign-posted Armenzano. When you reach Armenzano, the hotel is well-marked.

ROMANTIK HOTEL "LE SILVE DI ARMENZANO"
Manager: Daniela Taddia
06081 Località Armenzano, Assisi (PG), Italy
tel: (075) 80 19 000, fax: (075) 80 19 005
15 rooms: Double Lire 260,000-420,000
Closed January and February
Credit cards: all major
Restaurant open daily
Located 15 km E of Assisi
U.S.A. Rep: Euro-Connection 800-645-3876

The Villa Cipriani is just as I had envisioned in every dream of Italy: an old villa snuggled on a hill, her softly faded exterior emphasized by dark green shutters, masses of roses creeping over trellises, columns adorned with vines, lazy views over rolling green hills, faded ocher-colored walls half hidden by tall cypress trees dotting nearby hilltops, birds singing in the garden, the sentimental rhythmical peal of church bells, a pianist on the terrace playing old love songs, the fragrance of flowers drifting through the air like the finest perfume, a balmy night under the stars—perfection. My impression of a romantic paradise must not have been a unique experience for in the garden was a wedding party. A beautiful bride, a handsome groom; they had fallen in love at the Cipriani and had returned with family and friends from the United States for their marriage. The Villa Cipriani is located in Asolo, a charming, small, medieval, walled hill town less than two hours northwest of Venice. It has an atmosphere so delightful that Robert Browning chose it as a residence. And the home he chose? The Cipriani. Luckily, his home is now a hotel and you, too, can live in Asolo. Although the Villa Cipriani is a sophisticated, polished hotel, the warmth of reception is as gracious as in a small, family run inn: the manager, Giuseppe Kamenar, personally sees that all of his guests are properly pampered.

HOTEL VILLA CIPRIANI
Manager: Giuseppe Kamenar
Via Canova, 298
31011 Asolo (TV), Italy
tel: (0423) 95 21 66, fax: (0423) 95 20 95
31 rooms: Double Lire 375,000-430,000
Open all year
Credit cards: all major
Restaurant open daily
65 km NW of Venice, 14 km E of Bassano
U.S.A. Rep: CIGA 800-221-2340
Relais & Chateaux member

Asolo is a beautiful medieval town in the low lying hills northwest of Venice, dominated by castle ruins on the hillside above, and filled with charming streets, gothic arcades, and frescoed facades. It is here in this magical town where one of our favorite hotels in Italy, the Villa Cipriani, is secreted in a garden just a short stroll from the center of the village. But since the price tag at the Cipriani does not fit everyone's budget, for those who do not want to splurge on accommodations, an alternate choice is the Hotel Duse. Although lacking the romantic ambiance of the Villa Cipriani, its location is superb—right in the very heart of Asolo, surrounded by quaint streets lined with elegant shops. The Hotel Duse's management is very personalized yet very professional—friendly, helpful, and eager to please in every way. There is just a tiny reception lobby leading up to the guest rooms, which are not outstanding in their decor, but certainly adequate if you are not expecting old world charm. They are furnished in a modern mode and are exactly the same except for the color scheme—color coordinated fabrics with matching drapes, spreads and chairs, in reds, greens or blues. Each bedroom has air conditioning, television, direct dial phone, mini bar, and a spotlessly clean bathroom. Ten new rooms are in the works that might have been completed by the time of your arrival.

HOTEL DUSE
Manager: Luigi Prudente
Via Browning, 190
31011 Asolo (TV), Italy
tel: (0423) 55 241, fax: (0423) 95 04 04
12 rooms: Double Lire 150,000
Open all year
Credit cards: all major
No restaurant, breakfast only*
*Hosteria Ca Derton restaurant, same ownership
65 km NW of Venice, 14 km E of Bassano

The Hotel Subasio is located in Assisi with one wall forming part of the ancient square in front of the Basilica of St Francis. The hotel is linked to the Basilica by an arched colonnade. The setting is marvelous, with the rear of the hotel facing the beautiful Umbrian countryside. On the lower level there are several glorious terraces romantically shaded by vines. Many of the rooms also have splendid vistas over the Umbrian valley. Request one of the deluxe rooms with a balcony—these are delightful. The public rooms of the Subasio are pleasant, but rather stilted and formal. However, you will not be inside much anyway. The terraces are magic: to sit and watch the lovely fields mellow in the evening sun with that very special glow that is so characteristic of Umbria is certainly one of life's real pleasures. It is no wonder that many celebrities have chosen the Hotel Subasio for residence when visiting Assisi; such famous names as Charlie Chaplin and James Stewart grace the guest book. Andrea Rossi personally oversees the management of the hotel. There is a friendliness in the air from the gentle maid who turns down your bed in the evening to the charming waiter who helps select your local wine with dinner.

HOTEL SUBASIO
Owner: Sergio Elisei
Via Frate Elia, 2
06081 Assisi (PG), Italy
tel: (075) 81 22 06, fax: (075) 81 66 91
56 rooms: Double Lire 230,000-250,000
10 suites: Lire 300,000-320,000
Open all year
Credit cards: DC, VS
Restaurant open daily
177 km N of Rome, 26 km E of Perugia

For a moderately-priced place to stay in the heart of Assisi, the Hotel Umbra is an unbeatable choice. The hotel is located just a few steps down a narrow little alley that leads off from the Piazza del Commune—one of the central plazas in town. The entrance is through wrought iron gates that open to a tiny patio. Here you are treated to an idyllic oasis where tables are set under a trellis covered by vines that paint a lacy pattern of shadows. From this intimate terrace there is a lovely view. After passing through the patio, you enter into a lounge/reception area with doors opening into the dining room where very good meals are served. The public rooms have accents of antiques, but have a homey rather than grand ambiance. Steps lead to the simple bedrooms that are individually decorated. Most have been recently refurbished and are very pleasant. Splurge and ask for a room (such as 34) with a panoramic vista of the Umbrian valley. However, do not be disappointed if one is not available—the rooms overlooking the jumble of tiled roofs (such as 35) are also very nice. If you like small, family-run hotels that are not decorator perfect in every detail, but offer great heart and hospitality, the Hotel Umbra is an excellent choice. The delightful Alberto Laudenzi family oversee every detail of their small inn and make guests feel at home. The staff too is extremely gracious and accommodating. Best of all, the location is absolutely perfect.

HOTEL UMBRA
Owner: Alberto Laudenzi Family
Via degli Archi 6-Piazza de Comune
06081 Assisi (PG), Italy
tel: (075) 81 22 40, fax: (075) 81 36 53
26 rooms: Double Lire 145,000-180,000
Closed mid-January to mid-March
Credit cards: all major
Restaurant closed Tuesdays
Central location off main square
177 km N of Rome, 26 km E of Perugia

The Hotel Villa Bellago is a central, easily accessible base for exploring Umbria. Although the construction looks new, the Villa Bellago is constructed from three 19th-century farm buildings. Not many traces of the inn's early heritage are apparent, although if you look carefully, there are indications of its rustic origins in details such as the arched brick doorways in the dining room (which at one time was the stables). The core of the hotel is the central building that houses the reception, lounges, bar, and restaurant. Flanking the main house are two smaller buildings where all of the bedrooms are located. The furnishings are contemporary—the public rooms and guest rooms are decorated with non-descript, modern, hotel-looking furniture. You do not need to splurge. Unless you want a fireplace, the regular guest rooms are as nice as the suites, just a little smaller. Although the hotel does not exude an antique ambiance, it has many features that make it an outstanding value: the setting overlooking Lake Corbara is lovely, there is a 20-meter swimming pool, tennis courts, a well-equipped exercise room, and an outstanding terrace where guests can dine on overlooking the lake. And, speaking of dining, the food is excellent. This is not surprising as the hotel was opened by George Harpootlian, a well-known American restaurateur. The hotel is now managed by an Italian family, including Maria Sabrina, the charming fiancée of Harpootlian's son.

VILLA BELLAGO
Manager: Maria Sabrina Dorsaneo
Baschi-Todi Strada, SS 448
05023 Baschi (TR), Italy
tel: (0744) 95 05 21, fax: (0744) 95 05 24
12 rooms: Double Lire 130,000-215,000
Open all year
Credit cards: all major
Restaurant open daily
Not located in town of Baschi, but nearby
10 km from A1 (Orvieto exit) on road to Todi

The Hotel Florence is a moderately-priced hotel in the charming ancient port of Bellagio. The location is prime—right on the main square. Across the street, next to the lake is a lovely, wisteria-covered terrace where you can have a snack while watching the boat traffic. If you are lucky enough to snare a front room with a balcony, you can step out through your French doors and be treated to a splendid view of Lake Como. There is a small reception area and, down a few steps to your left, an intimate lounge with a fireplace, beamed ceiling and chairs set around tiny tables. A staircase leads to the upper floor where the guest dining room is located—it has no view of the lake, but does have a fireplace to warm the room on chilly days. The guest rooms are also located upstairs. Most of the guest rooms have been redone with pretty new fabrics, and some with antique furnishings. Splurge and ask for the corner room with French doors opening onto a large terrace with lounge chairs invitingly set for viewing the lake. If you want to economize, room 19 is a very sweet standard room. The hotel is owned by the Ketzlar family, who are real pros—the inn has been in their family for 150 years. It is now managed by Freidl Ketzlar, her daughter, Roberta, and son, Ronald—all speak excellent English, and treat their guests with genuine, old-fashioned hospitality.

HOTEL FLORENCE
Owner: Ketzlar Family
Piazza Mazzimi 42
22021 Bellagio-Lake Como (CO), Italy
tel: (031) 95 03 42, fax: (031) 95 17 22
38 rooms: Double Lire 160,000-165,000
Suite 200,000
Open mid-April to mid-October
Credit cards: EC, MC, VS
Restaurant open daily
Lakefront location
80 km N of Milan, 31 km NE of Como

The Grand Hotel Villa Serbelloni is certainly appropriately named. It definitely is *GRAND*. In fact, the public rooms are almost overwhelming, with intricately painted ceilings, gold mirrors, fancy columns, Oriental rugs, gilded chairs, massive chandeliers, and a sweeping marble staircase. The bedrooms are quite nice, although I did not think the decor outstanding. However, the quality is superb: lovely percale sheets, soft down pillows, and large towels. The service, too, is excellent. Located in the gardens by the lake there is a large swimming pool. If you prefer sightseeing or shopping to swimming, the colorful old port of Bellagio is just steps from the hotel. If you tire of exploring the town of Bellagio, the ferry is only a few minutes away. If you want to be discreet, the concierge can arrange a special boat to pick you up at the private pier in front of the hotel. For sport's enthusiasts, the Grand Hotel Villa Serbelloni has added a fitness and beauty center, squash court and two tennis courts. Perhaps the original grandeur of the Grand Hotel Villa Serbelloni has faded a little, but if opulent surroundings and the feeling of living in a masterpiece of a palace appeal to you, I think you will enjoy your stay here. Pretend you are a guest at a weekend house party—given by royalty, of course.

GRAND HOTEL VILLA SERBELLONI
Owner: Bucher Family
Manager: Giuseppe Spinelli
22021 Bellagio-Lake Como (CO), Italy
tel: (031) 95 02 16, fax: (031) 95 15 29
98 rooms: Double from Lire 374,000
13 apartments with cooking facilities
Lire 900,000 week for 2 persons
Open April 10 to October 20
Credit cards: all major
Restaurant open daily
78 km N of Milan, 31 km NE of Como
U.S.A. Rep: Premier World Marketing 800-877-3643

When visiting the charming medieval village of Bellagio, most travelers make a bee-line for a hotel steps from Lake Como. However, if you are looking for a very reasonably priced place to stay that affords a breathtaking view, then Il Perlo Panorama, located on the hill above Bellagio, certainly fits the bill. Although the oldest part of the hotel dates back to the early 1900's, the construction of this boxy, three-story building looks new. The interior is modern with rather non-descript furnishings both in the public rooms and in the guest rooms. (Number 16 is one of the best—a pleasant corner room with a balcony.) However, although the decor is bland, there is certainly nothing commonplace about the view. You might never leave the concrete terrace that stretches in front of the hotel. From here a stunning, bird's eye panorama spreads out before you: wooded hills extending steeply down to Lake Como and on beyond to a back drop of soaring mountains. This prime piece of real estate has been handed down through the Sancassano family. Today it is managed by the gracious Piera Sancassano who speaks not only Italian, but a little English, German, and French. She personally sees that all of her guests are well taken care of. Remember, this hotel is inexpensive so don't expect luxury. But, if you are on a budget and yet want the romance of an awesome view of Lake Como, this just might fill the bill.

IL PERLO PANORAMA
Manager: Piera Sancassano
Via Valassina, 180
22021 Bellagio, Lake Como (CO), Italy
tel: (031) 95 02 29, fax: (031) 95 15 56
13 rooms: Double Lire 90,000
Open Easter to October
Credit cards: none accepted
Separate restaurant just below the hotel
3 km south of Bellagio
80 km N of Milan, 31 km NE of Como

Although surrounded by a sprawling, uninteresting concrete metropolis, the center of Bologna shelters a fascinating maze of ancient twisting streets, arcaded passageways, marvelous shopping under porticoed walkways and some of the best food in all of Italy. The Corona d'Oro, located in the heart of the medieval quarter, is a small, well-managed hotel whose elegantly designed construction conserves architectural elements of various periods. In the inner courtyard (covered over with a skylight that rolls back to allow the room to return to its original open-air status) you can admire a portico that dates back to the 14th Century. The hall and stairwell, exquisitely done in the Liberty style of the early 1900s, leads up to the bedrooms that are individually decorated, mostly with modern furnishings, but with a touch of the traditional in the sedate color schemes and prints nicely displayed on the walls. Some of the rooms have recessed block panel ceilings with paintings of coat-of-arms and landscapes dating back to the 15th and 16th Centuries. The hotel does not charge a premium for the few rooms that have small balconies or terraces.

HOTEL CORONA D'ORO 1890
Manager: Mauro Orsi
Via Oberdan, 12
40126 Bologna, Italy
tel: (051) 23 64 56, fax: (051) 26 26 79
35 rooms: Double Lire 300,000-400,000
Closed August
Credit cards: all major
No restaurant, breakfast only
Located in heart of Bologna

In 1550, King John of Portugal decided to give a little gift to the Emperor Ferdinand of Austria, so he purchased an elephant in India, shipped it to Genoa, then planned to walk it to Austria. This giant beast grew weary about the time it reached Bressanone and was stabled for two weeks at the Am Hohen Feld Inn. Young and old came from miles around to see this impromptu circus. The proprietor of the Am Hohen Feld was obviously a master at marketing: to maintain the fame of his establishment, he promptly renamed his hotel—you guessed it—the Elefant. A picture of our friend the elephant was painted on the front of the building commemorating the sensational event. But even without an elephant story this hotel is a winner. Although the bedrooms themselves are a little drab, they are immaculately clean and comfortable. In contrast to the simplicity of the bedrooms, the reception areas and dining rooms are fantastic, incorporating beautiful antiques, museum quality paintings and magnificent paneling. But, even if there were no elephant story nor an antique ambiance to the hotel, the Elefant would have another tremendous attribute: the food is fantastic. Most of the eggs, butter, milk, fruit, and vegetables, and even the wine, come from the hotel's own farms. *NOTE:* Bressanone is called Brixen on some maps.

HOTEL ELEFANT
Manager: K. Falk
Via Rio Bianco, 4
39042 Bressanone (Brixen) (BZ), Italy
tel: (0472) 83 27 50, fax: (0472) 83 65 79
43 rooms: Double Lire 220,000-290,000
Open March to November and Christmas
Credit cards: EC, MC, VS
Restaurant closed Mondays
40 km NE of Bolzano, near Brenner pass

The Cenobio dei Dogi was formerly the summer home of the Genoese Doges, so it is no wonder that it has such an idyllic location nestled on a small hill that forms one end of Camogli's miniature half-moon bay. From the hotel terrace there is an enchanting view of the tiny cove lined with marvelous narrow old fishermen's cottages painted in all shades of ochre's and sienna's. The hotel has a very nice swimming pool, plus a private (though pebbly) beach. Many of the bedrooms have balconies that boast romantic views of this storybook scene. For tennis buffs, there is a tennis court, although I cannot imagine anyone wanting to play tennis with all the beautiful walking trails that make enticing spider web designs on the peninsula. The Cenobio dei Dogi is a larger, less personalized hotel than most that appear in this guide. And, although its decor seems a bit dated, it possesses a solid, comfortable, no-nonsense kind of charm. It is not chic in the jet set style of hotels frequently found on the Riviera. However, if you relate to lovely flower gardens, exceptional views, and slightly faded old world comfort, you will like this hotel.

HOTEL CENOBIO DEI DOGI
Manager: Gianluca Bungaro
Via Nicolo Cuneo, 34
16032 Camogli (GE), Italy
tel: (0185) 77 00 41, fax: (0185) 77 27 96
89 rooms: Double Lire 240,000-370,000
Closed January and February
Credit cards: all major
Restaurant open daily
Near Portofino–Italian Riviera
20 km SE of Genoa, 14 km NW of Portofino

As an alternative to staying in downtown Florence, you might want to consider instead the Villa La Massa that is located on the banks of the Arno about a 15-minute drive from town. The Villa La Massa is actually composed of three buildings—each old and each having its own unique charm. This beautiful estate originally belonged to the rich and powerful Giraldi family: inscribed tombstones, underground tunnels and a chapel still remain from this period of the villa's history. Although the Villa La Massa is very old, the hotel offers all of the modern amenities including tennis courts, a swimming pool, air conditioning, refrigerators in the guest rooms. The restaurant, Il Verrocchio, has a beautiful terrace for outdoor dining overlooking the Arno river and offers the best of Tuscan specialties. If you have a car, then the Villa La Massa might make an appealing alternative to staying in the heart of Florence: especially in summer when you can do your sightseeing during the day and return to a pool and garden setting at night—there is free courtesy bus service to and from Florence.

HOTEL VILLA LA MASSA
Owner: Carlo Grillini
Manager: Daniela Parrini Grillini
50012 Candeli (FI), Italy
tel: (055) 65 10 101, fax: (055) 65 10 109
40 rooms: Double Lire 420,000-490,000
Open all year
Credit cards: all major
Restaurant open daily
Located on Arno River
7 km E of Florence

The Hotel Flora in the center of Capri is truly a delight. Just beyond the landmark Quisisana Hotel is the stark white building reflecting the sun's rays and trimmed with lush deep purple bougainvillea vines. Signora Vuotto runs her hotel with great care and attention—striving to make her guests feel the Hotel Flora is their home away from home. She has succeeded. The small 24-room hotel has become known above all for its impeccable yet friendly service. The prim dining room with its smart striped yellow and green armchairs and colorful ceramic plates lining the walls, opens out to a large terrace overflowing with potted Mediterranean flowers and miniature palms. Guests linger over their morning cappuccino to take in the view over the San Giacomo ancient monastery to the sea from cushioned wicker chairs. Chef Giorgio practices his culinary expertise for dinner guests in the well known restaurant. Meals are usually served outside on the romantic terrace where Signora Vuotto mingles among her guests, making sure all are lovingly looked after. There is a fresh, perfumed air about this elegant jewel of a hotel that is carried out through the lovely bedrooms and suites finely decorated with antiques, and colorful Pierre Deux fabrics. Each of the bedrooms has television, a small refrigerator and, best of all, a terrace with a view of the famous Faraglioni rocks. Spotless bathrooms are tiled in typical Caprese style.

HOTEL FLORA
Owner: Virginia Vuotto
Via Federico Serena, 26
80073 Capri (NA), Italy
tel: (081) 83 70 211, fax: (081) 83 78 949
24 rooms: Double Lire 250,000-350,000
7 suites: Lire 400,000
Open Easter to October
Credit cards: all major
Restaurant open daily
Island of Capri, ferry from Sorrento or Naples

The Grand Hotel Quisisana conjures up the image of a Hollywood setting where the jet-set gather. The women, adorned in jewels and the latest swimming ensembles, sit in the sun and gossip about the latest scandal while their husbands (or boyfriends?) sit pool-side drinking Scotch and playing the game of grown boys—discussing their latest business ventures. But it is all great fun and quite in the mood of Capri that has been a playground for the wealthy since the time of the early Romans. The Grand Hotel Quisisana is a deluxe hotel with a gorgeous oval pool overlooking the blue Mediterranean. The air of formal elegance appears as soon as you enter the lobby decorated with marble floors, soft green velvet chairs, Oriental carpets, ornate statues, crystal chandeliers and beautiful paintings. All the bedrooms are well appointed and the deluxe rooms even have separate his and hers half-baths. Room rates include breakfast and lunch or dinner and you can choose from almost anything on the menu. The Grand Hotel Quisisana most definitely provides a setting and atmosphere to reflect the image of, and cater to, their jet-set clientele.

GRAND HOTEL QUISISANA
Manager: Gianfranco Morgano
Via Camerelle, 2
80073 Capri (NA), Italy
tel: (081) 83 70 788, fax: (081) 83 76 080
150 rooms: Double Lire 380,000-600,000
Open April to October
Credit cards: all major
Restaurant open daily
Island of Capri, ferry from Sorrento or Naples
U.S.A. Rep: LHW 800-223-6800

The Hotel Luna savors one of the most beautiful locations on the Island of Capri. It is just a short walk from the village, yet, in atmosphere, it seems far away from the bustle and noise. To the left of the path as you approach the hotel, you see the Luna's large, swimming pool surrounded by flowers and a view to the sea. The hotel is perched on the cliffs overlooking a spectacular coastline of green hills that drop straight into the sea, from which emerge giant rock formations. On two sides of the hotel there is a terrace with comfortable chairs where guests may enjoy this spectacular view. Just below the terrace, is one of the most outstanding features of the hotel—an open-air restaurant set on a balcony that hangs out over the cliffs with an unsurpassed panorama of the sea. The guest rooms and lounges are decorated in pastel colors. The furnishings are reproduction, formal antiques. The ambiance is similar to what is found in many commercial hotels. Splurge and ask for one of the best guest rooms that face the sea. Although these cost a bit more, the vista is memorable. The overall mood at the hotel is set by its delightful approach, a covered trellis pathway that, in summer, is completely shaded by brilliant bougainvillea and grape vines and bordered by flowers: a wonderful introduction to the Hotel Luna and to a restful interlude by the sea.

HOTEL LUNA
Manager: Luisa Vuotto
Viale Giacomo Matteotti, 3
80073 Capri (NA), Italy
tel: (081) 83 70 433, fax: (081) 83 77 459
44 rooms: Lire 230,000-430,000
Open April to October
Credit cards: all major
Restaurant open daily
Island of Capri, ferry from Sorrento or Naples

Hugging a hillside with a ship's prow position overlooking the sea, the Hotel Punta Tragara is definitely one of the Capri's landmarks. Whereas most of the island's villas and hotels have white facades that sparkle in the sunlight, the Hotel Punta Tragara is painted a deep sandy beige, accented by wrought iron grills, dark green shutters, and, of course, the profusion of flowers and greenery that make Capri so special. The hotel is reached by a pleasant 15-minute walk from the center of town—a path that dead-ends at the point where the hillside drops steeply down to the sea. Here the picturesque Faraglioni islands thrust their jagged peaks just below the hotel, affording fabulous views. Perhaps this spectacular setting is what made Eisenhower and Churchill choose the Hotel Punta Tragara for accommodation when they visited Capri. There is a certain formality to this small hotel—the staff seems professionally accommodating, but there is not the warmth often found in a small, family-run establishment. Sea chests, paintings of old sailing vessels, aged-bronze divers' helmets, ship's bells, and antique maps create a pleasing, nautical theme. It is not the decor, but rather the setting that make Hotel Punta Tragara special. Request a deluxe room with a view. However, even if your room is not one of the deluxe category, you can settle by one of the two swimming pools and soak up the sun and scenery

HOTEL PUNTA TRAGARA
Owner: Ceglia Goffredo
Via Tragara 57
80073 Capri (NA), Italy
tel: (081) 83.70.844, fax: (081) 83.77.790
35 rooms: Double Lire 320,000-450,000
Open Easter to mid-October
Credit cards: all major
Restaurant open daily
Island of Capri, ferry from Sorrento or Naples

The Villa Brunella is a small jewel located on the most picturesque and peaceful street of Capri, the Tragara, only a 10-minute walk to the center of town. The modern hotel, overlooking the Marina Piccola, squeezes the greatest advantage from its narrow, very deep lot. The hotel is built on levels starting at the street level with the terrace restaurant and stepping down the steep hillside to the blue swimming pool—at this point, only halfway down to the sea level (the beach is only about a 5-minute walk down the hill). The hotel is run more like a private home than a commercial hotel. The ever-gracious Vincenzo and his wife Brunella take great pleasure in entertaining guests and making them feel welcome. The 20 bedrooms, each with private bath, telephone, mini-bar, and air conditioning, are tastefully put together with pretty pink or powder blue floral bedspreads and matching curtains. The cool ceramic tiled floors, creamy white walls and potted plants add to the charm. Decoration in the rooms is really superfluous as the eye can hardly be torn away from the spectacularly dramatic views of the sea and island from one's own terrace. Simply heavenly.

VILLA BRUNELLA
Hosts: Brunella and Vincenzo Ruggiero
Via Tragara 24
80073 Capri (NA), Italy
tel: (081) 83 70 122, fax: (081) 83 70 430
20 rooms: Double Lire 324,000
Suite Lire 390,000
Open: Easter to October
Credit cards: all major
Restaurant open daily
Island of Capri, ferry from Sorrento or Naples

If you are approaching Florence from the west, perhaps on your way from Milan to Florence, we highly recommend stopping en route, just before you reach Florence, at the Paggeria Medicea. The hotel's address is Artimino, but the town is so small that I doubt you will find it on any map. Mark instead Carmignano on your map and when you arrive there you will find signs to Artimino, only a few minutes' drive farther on. The hotel is cleverly incorporated into what were once the pages' quarters for the adjoining 16th-century Medicea Villa La Ferdinanda. The long, narrow structure has been cleverly restored, preserving the many original chimneys that adorn the heavy, red-tiled roof. An open corridor whose heavily beamed ceiling is supported by a stately row of columns forms a walkway in front of the rooms. All of the guest rooms are simple, but very inviting, with tiled floors, pretty prints on the white walls, hand-loomed-looking white drapes hanging from wooden rods above the windows, and attractive antiques or copies of antiques as accents in each room. There is a snack bar in the same wing as the hotel, but the main restaurant, *Biagio Pignatta* (which serves simple but delicious Italian cooking), is located in a nearby building which at one time housed the butler for the villa. If you are a guest at the hotel, there is a swimming pool, two tennis courts, a running track, plus you have access to a delightful small Etruscan museum situated in the vaults of the adjoining Medicea Villa La Ferdinanda.

PAGGERIA MEDICEA
Manager: Alessandro Gualtieri
Viale Papa Giovanni XXIII
50040 Carmignano-Artimino (FI), Italy
tel: (055) 87 18 081, fax: (055) 87 18 080
37 rooms: Double Lire 180,00-240,000
Open all year
Credit cards: all major
Restaurant closed Wednesdays
20 km SW of Florence, 15 km S of Prato

We happened upon this inn during our exploration of Italy's glorious Tuscany region, well known for its rolling, vineyard covered hills. Just as the road curved into the small town of Castellina in Chianti, we noticed an inn we had never seen before and stopped for an inspection at the Hotel Il Colombaio. The building is very old—probably at one time a farmer's home with its typical heavy tiled roof, thick walls and courtyard. This comfortable inn is owned by the Baldini family and Roberta Baldini, the gracious daughter, is the manager. She speaks very good English and gave us a complete tour of the small hotel. The guest rooms are quite inviting, many with wrought iron beds and antique accents giving an appealing country flavor. There are 15 rooms and one suite in the main house, plus a small annex across the street with 6 more rooms. All have private bathrooms and are fresh and pretty. The dining room is especially cozy, again decorated with a rustic motif in keeping with the Tuscany countryside. A continental breakfast is the only meal served here, but Roberta is happy to recommend a good local *ristorante* for dining. On hot summer days, a welcome bonus is the swimming pool, located on a terrace behind the inn. (As a reader pointed out, the pool is nice, but not as dramatic as the one depicted in the hotel brochure.) For a reasonably priced place to stay with an old world ambiance, the Hotel Il Colombaio is a welcome addition to the Tuscany region.

HOTEL IL COLOMBAIO
Owner: Baldini Family
Via Chiantigiana, 29
53011 Castellina in Chianti (SI), Italy
tel: (0577) 74 04 44, fax: (0577) 74 04 44
22 rooms: Double Lire 100,000-120,000
Closed November
Credit cards: all major
No restaurant, breakfast only
21 km N of Siena on road 222

The Tenuta di Ricavo is unique—not a hotel at all in the usual connotation, but rather a tiny village with peasants' cottages that have been transformed into delightful guest rooms. The stables are now the dining room and the barn is now the office. Unlike many of the over-renovated hotels in Tuscany where much of what you see is almost 100% new construction, Ricavo is ALL real, an authentic Tuscan hamlet of stone cottages (attractively furnished with antiques) that have been lovingly restored to retain their original rustic charm. You enter the large property along a lane that leads through a huge pine forest where small cottages are nestled in amongst the trees. Gardens are everywhere and roses embellish the weathered stone cottages, giving them a fairy-tale appearance. The total effect is absolutely enchanting. Before it became a hotel, the village was the summer-holiday-home of a Swiss family, who, after World War II, transformed it into an exquisite resort. The family seeks no publicity. They do not need it: the hotel is always filled with fortunate guests who have discovered this paradise. However, the Tenuta di Ricavo is not for everyone. It is quiet. It is remote. It is unstructured. But it is a haven for the traveler for whom a good book, a walk through the forest, a swim in the pool, a drink at sunset, and a delicious dinner are fulfillment. Excellent English is spoken—especially by the gracious Christine Lobrano.

ROMANTIC HOTEL TENUTA DI RICAVO
Owner: Lobrano-Scotoni Family
53011 Castellina in Chianti (SI), Italy
tel: (0577) 74 02 21, fax: (0577) 74 10 14
23 rooms: Double Lire 200,000-360,000*
*3 night minimum
Open mid-March to October
Credit cards: EC, MC, VS
Restaurant closed Mondays
21 km N of Siena on road 22, 50 km S of Florence
U.S.A. Rep: Euro-Connection 800-645-3876

Castelrotto, a medieval village abounding in old world character, is located in the heart of the Dolomite mountains in north-eastern Italy. In the center of town, the Hotel Cavallino d'Oro faces the market square which highlights an especially quaint, colorfully painted fountain. The entrance to the hotel is signposted with a Golden Horse, reflecting the name of this 14th-century inn. The facade is a deep-mustard-color highlighted by dark green shutters and flower boxes overflowing with cheerful geraniums. There is a traditional old world atmosphere throughout this small inn. All of the guest rooms are individual in decor, and nicely furnished in a typical Tyrolian style. Three rooms are especially pretty with light pine, four poster beds. From the beginning the Hotel Cavallino has always provided accommodations. When first documented in 1393, the inn was a coaching station with facilities to care for the horses, and also, of course, food and rooms for the weary traveler. The original hospitality is certainly on-going. Stefan and Susanne (both of whom speak excellent English) have now taken over as the third generation of the Urthaler family to run the hotel. Not only do they exude a boundless, youthful enthusiasm and a gracious warmth of welcome, they are also constantly upgrading their small hotel by incorporating more antiques into the decor and renovating guest rooms. The dining room was closed on the day of my visit, but Stefan tells me the kitchen is excellent with the chef specializing in regional dishes.

HOTEL CAVALLINO D'ORO
Owners: Susanne and Stefan Urthaler
39040 Castelrotto (Kastelruth) (BZ), Italy
tel: (0471) 70 63 37, fax: (0471) 70 71.72
24 rooms: Double Lire 80,000-145,000
Open all year
Credit cards: all major
Restaurant closed Tuesdays
140 km S of Innsbruck, 24 km NE of Bolzano

Of the many magnificent old villas dotting the countryside near Venice, some have fallen into disrepair, some are still maintained as private residences, and a few have been converted into hotels. We looked at many of these fascinating villa-hotels but because of the expense of maintaining them, many are just too shabby to include. One however, the Villa Corner della Regina, still has an elegant, though slighted faded, appeal. Once home to Caterina, Queen of Cyprus, the villa dates from the beginning of the 16th Century and was later reconstructed around 1700 in the well-known Palladian-style. It is set in extensive manicured formal gardens and surrounded by vineyards. A pool is located to the left of the main building while the wing to the right, which originally housed the stables, has been converted to guest rooms and also some time-share condominiums. The decor in the side stable annex is nothing special, just standard hotel-like furnishings, but the suites in the villa abound with antiques—very grand and ornate, even somewhat overly fussy for my taste. There are several dining rooms in the villa: my favorite is a charming room with salmon-colored marble walls enhanced by color-coordinated tablecloths and draperies—formal yet cozy and not the least bit intimidating. The food served at the villa is excellent and the wines are produced on the estate. *NOTE:* Cavasagra is located between the towns of Ospedaletto and Albaredo on the Hallwag map.

VILLA CORNER DELLA REGINA
Owner: Count Dona delle Rose
Via Corriva, 10
Near Ospedaletto
31050 Cavasagra (TV), Italy
tel: (0423) 48 14 81, fax: (0423) 45 11 00
30 rooms: Double Lire 250,000-480,000
Open all year
Credit cards: all major
Restaurant open daily
45 km NW of Venice, 3 km W of Ospedaletto

A book on the most charming hotels in Italy would not be complete without including one of world's premier hotels, the Villa d'Este. Originally the hotel was a private villa built in 1568 by the Cardinal Tolomeo Gallio. He obviously had elegant (and expensive) taste, for the Villa d'Este is truly a fantasy come true. From the moment you enter the enormous lobby with the sweeping staircase, marble, crystal, soaring ceilings, statues, and columns surround you. Everything is elaborate and ornate. The bedrooms are all elegantly furnished—no two are alike, but all are beautiful with color-coordinated carpets, wall-coverings and bedspreads. Some of the bedrooms have prime locations overlooking the lake. Although the interior is lovely, it is the outside where the fun really begins. The hotel opens onto a large terrace where guests relax with refreshing drinks. Just a short distance beyond the terrace is the lake where there is a dock for boats and a very large swimming pool that extends out over the water. Tucked away in the park there are eight tennis courts, and within the nearby area, seven golf courses. However, the most stunning feature of the Villa d'Este is the park. It surrounds the hotel with lovely pathways winding between the trees, a jogging course, glorious flower gardens, statues and even a formal garden with dramatic mosaic colonnade.

VILLA D'ESTE
Manager: Marco Sorbellini
22010 Cernobbio, Lake Como (CO), Italy
tel: (031) 34 81, fax: (031) 34 88 44
158 rooms: Double Lire 550,000-870,000
Open March to November
Credit cards: all major
Restaurant open daily
53 km N of Milan, 5 km N of Como (town)
U.S.A. Rep: LHW 800-223-6800

Conveniently located about mid-way between Rome and Florence, La Frateria di Padre Eligio makes an excellent base for exploring the beauties of Tuscany and Umbria. However this very special hotel is so utterly bewitching, that you will be tempted to forego any idea of sightseeing and not set foot from the property. The guest rooms in this 13th-century convent (founded by St Francis) are housed in the original guest quarters where the friars lodged passing pilgrims. They are simply, yet tastefully, furnished with antiques. There is nothing to interrupt the enchantment—bathrooms and telephones are the only concessions to the modern era. The silence is sweetened by the song of birds and the air by the fragrance of flowers. A centuries-old forest surrounds the hotel with beckoning paths where you can stroll in perfect stillness. The restoration of this masterpiece of history, is superb. But the miracle is how it was accomplished. La Frateria di Padre, in addition to housing a deluxe hotel, is home to a commune of once-troubled young people. They toiled for 12 years to bring the Convento San Francesco back to its former beauty. Today these remarkable young men and women awaken at 6:00 am to begin long days of labor. They meticulously groom the gardens, tend the vegetable garden, run the hotel, bake the fresh breads, prepare the meals (exclusively using produce from the farm), and serve in the restaurant.

LA FRATERIA DI PADRE ELIGIO
Manager: Maria Grazia Daolio
Convento San Francesco
53040 Cetona (SI), Italy
tel and fax: (0578) 23.80.15 or 23.82.61
7 rooms: Double Lire 280,000-380,000
Open mid-February to January 6
Credit cards: all major
Restaurant open daily
89 km SE of Siena, 62 km NW of Orvieto

The Villa Anna Maria is located in Champoluc, a small town at the end of the beautiful Ayas Valley that stretches north into the Alps almost to the Swiss border. The glaciers of the Monte Rosa (one of the 4,000 meter peaks of the Alps) provide a glorious backdrop as you drive up the valley. Champoluc is a well-known ski center in winter as well as a favorite mountain summer resort. As you drive through Champoluc you see a small sign for the Villa Anna Maria on the right side of the road just before you leave town. Turn right on this little lane that winds up the hill and look for the Anna Maria on your right, set in a serene pine grove. The Villa Anna Maria is not a luxury hotel, but rather an old mountain chalet that is now a simple, but very charming, inn. A large deck for sunning stretches across the entrance. Inside there is a lovely dining room—my favorite room— which exudes warmth and coziness with its wooden Alpine-style country chairs, wooden tables, and gay red checked curtains at the windows. Upstairs the bedrooms are not luxurious but most agreeable, with wooden paneling on the walls and a rustic ambiance, and each one with a private bathroom. The atmosphere is homey—wonderful for those seeking a friendly country inn in a mountain village.

VILLA ANNA MARIA
Owner: Miki Origone
Via Croues, 5
11020 Champoluc, Monte Rosa (AO), Italy
tel: (0125) 30 71 28, fax: (0125) 30 79 84
20 rooms: Double Lire 160,000
Open June 20 to mid-September
December 10 to mid-April
Restaurant open daily, only for guests
Mountain location–NW Italy
175 km NW of Milan, 100 km N of Turin

The Ca'Peo, a well known restaurant serving some of the finest food in Italy, is located high in the coastal hills south of Genoa. You might think you will never arrive as the road winds ever upward through groves of olive and chestnut trees. But the way is well signposted, and just about the time you might be ready to despair, you will find a wonderful old farmhouse, owned by Franco Solari, who is host and in charge of the wines, and his wife, Melly, who is the chef. As we checked in, the entire family was in the kitchen busily chopping vegetables, rolling out pastry and preparing the fish for the evening meal. The dining room, enclosed on three sides by large arched windows, takes advantage of a sweeping view to the sea. Be aware that the meals are VERY expensive, but if you appreciate fine food and wines, superb. Dining is definitely the main feature; however, in a modern annex there are five suites available for guests who want to spend the night. The decor here is not antique, but each of the large suites is pleasant, and after lingering over a wonderful meal accompanied by delicious wines, how nice to walk just a few steps to your bed. A final note the Ca'Peo is only about half an hour's drive from the popular resort of Portofino, so you might want to stay here instead or at least treat yourself to a memorable meal—but call ahead as reservations are necessary.

CA'PEO
Owners: Franco and Melly Solari
Via dei Caduti, 80
16040 Chiavari a Leivi (GE), Italy
tel: (0185) 31 96 96, fax: (0185) 31 96 71
5 suites: Lire 180,000
Closed November
Credit cards: VS
Restaurant closed Mondays
6 km N of Chiavari toward Leivi
44 km SE of Genoa, 22 km NE of Portofino

I was puzzled to receive a hotel questionnaire response postmarked St Simon's Island, Georgia. But quickly all was explained. It was from James Adams who had been living in Europe, perfecting his Italian cooking skills at one of the finest restaurant-hotels in Italy, the Locanda del Sant'Uffizio—Ristorante da Beppe. The owner, Giuseppe Firato (Beppe), speaks no English so when our request for information arrived, he asked his American protégé to respond. After visiting the hotel, I can only say that it was more perfect than anticipated. Below is James' wonderful letter describing so superbly his home away from home. "Originally in the 1500s the Locanda del Sant'Uffizio was a Benedictine monastery and served as such up until the mid 1800s after which time it passed into private hands serving as a farm. In 1972, Signor Giuseppe Firato (Beppe), a man from the village, bought the farm and slowly began converting it into its present form. Naturally at first there were only several rooms while the rest of the buildings were used for farming and wine growing. Through the years rooms have been added very carefully, with great respect for the traditional aesthetics, and now there are 35 guest rooms. All furnishings are antique and every detail of the decor has been rigorously overseen personally by Signor Beppe and his wife, Carla, with the result being a very tasteful, elegant, yet relaxed hotel cozily nestled amongst the vineyards in the hills of Monferrato. Other features include a tennis court, a swimming pool (in front of which one can have breakfast and lunch in the warm months) and, last but not least, there is the Ristorante da Beppe, an exquisite restaurant serving the finest of Piemontese cuisine. It is of course owned and operated by the Firato family, and, in fact, the restaurant preceded the hotel. It has earned one Michelin star and has been rated highly in notable Italian guides such as Espresso and Veronelli. When one combines the charm and relaxation of this elegant hotel with the pleasures of such a refined table, one is left with a very memorable experience."

There are many features that make the Locanda del Sant'Uffizio very special, but, without a doubt, the Firato family is responsible for the ambiance of warmth and hospitality that radiates throughout the hotel. Signor Beppe was born in the tiny village (population 50) where the hotel is located. When his father who owned a bar died, Beppe took over—although he was only a boy at the time. The rest is history: the bar grew into a restaurant, the restaurant into a tiny hotel, the small hotel into a delightful resort. Such a success story is not surprising when you meet Signor Beppe. He speaks no English. He does not need to. His charismatic charm transcends all language barriers. It is no wonder his restaurant—isolated in the countryside—is filled each night with chicly dressed Italian clientele: Beppe greets each of them with an exuberant warmth, and the food is outstanding, truly a gourmet delight. Since we originally visited the Locanda del Sant'Uffizio, Beppe and his wife have been joined in the operation of the Locanda del Sant'Uffizio by their two sons: Fabio, a chemical engineer, collaborates with the chef and Massimo, an architect, assists his father in the welcoming of guests. Happily for the visitors from abroad, both sons speak English and French. Be aware that the meals and wine are VERY expensive.

LOCANDA DEL SANT'UFFIZIO
RISTORANTE DA BEPPE
Owner: Giuseppe Firato
Near Moncalvo
14030 Cioccaro di Penango (AT), Italy
tel: (0141) 91 271, fax: (0141) 91 60 68
*35 rooms: Double Lire 480,000 **
*Rate includes breakfast and dinner
Closed January and August 10-20
Credit cards: EC, MC, VS
Restaurant open daily
5 km SE of Moncalvo, 60 km E of Turin
21 km N of Asti toward Moncalvo

The Hotel Menardi dates back over 200 years. Originally it was a peasant's farmhouse, but as Cortina's popularity as a fabulous ski center has spread so has the town, and now the farm is located right on the outskirts of town on the main road heading north. Nevertheless, the Menardi family, who have owned the home for a century and a half, have managed to maintain the country flavor through the use of many antiques, nostalgic prints on the walls, old clocks, giant dowry chests, Oriental carpets, and beautiful hanging cupboards—all set off by the warmth and gaiety of flowers everywhere. The dining room is appealingly cozy and the delicious food is impeccably served. The individually decorated bedrooms are all attractive. In addition to the original inn that has 40 bedrooms, there is a new house in the back garden with an additional 15 rooms. It seems that, due to its location on the main road, the Menardi farm just naturally evolved into a hotel. At first it gave shelter to the men carting loads over the Cimabanche Pass who needed a place to sleep—more often than not in the hay loft. Today the inn is a simple, but wonderful, small hotel whose special ingredient is the old-fashioned warmth and hospitality of the gracious Menardi family who personally see that every guest is made to feel welcome.

HOTEL MENARDI
Owner: Menardi Family
112 Via Majon
32043 Cortina d'Ampezzo (BL), Italy
tel: (0436) 24 00, fax: (0436) 86 21 83
55 rooms: Double Lire 160,000-280,000
Open July to September
and Christmas to March
Credit cards: VS
Restaurant open daily
133 km E of Bolzano
71 km N of Belluno

Corvara, a mountain village in northeastern Italy, is popular with guests who enjoy walking through high alpine meadows in summer and skiing down snow covered slopes in winter. Although the Dolomite region is one of the most beautiful in Italy and offers many hotels, there is not a rich choice for visitors who prefer small inns with an old world, antique ambiance. Luckily, La Perla, located in the center of Corvara, offers not only a convenient place to stay, but also a cozy ambiance. This small inn is owned and managed by the Costa family who lovingly oversee every detail. The day I visited, Signora Costa was busily engaged in supervising the table arrangements to be sure everything was perfect. You enter into a large reception lobby where heavy wooden beams, Oriental carpets on tiled floors, fresh plants and country-patterned drapes set the mood. But the real winners are the dining rooms. There are a series of lovely places to eat: each with its own personality—all absolutely oozing with cozy charm. Antique clocks, tiled ovens, low beamed ceilings, painted chests, warm antique wood paneling, abundant accents of copper plus handsome linens, fresh flowers and candlelight make each room a dream. The guest rooms have all the modern amenities, but do not display the old world ambiance of the public rooms.

ROMANTIK HOTEL LA PERLA
Owner: Costa Family
39033 Corvara (BZ), Italy
tel: (0471) 83 61 32, fax: (0471) 83 65 68
50 rooms: Double Lire 290,000-510,000
Open July to September
and mid-December to Easter
Credit cards: VS
Restaurant open daily
65 km E of Bolzano, 47 km W of Cortina
U.S.A. Rep: Euro-Connection 800-645-3876

The Punta Est is a lovely old villa perched on a hilltop overlooking the sea. When the home was converted to a villa, an annex was added to provide more bedrooms. However, it still gives the friendly feeling of a private home. This warmth of reception and attention to detail are the result of the management of the Podestà family who own and manage the inn. They seem dedicated to making your stay as enjoyable as possible— even their German Shepherd seems to want to welcome you. There are little terraces with lovely views snuggled at various levels among the trees and on one of these terraces is a swimming pool. There is also access to the public beach of Finale Ligure that can easily be reached by walking down the path to the main highway and following the tunnel beneath the highway to the beach. The rooms in the main villa are smaller and more old-fashioned than those in the newer annex that are more reminiscent of an American motel. There is a small dining room for breakfast that is especially inviting with its blue and white English bone china service. This is just one example of a very nice touch offered by owners who really want to please.

HOTEL PUNTA EST
Owner: Podestà Family
Manager: Attilio Podestà
Via Aurelia N.1
17024 Finale Ligure (SV), Italy
tel: (019) 60 06 11, fax: (019) 60 06 11
37 rooms: Double Lire 300,000-360,000*
*Rate includes breakfast and lunch or dinner
Open May to October
Credit cards: AX, VS
Restaurant open daily
72 km SW of Genoa, 75 km E of San Remo

The Grand Hotel Villa Cora is a mansion, originally built during the 19th Century by the Baron Oppenheim as a gift for his beautiful young bride. Among the many romantic tales of the Villa Cora is the one about Oppenheim's wife who, so the story goes, became enamored of one of her many admirers. The jealous baron was so enraged that he threatened to burn the entire mansion. Luckily for you and me, he was stopped in time from this mad endeavor by his friends, and today this magnificent villa is a stunning hotel. Although only about a 5-minute taxi ride from the center of Florence (or a 15-minute walk), the Grand Hotel Villa Cora is eons away in atmosphere. You feel more like a guest on a country estate rather than in a city hotel. The villa is set in intricate gardens and even has a pool. The interior of the hotel is rather ornate and sumptuous. You can almost hear the sounds of laughter and music drifting through the gardens, and indeed the mansion has always been famous for its dramatic parties: at one time the villa was the residence of Napoleon's wife, Empress Eugenia, whose gay entertaining was the talk of Florence. Now this grand palace-like home can be yours for days of dreams and romance. There is free limousine service for guests to and from Florence.

GRAND HOTEL VILLA CORA
Manager: Valerio Rastrelli
Viale Machiavelli, 18/20
50125 Florence, Italy
tel: (055) 22 9 8451, fax: (055) 2 29 086
48 rooms: Double Lire 448,000-587,000
Open all year
Credit cards: all major
Restaurant open daily
15-minute walk from the heart of Florence

After being closed for two years for complete renovation, the Hotel Helvetia and Bristol reopened in late 1989 and instantly became, in my estimation, the finest luxury hotel in the center of Florence. Nothing has been spared to make this showplace a true beauty. The decor is outstanding. The lounges, exquisitely decorated with an elegant, yet extremely comfortable, home-like ambiance, exude quality without flamboyance. Each of the guest rooms is also superbly decorated, and, as in a private home, no two are alike. Abundant use of exquisite padded fabric wall coverings, with color-coordinated draperies, upholstered chairs and bedspreads along with lovely antiques make each one special. I fell in love with each of the rooms. But my very favorites were the mini suites: room 257 in gorgeous shades of muted green, and room 363 in lovely golds, creams, and dusty pinks, with a sumptuous marble bathroom with Jacuzzi tub, heated towel racks, plus the added bonus of a tiny terrace. The dining room, cozy yet elegant with dark walls and soft lighting, features Tuscan cuisine. For light refreshments, a cool drink or just relaxing, the *Giardino d'Inverno* (Winter Garden) is a marvelous retreat—light and airy with a domed, old-fashioned skylight, potted plants and nostalgic wicker furniture. The Helvetia and Bristol is expensive, but no more so than the other luxury hotels in Florence, and for those who appreciate quality and refinement, it is unsurpassed.

HOTEL HELVETIA AND BRISTOL
Manager: Franco Ensoli
Via dei Pescioni, 2
50123 Florence, Italy
tel: (055) 28 78 14, fax: (055) 28 83 53
52 rooms: Double Lire 466,690-574,040
Open all year
Credit cards: all major
Restaurant open daily
In the heart of Florence
Relais & Chateaux member

Each time we visit the Loggiato dei Serviti, we are again impressed with what a pleasant small hotel this is for the money. Many of the hotels in Florence are lovely, but fabulously expensive: others are reasonably priced, but shabby and dark. So it is an exceedingly happy surprise to find a light, airy, antique-filled small hotel—at a reasonable rate. This is not a deluxe hotel, but we think you will be well pleased. The building dates back to the 16th Century when it was built for the order of the Serviti fathers. The character of the original building has been meticulously maintained adding greatly to the charm of the hotel. The location is superb: right in the heart of Florence on the historical Piazza SS. Annunziata. There is a small reception area as you enter, beyond which is an intimate little bar where snacks are served (there is no restaurant at the hotel). A miniature elevator—just large enough for two people to squeeze into—takes you upstairs to the spacious bedrooms, each with private bath and each individually decorated in excellent taste with liberal use of antiques. There are four suites, one of which even has two bedrooms and two bathrooms. Although of course more expensive than the standard double room, these suites are most attractive and a good value for a family.

LOGGIATO DEI SERVITI
Owner: Budini Gattai
Piazza SS. Annunziata, 3
50122 Florence, Italy
tel: (055) 21 91 65, fax: (055) 28 95 95
29 rooms: Double Lire 235,000
4 suites: Lire 270,000-450,000
Open all year
Credit cards: all major
No restaurant, breakfast only
In the heart of Florence

The Lungarno Hotel is superbly located directly on the Arno River and only a few minutes' walk from the Ponte Vecchio. Although most of the hotel is of new construction, the architect cleverly incorporated an ancient stone tower into the hotel so it is easy to rationalize including this hotel—one of my favorites in Florence—into this travel guide. The interior of the hotel is traditional rather than antique in decor, but the decorating is done with excellent taste and the effect is most pleasing. Lovely soft colors are used throughout with beautiful prints on the wall and many fresh flowers. The bedrooms are very comfortable and those who book well in advance can request one of the rooms overlooking the Arno. Those who really plan ahead might even be lucky enough to secure one of the few rooms with a large terrace overlooking the river—these rooms are very special and well-worth the extra cost. What a treat to sit on your own terrace in the evening and watch the Arno fade into gold and the Ponte Vecchio glow in the setting sun. There are several rooms in the tower itself, one of which is especially romantic with its old stone wall and its staircase that leads up to a little balcony and a third bed. Several of the other rooms in the new portion of the hotel also have lofts that can be used as sleeping alcoves.

LUNGARNO HOTEL
Manager: Nedo Naldini
Borgo San Jacopo, 14
50125 Florence, Italy
tel: (055) 26 42 11, fax: (055) 26 84 37
66 rooms: Double Lire 270,000-370,000
Open all year
Credit cards: all major
No restaurant, breakfast only
Short walk to Ponte Vecchio
Directly on the Arno River

Mario's came highly recommended to us by several readers, and after seeing the hotel for ourselves, we agree that it is a delightful small hotel, moderately priced for Florence. It is conveniently located two blocks from the train station, and within easy walking distance to the city's major sightseeing. From the street, the appeal of the hotel is not readily evident as it is housed in a rather nondescript building. But after ascending the stairs to the second floor and stepping into the cozy, beamed-ceilinged lobby, you know you've arrived at a well-tended small hotel with an old Florentine ambiance. Facing the reception desk is an inviting sitting area with sofas arranged under a wall of pictures, Oriental carpets enhancing the dark tile floors, and artfully arranged pictures and plants setting off the cream colored walls. Each of the guest rooms has a country fresh feeling with antique armoires, wrought iron headboards, rustic wooden desk and chairs and pretty bedspreads. The rooms are not large, but are very pleasing and immaculately tidy. A copious breakfast is served family-style at long dining tables in a charming room whose walls are hung with many pictures. Guests choose from a wonderful selection of breads, cheese, cereal, boiled eggs, coffee, tea, and chocolate. The nicest aspect of this hotel is the fact that it is small enough to be very personalized and Mario sees to it that every guest feels special.

MARIO'S
Owner: Mario Noce
Via Faenza, 89
50123 Florence, Italy
tel: (055) 21 68 01, fax: (055) 21 20 39
16 rooms: Double Lire 120,000-170,000
Open all year
Credit cards: all major
No restaurant, breakfast only
2 blocks from the Florence train station

The Monna Lisa, located about a five-minute walk from the heart of Florence, is a real gem. Facing directly onto a small side street, the simple exterior gives no hint of the appealing small hotel secreted behind the heavy doors. The present owners, the Ciardi-Dupre family, are direct descendants of the very famous sculptor, Giovanni Dupre. This heritage undoubtedly accounts for the many art treasures found accenting every nook and cranny of this little inn. Many elegant, family antiques are also displayed throughout the Monna Lisa. The hotel has only 20 rooms. They vary in size—ask for one of the larger rooms as some are quite small. The decor varies too, but many have handsome antique beds and massive beamed ceilings. A few have balconies overlooking the pretty back garden. The exceptional appeal of the hotel, however, is not the guest rooms, but the public areas: the beautiful lounge, cozy bar, small parlor and spacious reception area from which a dramatic stone staircase gracefully sweeps up to the second floor guest rooms. The Monna Lisa is very home-like; in warm weather guests usually relax in the secluded back garden. Another real bonus if you are arriving by car: to the rear of the property is a parking area (access is from Via della Pergola, a one-way street that runs behind the hotel). The Monna Lisa was originally an elegant Renaissance palace and you will certainly feel like nobility while a guest at this hotel.

HOTEL MONNA LISA
Owner: Ciardi-Dupre Family
Manager: Riccardo Sardei
Borgo Pinti, 27
50121 Florence, Italy
tel: (055) 24 79 751, fax: (055) 24 797 55
20 rooms: Double Lire 250,000-355,000
Open all year
Credit cards: all major
No restaurant, breakfast only
5-minute walk from the heart of Florence

The Regency is located on a small park-like square only a ten-minute walk from the heart of Florence. It is, however, a world away in atmosphere—instead of the noise of motorcycles and the bustle of tourist-filled streets, you have a peaceful, quiet, elegant setting. The mood of being away from it all is enhanced as you enter the hotel. Again you are protected: the front door is usually kept locked and only guests of the hotel are allowed inside. You ring the front door bell just as you would in a private home. Although small, the Regency is a deluxe hotel and, in fact, it is quite amazing that with only 38 rooms the Regency can offer so many of the luxuries that are usually found only in larger hotels, such as a concierge to assist you with any of your personal needs and an intimate restaurant in a gorgeous wood paneled dining room. A larger restaurant will soon be open in an adjoining townhouse. The bedrooms are spacious and luxurious, with excellent lighting and elegant bathrooms. I would prefer a few more antiques, but these are found mostly in the lounges and the dining room. At the present time, the Regency spreads into several adjacent homes with a garden connecting the wings.

HOTEL REGENCY
Owner: Amedeo Ottaviani
Manager: Pietro Panelli
Piazza Massimo d'Azeglio, 3
50121 Florence, Italy
tel: (055) 24 52 47, fax: (055) 24 52 47
38 rooms: Double Lire 350,000-520,000
Open all year
Credit cards: all major
Restaurant open daily
10-minute walk to the heart of Florence
U.S.A. Rep: LHW 800-223-6800
Relais & Chateaux member

The Torre di Bellosguardo is a romantic villa, nestled on the shelf of a hill with an unsurpassed view of Florence. Below the hotel, the tiled rooftops, steeples, towers and domes of the city seem like a fairyland at your fingertips. It is not surprising the setting of the Torre di Bellosguardo is so fabulous. It was chosen by a nobleman, Guido Cavalcanti (a friend of Dante's), as the most beautiful site in Florence on which to build his home. The villa is owned today by Amerigo Franchetti who inherited the fabulous property from his grandmother, a baroness. All of the guest rooms are decorated in antiques and vary in size as they would in a private home. The most splendid feature of the hotel is its gorgeous setting and meticulously groomed garden that highlights a swimming pool set on a terrace overlooking Florence. What a delight to relax after a day of sightseeing and watch the beautiful buildings below you melt in the twilight, to reappear as a panorama of twinkling lights. Unfortunately breakfast is the only meal served, so guests must wind back down a narrow twisting road to go to a restaurant. However, many guests feel this is a small price to pay for the opportunity to live in a secluded villa, away from the hustle and bustle of the city.

TORRE DI BELLOSGUARDO
Owner: Amerigo Franchetti
Via Roti Michelozzi, 2
50124 Florence, Italy
tel: (055) 22 95 29, fax: (082) 22 90 08
16 rooms: Double from Lire 380,000.
Suite Lire 580,000
Open all year
Credit cards: all major
No restaurant, breakfast only
5-minute drive to the heart of Florence

The Bencista is a real find for the traveler looking for a congenial, appealing, family run hotel near Florence that has charm and yet is reasonably priced. This delightful old villa, romantically nestled in the foothills overlooking Florence, is owned and managed by the Simoni family who are always about, personally seeing to every need of their guests. Simone Simoni speaks excellent English, and on the day of my arrival he was patiently engrossed in conversation with one of the guests, giving him tips for sightseeing. Downstairs there are a jumble of rooms, each nicely decorated with rather dark, Victorian furniture. Upstairs are the bedrooms that vary in size, location, and furnishings. Some are far superior to others; however, they are all divided into only two price categories: with or without private bathroom. Many people return year after year to their own favorite room. During the season, reservations are usually given only to guests who plan to spend several days at the hotel—this is an easy requirement because the hotel is beautifully located for sightseeing in both Florence and Tuscany. (If you do not have a car, there is a bus at the top of the road that runs regularly into Florence.) Two meals (breakfast and a choice of lunch or dinner of family-style Italian cooking) are included in the price. One of the outstanding features of the pensione is its splendid terrace where guests can enjoy a sweeping panorama of Florence.

PENSIONE BENCISTA
Owner: Simone Simoni
50014 Fiesole (FI), Italy
tel: (055) 59 163, fax: (055) 59 163
43 rooms: Double Lire 230,000*
Double without private bath Lire 190,000*
*Rates include breakfast and lunch or dinner
Open all year
Credit cards: none accepted
Restaurant open daily, only for guests
8 km NE of Florence

It would be difficult to find another hotel with as many attributes as the Villa San Michele. In fact, almost impossible. How could one surpass a wooded hillside setting overlooking Florence, a stunning view, gorgeous antiques, impeccable management, gourmet dining, and, as if this were not enough, a building designed by Michelangelo. The Villa San Michele was originally a monastery whose inner courtyard dates back to the 15th Century. No expense has been spared in the reconstruction of this fabulous building to maintain the ancient ambiance. There are only 26 guest rooms, and, although not large, they are decorated with elegant taste. In addition, there are ten suites. Two are located in the Villa San Michele, six are in the Italian garden, and two are located in the *Limonaia*. All have stunning views of Florence and the Arno valley. The lounges, dining rooms, terraces and gardens are also exquisite. Breakfast and either dinner or lunch are compulsory, but this is no problem since the food is delicious. Meals can be enjoyed either in a beautiful dining room or on a lovely veranda that stretches along the entire length of the building. A swimming pool has been built on a secluded little terrace above the hotel, and, as with every feature of the Villa San Michele, it is beautiful, perfectly situated to capture the view and surrounded by fragrant gardens.

VILLA SAN MICHELE
Manager: Maurizio Saccani
Via Doccia, 4
50014 Fiesole, (FI), Italy
tel: (055) 59 451, fax: (055) 59 87 34
36 rooms: Double Lire 870,000
Open April to November
Credit cards: all major
Restaurant open daily
7 km NE of Florence
U.S.A. Rep: LHW 800-223-6800
Relais & Chateaux member

Across the street from the 12th century Abbazia di Follina, in the small town of Follina (less than an hour's drive north of Venice), there is a jewel of a small hotel, the Romantik Hotel Abbazia. As you enter into the spacious lobby with its subdued lighting, Oriental carpets, and fine antique furniture, you will feel as if you are entering a private home rather than a commercial hotel. There are only 17 guest rooms, each superbly decorated in an individual style reflecting an English country manor ambiance. All of the bedrooms are decorator perfect with color coordinating wallpapers, draperies, bed coverings and carpets. Accents of antiques, beautifully framed pictures, and bouquets of flowers make each room special. Particularly appealing are rooms 4, 5 and 6 that have large flower-decked terraces that overlook the garden in the central courtyard. There isn't a restaurant. However, just a few-minute's-drive away is the superb *Ristorante da Gigetto*, a delightful villa, brimming with country antiques where, you can dine exquisitely (restaurant closed Mondays and Tuesdays). In the cellar is an outstanding wine collection—a truly incredible selection of priceless wines beautifully displayed in a museum-like setting—ask the owner, Gigetto, if he has time to give you the tour. Just 20 km from Follina is the charming town of Asolo, plus, in the area there are numerous Palladian villas to admire.

ROMANTIK HOTEL ABBAZIA
Owner: Zanon Family
Via Martiri della Liberta
31051 Follina (TV), Italy
tel: (0438) 97 12 77, fax: (0438) 97 00 01
17 rooms: Double Lire 195,000-250,000
Open all year
No arrivals Mondays or Tuesdays
Credit cards: all major
No restaurant, breakfast only
90 km S. of Cortina, 60 km NW of Venice
U.S.A. Rep: Euro-Connection 800-645-3876

I was enchanted with the Villa Fiordaliso (a fetching pink and white villa superbly located on the shore of Lake Garda) when I spent the night in one of its antique-filled bedrooms overlooking the lake several years ago. At that time, I wrote a glowing description of this beautiful little hotel, only to learn from the manager that I was one of the last guests—the villa was closing to the public. Nevertheless, when researching for a later edition, I went by the Villa Fiordaliso for old times' sake and, to my delight, found it open again as a small hotel. Although the emphasis now is definitely on dining (the meals are expensive, but excellent), there are seven bedrooms—each unique in decor, yet each with every modern comfort. The rooms facing the lake have a lovely view, and are quieter since they are away from the noise of the street. Throughout the interior there is a blend of antique and stylish modern furniture, nicely set off by ornate parquetry floors, cool marble pillars, and magnificent gilded and painted ceilings. For history buffs, the villa offers a bit of romance—the Villa Fiordaliso was a gift of Mussolini to his mistress, Claretta Petacci. In fact, Claretta's bedroom is one of the rooms available and is a real winner with an enormous marble bathroom. The Villa Fiordaliso is owned and managed by the Tosetti family whose warmth of welcome mellows the sophisticated ambiance of this small hotel.

VILLA FIORDALISO
Owner: Giuseppe Tossetti
Via Zanardelli, 132
Lake Garda, 25083 Gardone Riviera (BS), Italy
tel: (0365) 20 15 8, fax: (0365) 29 00 11
7 rooms: Double from Lire 200,000
Suites to Lire 600,000 (Claretta's suite)
Open March to October
Credit cards: all major
Restaurant open daily
130 km E of Milan, 66 km W of Verona

La Foresteria Serègo Alighieri is in a working farm producing wine and olive oil. Only a discreet brass sign on the gate hints at any commercialism, yet it is indeed a fabulous place to stay. Each reasonably-priced guest room is a one or two-bedroom apartment with a well-equipped kitchen, charming living room, and a large bathroom tiled in local marble. The decor throughout reflects tasteful, elegant simplicity—white-washed walls set off country antiques, and comfortable sofas are upholstered in Venetian pure cotton fabrics in green and cream stripes. Soft green is repeated in the pretty cotton drapes and bed spreads. It is not surprising that La Foresteria has been developed with such love and meticulous care to maintain the estate's authentic charm—the present owner, the gracious Count di Serègo Alighieri, is the 20th generation to own the property! Family records indicate the first ancestor to own the land was the poet Dante's son, who purchased the estate in 1353. This vast farm was almost doomed at the end of World War II when the receding armies had orders to destroy it. As a forestalling tactic, the present count's father invited the commanding officers to a magnificent party. Perhaps it was the abundance of the excellent wines served, but happily the officers forgot their orders. To celebrate this miracle of the saving of the town, every April, the local town people make a pilgrimage to the estate to celebrate mass—followed of course by a little wine.

LA FORESTERIA SERÈGO ALIGHIERI
Owner: Count Pieralvise di Serègo Alighieri
Via Stazione 2
37020 Gargagnago di Valpolicella (VR), Italy
tel: (045) 77 03 622, fax: (045) 77 03 523
8 apartments: Double Lire 210,000-270,000
Open February to December
Credit cards: all major
No restaurant, breakfast on request
18 km NW of Verona, 20 km E of Lake Garda

When we first saw the Hotel Villa Giulia it was rated by the government as a third class pensione. However, the hotel is no longer a simple pensione. On our last visit we were pleased to note that all the rooms now have a private bathroom and even a swimming pool has been built into the garden. The inn is a Victorian-style villa in a large park that extends down to Lake Garda. A dramatic staircase at the end of the hallway leads to the simple bedrooms. In addition to the rooms in the main villa, guest rooms are available in a modern annex. On the same level as the entrance hall is a dining room that is quite appealing with enormous chandeliers and antique-style chairs. On a lower level, opening out onto the garden, is another dining room that is quite modern and lacking in charm. When the weather is warm, the favorite place to dine is on the terrace where tables are set to enjoy the sun and a view of the lake. Wherever you choose to dine, you will enjoy good home-style Italian cooking—it is not surprising that the food is well prepared since Signora Bombardelli, the owner, is usually bustling about in the kitchen personally overseeing the preparation of the next meal. She does not speak much English, but is extremely gracious and is always about seeing that her guests are happy. Although not fancy, all of the rooms offer satellite television, mini-bar, and safe. The Hotel Villa Giulia offers a pleasant stay at reasonable prices and a superb lakefront location.

HOTEL VILLA GIULIA
Owner: Rina Bombardelli
Via Rimembranza, 20
25084 Gargnano, Lake Garda, (BS), Italy
tel: (0365) 71 289, fax: (0365) 72 774
30 rooms: Double Lire 180,000-220,000*
*3 night minimum
Open April to October
Credit cards: all major
Restaurant open daily
140 km E of Milan, 78 km W of Verona

The entrance to Baia d'Oro is off the narrow, cobbled street that runs through the quaint lake-side town of Gargnano-Villa. Once inside, there is a small lounge, intimate bar, and a dining room. To truly appreciate the attributes that make this small inn so very special, you must step outside to the terrace that stretches out over the water. In the daytime this sun-drenched oasis is a favorite with the luncheon crowd. In the evening as the sun sets, fresh flowers and candles are placed on small tables dressed with fresh linens: a romantic scene that will beckon you again and again to the Baia d'Oro. The food lives up to all expectations: the pasta is home-made in the kitchen, the fish is fresh from the lake. As you dine, here is a constant parade of beautiful yachts pulling up to the dock, unloading their cargo of laughing, chicly dressed, obviously well-to-do Italians who have come to dine. After dinner, you go a narrow staircase to the basic bedrooms that are perfect for the young of heart who are not expecting decorator perfect furnishings. Our favorite is 14, an old-fashioned room with an antique dresser, a fancy upholstered king sized-bed, a couple of frumpy little chairs, and two large windows opening onto the lake. The Baia d'Oro is owned by the Terzi family (Gianbattista Terzi is a well-known artist). In recent years, their son, Gabiele, has taken over the management. He does a superb job personally orchestrating the dinner each evening and seeing that all overnight guests are happy.

BAIA D'ORO
Owner: Terzi Family
Manager: Gabriele Terzi
Via Gamberera, 13, 25084 Gargnano-Villa
Lake Garda (BS), Italy
tel: (0365) 71 17 1, fax: (0365) 72 56 8
13 rooms: Double Lire 286,000*
*Rate includes breakfast and dinner
Open April to October
Credit cards: all major
Restaurant open daily
140 km E of Milan, 78 km W of Verona

Romantically surrounded by a vast estate of olive trees, vineyards, and long avenues of towering cypress trees, the Castello di Uzzano is ideally located in the heart of Tuscany. Without disturbing the authentic charm of the 12th-century castle, six apartments (facing the fortified courtyard) have been incorporated into the walls of the castle. Each apartment has a complete kitchen so breakfast is not included in the price of the room (although upon prior notice, breakfast can be ordered, also lunch or dinner for small groups). However, most guests seem to prefer buying fresh produce in the local markets and fixing simple meals at home. Each of the one or two-bedroom apartments is decorated using color coordinated fabrics and handsome antiques. One of my favorite apartments (the least expensive) is *Il Madonninio* with a country-cozy living room and sweetly decorated bedroom. My other favorite (the most expensive) is *Nidcolò da Uzzano* whose spacious rooms are decorator perfect in every detail. There is a two-night minimum, but for guests who can stretch their stay, the rates go down. I have left the very best for last. Terraced below the 15th-century villa wing of the castle (the birthplace of Leonardo da Vinci's Mona Lisa) is an incredibly gorgeous, perfectly-tended, formal garden—it must be the most beautiful in Tuscany. This garden is so outstanding, it would be worth a stay at Castello di Uzzano on its merits alone.

CASTELLO DI UZZANO
Owner: Marion de Jacobert
Via Uzzano 5
50022 Greve in Chianti (FI), Italy
tel: (055) 85 40 32, fax: (055) 85 43 75
6 apartments: Double Lire 260,000-425,000*
*Breakfast not included, 2-night minimum
Open all year
Credit cards: all major
No Restaurant
27 km SE of Florence, 40 km N of Siena

Finally there is a very special place to stay near the Rome airport. However, to merely say that a void has been filled is totally inadequate for La Posta Vecchia without a doubt offers some of the most sensational accommodations in all of Italy—in all the world. Not that everyone will be able to afford to stay here for this is an expensive small inn—very expensive, but if you have the money, it is a real bargain. For this is the opportunity of a lifetime for those who want to taste the lifestyle of the rich and famous. La Posta Vecchia was the late John Paul Getty's home—his Italian villa nestled on the edge of the ocean just north of the Rome airport. Just imagine: there are only seventeen rooms, mostly suites, tucked into an enormous mansion, secluded by manicured gardens artfully created to emphasize the ruins of a Pompeii-like Roman villa whose beautiful mosaic floor peeks from between surrounding flowers and hedges. Within the villa, priceless antique furniture, statues, and fabulous fabrics adorn the rooms, artfully blended by Getty's interior designer to create an opulent, tasteful splendor. For Getty, nothing was too special, nothing too expensive. All has been retained as it was in Getty's day, the only changes being some cosmetic spiffing such as painting and new drapes (this was taking awhile because the factory in Paris where the original fabric had been woven had to be tracked down—but replacements were on the way at the time of our visit). The new owner has accomplished a remarkable feat of returning the villa to its original magnificence. The primary use of the villa is for small groups that book the entire hotel for private conferences, think tanks, seminars, and family reunions. If you want the entire villa for an exclusive holiday, you need have no worry about security since columns, discreetly positioned on each corner of the property, send out detector rays to keep anyone from the premises, plus of course bullet proof glass in the Getty bedroom and steel infrastructure in the walls. Also, should you want to bring your staff, the third floor is well equipped for your maids and butlers.

The latest renovation has artfully tucked bedrooms into the north tower wing. When Getty was renovating the villa for his personal use and installing the magnificent pool in the northern wing of the house, he found the villa dated back much earlier than he originally speculated. Beneath the house were the foundations of a Roman villa thought perhaps to be the weekend retreat of Julius Caesar. Getty, who was profoundly interested in archaeology, spared no expense to preserve this antiquity. The Roman ruins now encompass the lower level of the home and guests can wonder at the gorgeous mosaic floors, walls and pottery displayed like in a living museum. Parts of the museum can be viewed from the upper level where a panel of glass has been installed in the floor so the mosaic under-flooring can be viewed. There is even a workshop in this subterranean museum, where archaeologists under the supervision of the Department of Fine Arts continue to piece together the puzzle of this fascinating villa. Since La Posta Vecchia is sometimes rented to small groups there will be times when won't be available for individual bookings. But, if you are lucky and can snare a room, this is truly an experience of a lifetime.

LA POSTA VECCHIA
Manager: Harry Charles Mills Sciò
00055 Palo Laziale
Ladispoli (Roma), Italy
tel: (06) 99 49 500, fax: (06) 99 49 507
17 rooms: Double Lire 640,000-840,000
Suite Lire 1,340,000-2,140,000
Lunch or dinner Lire 120,000 per person
Credit cards: all major
Restaurant open daily, only for guest
2 km S of Ladispoli at Palo
25 km N of Rome Airport
Relais & Chateaux hotel

Cinqueterre is the name given to five villages (Monterosso, Riomaggiore, Vernazza, Manarola, and Cornigllia) that are built into the mountainous coast of Liguria. Several of these picturesque villages are accessible only by foot or train. A favorite base for exploring these tiny fishing hamlets is the modest resort of Levanto. The Hotel Stella Maris is a simple, two-star hotel, but it exudes such warmth and caring that it is highly recommended to the traveler who values true hospitality rather than decorator perfect accommodation. Not that the hotel is lacking in character. It is located on the second floor of a 17th-century palazzo. Remnants of its past grandeur remain. Many of the bedrooms feature high, elaborately frescoed ceilings and handsome antique beds. I think my favorite is number 4, an especially inviting room with a romantic wooden, French-style headboard. The dining room also has a frescoed ceiling and a fancy mural depicting a Maharajah and his elephant train. It is not the elaborate frescoes nor the antique decor in some of the bedrooms that make Hotel Stella Maris special. What pulls this little hotel above the ordinary is the true hospitality of the owners. Although only a little English is spoken, Renza and Sandro exude a rare, merry warmth that is sure to touch your heart. And, Renza is a wonderful cook, treating her guests each evening to good old-fashioned Italian home cooking—as you might expect, frequently featuring fresh seafood.

HOTEL STELLA MARIS
Owners: Renza and Alexandro Italiani
Via Marconi 4
19015 Levanto (SP), Italy
tel: (0187) 80 82 58, fax: (0187) 80 73 51
14 rooms: Double Lire 198,000*
*Rate includes breakfast and dinner
Closed November
Credit cards: EC, MC, VS
Restaurant open daily
83 km SE of Genoa, 36 km NW of La Spezia

Limone sul Garda is a small town tucked into a pocket of a hillside at the edge of Lake Garda. This very old town of pastel colored houses adorned with bougainvillea and twisting cobbled streets attracts so many visitors that in high season it is wall to wall tourists. But, the town is nevertheless very quaint, and especially appealing off season when you can avoid some of the crowds. There are several large, modern hotels on the hillside, but the Hotel Le Palme (in a building dating back to the 17th Century), is in the heart of town, directly on the lake. Whereas many of our suggestions in the Lake Garda area are intimate, family-operated inns, Le Palme is a hotel with more of a commercial ambiance. You enter into the lobby and go down a few steps to a small bar and an especially attractive dining room with handsome wooden, antique-style, high back chairs and beautifully set tables. From the dining room, French doors open onto an appealing outside dining room on a balcony overlooking the lake. Tucked along the side of the hotel is another, more casual place to eat in a garden terrace overlooking the lake. Here white wrought iron tables and chairs are set under the centuries-old palm trees with many plants and colorful flowers. The price is the same for all the guest rooms, but the ones overlooking the lake are prime. The rooms are pleasant and some have had a few antique pieces of furniture. The Risatti brothers who own Hotel Le Palme, own several hotels in town which is an advantage because guests can use the pool at their hotel La Pergola.

HOTEL LE PALME
Owner: Risatti Family
Via Porto, 36
25010 Limone sul Garda (BS), Italy
tel: (0365) 95 46 81
28 rooms: Double Lire 165,000
Open Easter to October
Credit cards: all major
Restaurant open daily
160 km NE of Milan, 97 km NW of Verona

The Albergo del Sole, located about an hour's drive south of Milan, came highly recommended to us as one of Italy's finest restaurants with rooms so we arrived eagerly for our first visit. Happily, this little inn surpassed our highest expectations, offering an elegantly rustic setting and delicious meals. This 600-year-old farmhouse is now a food connoisseur's dream come true. From the moment you enter this old stone home you are enveloped in a country ambiance enhanced by fine antiques, heavy beams, copper pots hanging on the walls and extravagant bouquets of flowers. The heart of the inn is its kitchen, long famous as one of Italy's finest, and well-deserving of its Michelin star. The food, featuring regional specialties prepared from the freshest of locally produced ingredients, is very expensive, but outstanding. If you cannot overnight here, the inn is well-worth a visit simply for its atmosphere and cuisine. However, if possible, plan to spend the night so you can linger over your dinner and savor the fine food and wines. Some of the guest rooms are in the main building, others are in rooms tucked around the back garden. Each of the bedrooms is nicely decorated, but with a much more modern mood than the dining rooms. Although the food and country style furnishings are outstanding, it is the traditional Italian welcome and caring warmth of the owners, Franco Colombani and his sons Francesca and Mario, that make the Albergo del Sole so special.

ALBERGO DEL SOLE
Owner: Franco Colombani and Family
Via Trabattoni 22
20076 Maleo (MI), Italy
tel: (0377) 58 142 fax: (0377) 45 80 58
8 rooms: Double Lire 290,000-320,000
Closed January and August
Credit cards: all major
Restaurant closed Sunday evenings and Mondays
60 km S of Milan, 23 km W of Cremona

Clinging to the steep hillside above the beautiful coast of Basilicata, Maratea is a charming village of very old, colorful houses and narrow cobbled streets. As the road loops ever-upward through the town, you soon come to the Locanda delle Donne Monache, carved into the rocky slope next to the tiny parish church of St Maria. Originally a nunnery dating to the early 1700's, the convent has been meticulously transformed into a deluxe, small hotel. Obviously no expense was spared in the reconstruction—every detail exudes quality and refinement. The exterior blends well with other houses in the village— salmon-colored stuccoed walls with white trim and rustic heavy tiled roof. Inside the color scheme continues with sky blue added for accent. The dramatically decorated bedrooms are tucked throughout the hotel, each taking advantage of its special vista. The largest guest rooms are designated as suites. Number 9 is especially enchanting with a stunning bath tub carved into the rocks and a pretty view out over the tiled roof tops. On the upper terrace next to the small church, a swimming pool seems to float in the air, suspended above the jumble of village roof tops. On balmy summer evenings guests enjoy superb meals outside under the stars. The quiet serenity that must have appealed to the nuns so long ago, greets the guests each morning as the sweet fresh air, the fragrance of flowers, the song of birds, and the church bells cast their spell.

LA LOCANDA DELLE DONNE MONACHE
Owner: Bruno Raffaele
Via Carlo Mazzei, 4
85046 Maratea (PZ), Italy
tel: (0973) 87 74 87, fax: (0973) 87 76 87
30 rooms: Double Lire 300,000-400,000
Open April to October
Credit cards: all major
Restaurant open daily
220 km S of Naples, 5 km W of Maratea

The Hotel Santavenere was a wonderful surprise. I had seen pictures of the hotel before I arrived and it looked rather like a motel—a long, narrow building with each floor a row of guest rooms. The photographs did not do it justice—the hotel is absolutely a knockout. From the moment you walk into the lobby, the gracious ambiance of an exquisite country home surrounds you. The living room is elegant, but not stuffy—soft, comfortable sofas and lounge chairs, slipcovered in an attractive country print, form cozy conversation nooks. Excellent antiques lend further charm. Plus, there are many nautical accents, such as models of sailboats, giving even more interest to the room. The dining room follows in excellent taste—a large, airy room with high-backed wooden chairs, fresh flowers on the tables, and white linen tablecloths. The bedrooms are beautifully decorated with excellent copies of antiques and have modern bathrooms. Each bedroom opens onto its own terrace or balcony with lovely sea views. The location too is exceptional: there is a lush lawn adorned with a swimming pool that stretches to the side of the hotel. Beyond the lawn the cliffs drop down a steep wooded hillside to the crystal-clear deep blue sea. A footpath leads winds down through the trees to a small pier. *NOTE:* As we go to press, the hotel is in the process of choosing a new manager.

HOTEL SANTAVENERE
Owner: I.T.G.P. S.p.A
Località Fiumicello di Santa Venere
85040 Maratea Porto (PZ), Italy
tel: (0973) 87 69 10, fax: (0973) 87 76 54
44 rooms: Double Lire 600,000*
*Rates includes breakfast and dinner
Open June to September 26
Credit cards: AX, VS
Restaurant open daily, only for guests
220 km S of Naples, 5 km W of Maratea

The siena and cream-colored, Liberty-style Villa Cheta Elite is located on the main coastal road just south of Acquafredda. A steep path winds up through the garden to the hotel, which has a series of tall French doors opening onto a shaded terrace where glimpses of the sea can be seen through the flowers and the trees. The hotel retains the genuine warmth and charm of a private home, without any hint of the formal commercialism of a hotel. Throughout there is a comfortable, lived-in, old-fashioned elegance. The exceptionally gracious owner personally supervises every detail in the operation of his small hotel, and welcome one and all as guests in a private home. Some of the staff speak English. Lamberto does not need to—his smile and infectious laughter transcends any language barrier. Each bedroom is individually decorated using homey, family antiques. When the weather is balmy guests eat dinner on the terrace whose white wrought-iron tables are prettily set with fresh linens and bouquets of flowers from the garden. The home-cooked meals are outstanding. If you prefer small, family-owned hotels to the sophisticated glamour of expensive resort-style hotels along this magical coast of Southern Italy, the Villa Cheta Elite will definitely win your heart.

ROMANTIK HOTEL VILLA CHETA ELITE
Owner: Lamberto Aquadro
Via Timpone, 46
85041 Acquafredda di Maratea (PZ), Italy
tel: (0973) 87 81 34, fax: (0973) 87 81 34
20 rooms: Double Lire 200,000-300,000*
*Rate includes breakfast and dinner
Open March 26 to October 23
Credit cards: all major
Restaurant, open daily, for guests only
1 km S of Acquafredda, 210 km S of Naples
U.S.A. Rep: Euro-Connection 800-645-3876

Once in a while a hotel is so perfect that it is tempting not to include it—selfishly fearful that if everyone knows how exceptional it is there might not be room in the inn when we return. The Castel Freiberg is just such a hotel, but conscience dictates sharing our Shangri-La with you. This fantasy castle cresting a hilltop in the mountains near Merano exudes charm. All of the public rooms are a decorator's dream where priceless antiques abound. The bedrooms, each individual in decor, are all tastefully furnished and some have balconies overlooking the mountains. Even if the setting were not perfect, this castle would be a winner because of its enchanting decor, but add to this a gorgeous restaurant in a richly paneled room with gourmet cooking, and what else could you possibly desire? Well, there is more. If you talk to the masterful and professional concierge, you will find that surrounding the Castel Freiberg is a maze of splendid walking paths. Also, of course, there is a beautiful pool in a garden setting with the mountains as a dramatic backdrop, as well as an inside pool, clay tennis courts, an exercise room, and more—you must go to see for yourself.

HOTEL CASTEL FREIBERG
Owner: Bortolotti Family
Via Labers
39012 Merano, (BZ) Italy
tel: (0473) 24 41 96, fax: (0473) 24 44 88
35 rooms: Double Lire 300,000-340,000
Open mid-April to November
Credit cards: all major
Restaurant open daily
In the countryside 7 km S of Merano
28 km NW of Bolzano
Relais & Chateaux member

Castel Labers (also called Schloss Labers) is a lovely old castle that dates back to the 11th Century. It has a picturesque setting on a hillside surrounded by vineyards and overlooking the beautiful Merano Valley that is framed by dramatic mountains. Although not luxurious, this castle has character and charm. Probably its major attribute is excellent management by the Stapf-Neubert family who oversee every detail of the operation and take personal responsibility to ensure that everyone is properly pampered. I spoke to Signor Neubert who told me that his great grandfather came from Copenhagen in 1885 and bought the castle which became so popular with his visiting friends that it soon became a prosperous hotel. The lounges and dining rooms are not fancy, but have a lived-in, comfortable ambiance. Many fresh foods are included in the menu and both red and white wines, produced from the inn's own vineyards, are served with meals. The central staircase dramatically leads upstairs where many of the bedrooms have lovely mountain views. The setting of this old castle is peaceful and quiet, and if you enjoy being in the countryside, you will delight in the marvelous network of walking paths that abound in this area.

HOTEL CASTEL LABERS
Owner: Stapf-Neubert Family
Via Labers, 25
39012 Merano (BZ), Italy
tel: (0473) 23 44 84, fax: (0473) 23 41 46
32 rooms: Double Lire 240,000-270,000
Open April to November
Credit cards: all major
Restaurant open daily, only for guests
In the countryside 3 km NE above Merano
28 km NW of Bolzano

If you love picturesque chalet-style hotels in quiet, isolated surroundings, then the Hotel Vigiljoch will definitely be your cup of tea. There is absolutely no highway noise: there are no cars. The only way to reach the hotel is by cable car that you take from the town of Lana that is near Merano in the mountains of northeastern Italy. The cable car rises quickly from the floor of the valley and presents breathtaking views of the vineyards and apple orchards. When the cable car reaches the top and slowly joggles into the terminal, you will see the Hotel Vigiljoch just to the left of the station. In summer, flowers cascade from every window box and umbrellas gaily decorate the front terrace. Inside you find quite simple bedrooms, many of which have balconies with a sweeping view of valley and mountains. The bedrooms are small but pleasantly furnished with furniture painted in an Alpine motif. A sprinkling of antiques highlights the lounges. My very favorite room is an intimate, wood-paneled dining room whose wonderful country prints of blue and red are complimented by attractive light-pine furniture. The gracious owner, Karl Gapp, is extremely knowledgeable about what to see and do in the area. He is very active with the tourist office and can assist guests with their various travel plans.

HOTEL VIGILJOCH
Owner: Karl Gapp
39011 Vigiljoch
Lana bei Merano (BZ), Italy
tel: (0473) 56 12 36, fax: (0473) 56 14 10
35 rooms: Double Lire 120,000-180,000
Open mid-March to mid-November
Credit cards: none accepted
Restaurant open daily
Accessible only by cable car
9 km S of Merano on route 238
24 km NW of Bolzano

Hotel Carrobbio is located on a narrow side street, just a few steps off the Via Torino—a major street leading to the Duomo. From the outside the hotel appears non-descript—a not-too interesting, modern, four-story building. However, I was glad I stopped to take a look because this small hotel has a lot to offer. Not that it can compare with its neighbor, the elegant Hotel Pierre Milan, but the prices are much lower. The reception area is small and guests are greeted warmly. According to the friendly reception manager, Franco Grassi, the hotel is small enough to know guests by name: they are never just a number. Beyond the reception area is a bar that leads into a lounge with the chairs and sofas upholstered in black leather. One end of the room is mirrored, reflecting puffy Austrian drapes and potted palms. A skylight, illuminating the core of the building, imparts a cheerful ambiance. A large buffet breakfast (served in a rather plain, white-walled room) is included in the room rate. Well-lit hallways lead to the bedrooms that are all similar in decor with built-in headboards, good reading lights, color coordinated bedspreads and chair coverings, mini bars, and television. Ask for one of the bedrooms on the top floor—three of these have spacious terraces with tables and chairs for sitting outside when the weather is nice. One of the nicest aspects of the Hotel Carrobbio is that it is so well kept. Everything looks fresh and new—not surprising as the hotel only opened in 1990.

HOTEL CARROBBIO
Manager: Franco Grassi
Via Medici 3
20123 Milan, Italy
tel: (02) 89 01 07 40, fax: (02) 80 53 334
35 rooms: Double Lire 290,000
Open all year
Credit cards: all major
No restaurant, breakfast only
Located about 10-minute walk from the Duomo

Milan has very few deluxe small hotels with character. But, since the Hotel Pierre Milan came on the scene a few years ago, that need has been superbly fulfilled. The Pierre Milan is expensive, but no more so than other hotels in the same category. You walk under the canopy, through a large glass entry flanked by two handsome statues of prancing horses, and into the spacious reception lounge decorated in tones of beige accentuated by cream-colored marbles. Even when the hotel is fully booked, there is an air of quiet refinement. An inner courtyard provides a garden effect for the chic dining room with just a handful of tables, exquisitely set with fine linens. A hallway leads to the American bar, which opens onto a sophisticated, intimate lounge with black leather sofas and a grand piano. The guest rooms are not large (except for the suites), but each is individually decorated in impeccable taste: walls covered with fine fabrics, color coordinating with the carpets, drapes and bedspreads. On the bedside table a control panel allows you to call house-keeping, turn off the lights, turn on the television, put a "do not disturb" sign outside the door, and even electronically lower the window shades without getting out of bed. Many rooms have an antique desk or writing table, one of my favorites, room 210 (with French blue walls and drapes) has an antique, wooden, king-sized sleigh bed. The Hotel Pierre is located in the historically interesting Sant'Ambrogio district.

HOTEL PIERRE MILAN
Manager: Lorenzo de Lodi
Via De Amicis, 32
20123 Milan, Italy
tel: (02) 72 00 05 81 fax (02) 80 52 157
47 rooms: Double Lire 370,000-500,000*.
*Weekend specials (on request) Double Lire 320,000
Closed August 1-21 and December 23-January 8
Credit cards: all major
Restaurant open daily
15-minute walk to the Duomo

We were delighted to find a hotel of character less than a ten-minute drive from the popular Milan Malpensa airport. And, although the Hotel Villa Malpensa is not inexpensive, you can stay here for a fraction of the cost of staying in a fancy hotel in Milan, with the added bonus of knowing you don't have to rush to catch your early morning flight. You can even squeeze in a quick swim in the pool before you leave for the airport. This stately, four-story formal mansion was once the home of the Counts of Caproni (one of the wealthiest families of northern Italy). You enter into a formal hallway painted a soft cream color, with a soaring ceiling, walls enhanced by ornate plaster sculpturing, marble floors, and oriental carpets. Throughout the original core of the hotel, the past magnificence of this 1931 villa lives on through ornate architectural features. However, throughout the rest of the hotel there is no great flair to the decor— the contemporary furnishings are typical of a commercial hotel. But, you cannot fault the amenities. All of the spacious guest rooms have built-in headboards with proper reading lights, comfortable mattresses, satellite televisions, mini-bars, direct dial telephones, hair dryers, and air conditioning. Some of the bedrooms have balconies where you can watch the planes taking off and landing.

HOTEL VILLA MALPENSA
Owner: Fausto Bonini
Via Don Andrea Sacconago, 1
21010 Vizzola Ticino (Varese), Italy
tel: (0331) 23 09 44, fax: (0331) 23 09 50
43 rooms: Double Lire 280,000
Open all year
Credit cards: all major
Restaurant open daily
4 km SW of Milan-Malpensa Airport

During the 17th and 18th Centuries it was fashionable for wealthy Venetian nobles to build palatial retreats along the cool banks of the Brenta River, thus the waterway became lined with sensational villas all the way from Venice to Padua. Today villages and commerce have built up in the area, but many of the mansions still survive, filled with statues, frescos, and Murano glasswork, attesting to the opulent life-style of days gone by. Some mansions are now open as museums, but for those who really want to experience living the noble life there is the lovely 17th-century Villa Margherita, an elegant small hotel. It is situated across the highway from the canal, just a short stroll from one of the villa museums, and a short drive from the others. Many converted villas in Italy are beautiful but faded, reflecting genteel neglect. Not so with the Villa Margherita where all is beautifully maintained; every detail is perfect. From the lounges with their elegant antiques to the guest rooms with color coordinated fabrics, each detail shows the care and involvement of the owners, Valeria and Remigio dal Corso. Far from the hubbub of Venice, yet only a 20 minute drive away, the Villa Margherita is an excellent hotel choice for those who prefer to avoid the hustle and bustle of the city. If you go into Venice, it's easiest to take the bus, thus avoiding the congestion of traffic and high cost of parking.

ROMANTIK HOTEL VILLA MARGHERITA
Owner: Valeria and Remigio dal Corso
Via Nazionale 416
30030 Mira (VE), Italy
tel: (041) 42 65 800, fax: (041) 42 65 838
19 rooms: Double Lire 200,000-240,000
Open all year
Credit cards: all major
Restaurant open daily
On canal 2 km W of Mira
20 km W of Venice
U.S.A. Rep: Euro-Connection 800-645-3876

Il Melograno is a rarity: a small, luxury hotel that is truly managed by the family—creating a warmth and cordiality seldom found in a hotel of this sophistication. Camillo Guerra oversees every detail of his hotel, ably assisted by his children. One daughter cordially manages the front desk, another oversees the health spa, while his son works behind the scene in the business office. White walls enclose a parcel of land whose core is a 16th-century, fortified farmhouse, which for many years was the holiday retreat of the Guerra family. In 1985, Signor Guerra (an antique and fine art dealer from Bari) decided to expand his home-away-from-home into a hotel. Taking meticulous care to preserve the ancient olive trees (one two-thousand years old), he built a series of superbly furnished guest rooms clustered in white, Moorish-style buildings facing intimate patios. The original farmhouse now houses the reception, romantic bar, beautiful dining room, and lounges that are exquisitely decorated in antiques. Cheerful, floral-slip-covered chairs and Oriental carpets accent stark white walls and floors. One of the inner patios is a fragrant small orange grove, watered by an ancient stone irrigation system. The dining room opens onto a pool-side terrace where meals are served overlooking the pomegranate and fig trees. Il Melograno makes an excellent, luxurious base for exploring the fascinating Apulia region of southern Italy.

IL MELOGRANO
Owner: Guerra Family
Contrada Torricella 345
70043 Monopoli (BA) Italy
tel: (080) 69 09 030, fax: (080) 74 79 08
37 rooms: Double Lire 260,000-680,000
Closed February
Credit cards: all major
Restaurant open daily
On the heel of Italy, 70 km NW of Brindisi
Relais & Chateaux member

For those who wish for accommodations with all the trimmings, yet still want to feel like a pampered guest in a private home, Villa Pambuffetti is an ideal choice. Situated in Umbria, the green heart of Italy, in the well-preserved hilltop town of Montefalco with its 13th-century Francescano frescoes, this splendid villa was once a private home. And although managed with professional skill, the gracious Pambuffetti family has a magic touch that that makes each guest feel very special. The decision to transform their country house into a 15-room inn seemed a natural choice when gracious Signora Pambuffetti's daughter, Alessandra, and her husband, Mauro, returned from the United States with a wealth of experience in the hotel and restaurant business. Alessandra demonstrates her culinary skills preparing Umbrian specialties for guests. Her delicious cakes, tarts, and homemade jams are part of the full breakfast served in the elegant cream and dusty rose colored dining room. Here guests are treated to the same spectacular panoramic view taking in Assisi, Perugia, Spoleto, Spello, as described by the Nobel-prize-winning author Herman Hesse in 1907. The actual villa is also mentioned, with its manicured gardens (which now have a swimming pool), and centuries-old cypress trees. Every small detail is tended to in the individually-decorated rooms with their travertine marble bathrooms. The room in the tower, the *Torre dell'Amore*, with its 360-degree vistas is always a favorite.

VILLA PAMBUFFETTI
Owner: Pambuffetti Family
Via della Vittoria 20
06036 Montefalco (PG), Italy
tel: (0742) 37 94 17, fax: (0742) 37 92 45
15 rooms: Double Lire 240,000-320,000
Open all year
Credit cards: all major
Restaurant open daily for dinner
30 km S of Assisi, 80 km NE of Orvieto

La Chiusa, nestled in the hills of Tuscany southeast of Siena, is an old stone farmhouse whose restaurant is so well known that guests come from miles away to enjoy the meals where everything is fresh, homemade, and delicious. Dania and Umberto Lucherini are the gracious owners and Dania is the talented chef. Almost all the vegetables, olive oil, meats, wines, and cheeses either come from the inn's own farm or from those nearby. The original wood burning oven still stands in the courtyard in front of the inn, emitting delicious aromas of freshly baking bread. The dining room is large and airy, with an uncluttered simple elegance enhanced by windows overlooking rolling hills. When the weather is balmy, meals are also served on the back terrace that is ideally positioned with a sweeping view. The emphasis here is definitely on the exquisite meals, but happily there are also bedrooms for guests who want to spend the night. Like the dining room, the guest rooms are perfectly in keeping with the ambiance of the old farmhouse, lovely in their rustic simplicity yet with every modern convenience. If you appreciate and are willing to pay for gourmet meals, this is a perfect base for exploring Tuscany.

LA CHIUSA
Owner: Lucherini Family
Manager: Sodi Franco
Via della Madonnina 88
53040 Montefollonico (SI), Italy
tel: (0577) 66 96 68, fax: (0577) 66 95 93
12 rooms: Double Lire 280,000-490,000
2 suites: Double Lire 420,000
Open mid-March to November 5
and December 7 to January 7
Credit cards: all major
Restaurant closed Tuesdays
60 km S of Siena, 10 km NW of Montepulciano

The Gasthof Obereggen, located in the Val d'Ega (Ega Valley) is very simple, but quite wonderful. The inn is situated on the side of a hill overlooking a gorgeous mountain valley in one of the most beautiful mountain regions of northeastern Italy. The town of Obereggen is a ski resort and the lift is just a few minutes' walk away. From the sun-drenched deck that extends generously out from the hotel, there is an absolutely glorious vista across the green meadows to the mountains. Behind the hotel even more majestic mountains poke their jagged peaks into the sky. Inside there is a cozy dining room. Signor Pichler must be a hunter, for trophies line the walls, and there is a typical tiled stove against one wall to keep the room toasty on a cold day. The inn has 12 bedrooms—those on the second floor open out onto lovely view-balconies. The greatest asset of this inn, and the real reason for its inclusion, is Signora Pichler: she is very special—running her little inn with such a warmth and gaiety that just being in the same room with her is fun. Signora Pichler speaks no English, but her hospitality crosses all language barriers, and her bountiful, delicious home style cooking speaks to all who love to eat. *NOTE:* Obereggen is not on most maps. If coming from Bolzano head southeast through the Val d'Ega for approximately 16 kilometers and turn to right for Obereggen. The closest town on the Hallwag map is Ega (Ega is also called San Floriano*)*.

GASTHOF OBEREGGEN
Owner: Pichler Family
39050 Obereggen (San Floriano)
Val d'Ega (BZ), Italy
tel: (0471) 61 57 22
12 rooms: Double Lire 112,000-120,000*
*Rate includes breakfast and dinner
Closed May and June
Credit cards: none accepted
Restaurant open daily
25 km SE of Bolzano, 3 km S of Nova Levante

The town of Orvieto, just off the main expressway between Rome and Florence, is one of the most picturesque of all the Umbrian hilltowns. The small city crowns the top of a hill—an intriguing sight that can be viewed from miles away. Less than a 10-minute drive south of Orvieto is a 12th-century Gothic abbey that has been converted into a hotel. Here you can stay surrounded by the romantic ruins of yesteryear. We have over-nighted at La Badia, enjoying the pool and the old-world atmosphere. Some readers have written they too liked their stay at La Badia, but we continue to receive some letters complaining of the aloof attitude of the personnel. Although La Badia does not seem to exude the caring management that makes staying at a hotel special, the location near the stunning town of Orvieto is excellent. The hotel itself is nice: the dining room is especially attractive with an enormous, high vaulted stone ceiling, wrought iron fixtures, heavy wooden beams, eye-catching copper accents and, at one end, a cavernous fireplace complete with a roasting spit. The bedrooms are not large, but are comfortable and many have a stunning view of the town of Orvieto. In the meadows behind the monastery there is a pool that makes a welcome respite from a day on the road.

LA BADIA
Manager: Luisa Fiumi
05019 Orvieto Scalo (TR), Italy
tel: (0763) 90 359, fax: (0763) 92 796
24 rooms: Double Lire 283,000
Open March to December
Credit cards: all major
Restaurant closed Wednesdays
4 km S of Orvieto
115 km N of Rome

The Villa le Barone was once the home of the famous Tuscan family, Della Robbia, whose delightful terra cottas are still seen throughout Italy. Most of the estate now has been beautifully converted into a deluxe small hotel, but the present owner, Duchessa Franca Viviani Della Robbia, still maintains a charming vine covered cottage for her own use. Although she is now in her eighties, the Duchessa comes frequently to the villa to ensure that her impeccable standards and exquisite taste prevail. Staying at the Villa le Barone is very much like being the fortunate guest in a private, elegant home set in the gorgeous Tuscany hills. There are only 25 guest rooms, all of which vary in size and decor, but each with an individual charm. In addition, there is a lovely pool on a terrace overlooking the vineyards and out to the mellow hills beyond. Wonderful little terraces are found secluded in the park-like setting where guests can find a quiet nook to read or just to sit and soak in the beauty. The food is divine and in balmy weather lunch can be taken in the garden and dinner inside in a charming dining room that formerly housed the stables. Reservations are accepted for a minimum of three nights, but that should be no problem—three nights will be too short an interlude to spend in this romantic paradise. *NOTE:* The closest town on the Hallwag map is Greve.

VILLA LE BARONE
Owner: Duchessa Franca Viviani Della Robbia
Manager: Caterina Buonamici
Via San Leolino, 19
50020 Panzano in Chianti (FI), Italy
tel: (055) 85 26 21, fax: (055) 85 22 77
25 rooms: Double Lire 340,000–390,000*
*Rate includes breakfast and dinner, 3 night minimum
Open Easter to October
Credit cards: AX
Restaurant open daily, only for guests
31 km S of Florence, 6 km S of Greve

Just five kilometers from the bustling city of Verona relax in the countryside at the exquisite Villa del Quar where you can enjoy excellent accommodations, gourmet dining, and the warmth and charm of a family-managed hotel. The gracious owner, Leopoldo Montresor, is a talented architect who spared no expense to assure that the end result of his personally-supervised renovation his estate exuded charm and taste. The Montresors live in one wing of the villa, conveniently close for Evelina Acampora-Montresor who manages the hotel. The property has been in the Montresor family for many generations—ever since Leopoldo's great, great, great grandfather won the land in a game of cards at the casino in Venice in the early 1800's. Your heart will be captivated from the moment you pass the family chapel and enter the reception lounge (formerly the storage barn), elegantly decorated with finely upholstered sofas in warm shades of pinks and mellow yellows. Sunlight floods the room through a wall of windows that open onto an inviting side terrace where guests dine in warm weather. There is also a most attractive, beamed ceilinged dining room where meals are elegantly served on tables set with fine linens. The guest rooms are equally appealing and furnished in antiques. As an added bonus, a large swimming pool is enchantingly set in a meadow with vineyards stretching almost to the edge of the pool.

HOTEL VILLA DEL QUAR
Owners: Evelina Acampora-Montresor
and Leopoldo Montresor
Via Quar N 12
37020 Pedemonte (VR), Italy
tel: (045) 68 00 681, fax: (045) 68 00 604
22 rooms: Double Lire 295,000-395,000
Open all year
Credit cards: all major
Restaurant open daily
10 km N of Verona, 15 km E of Lake Garda

How smug I felt at discovering the Castel Pergine, for here is a picture book castle perfect for the budget-minded tourist. No need to forfeit romance and glamour for even though the Castel Pergine is inexpensive, it has a fabulous location dominating a hilltop above the town of Pergine. Luckily, this castle has been delightfully transformed into a small hotel with incredible views out over the valleys and wooded hills. From the tower you can even see two small lakes in the distance which invite a picnic. The Castel Pergine is more famous as a restaurant than a hotel, in fact the Michelin guide gives the kitchen a two fork rating. The dining room has an engaging medieval decor, gorgeous views, and good food. In another wing of the castle the guest rooms offer accommodation ranging from rather basic to comfortably charming. About half of the 21 rooms have private baths; these are more expensive but also more appealingly decorated with handsome wooden paneling and rustic, country-style furnishings. All the guest rooms are pleasant, most offering lovely views, but room 27, a corner room, is especially large and pretty. The Castle Pergine is a real bargain for the price-conscious traveler, its secluded hilltop ambiance definitely a winner—especially if you are traveling with children who will love their own Disneyland-like castle.

CASTEL PERGINE
Managers: Verena and Theo Schneider
38057 Pergine (TN), Italy
tel: (0461) 53 11 58
21 rooms: Double Lire 176,000*
*Rate includes 3 meals a day
Open May to mid-October
Credit cards: none accepted
Restaurant open daily in high season
71 km S of Bolzano, 10 km E of Trento
2.5 km E of Pergine

I am such a romantic that, as the boat chugged across the lake from Stresa to the medieval fishing village of Isola dei Pescatori and I saw the Hotel Verbano with its reddish-brown walls, dark green shutters, and tables set on the terrace overlooking the lake, my heart was won—completely. To accommodate the many people who clamor off the excursion boats each day to visit the picturesque Isola Dei Pescatori (*Fisherman's Island*), the hotel has a large dining room with arched windows overlooking Lake Maggiore. However, when the weather is warm, the favorite place to dine is outside on the idyllic terrace overlooking nearby Isola Bella (*Beautiful Island*). In the evening, when most of the tourists have departed, the terrace becomes even more romantic—particularly a full moon reflecting on the rippling water. The food is excellent: featuring freshly-caught fish from the lake. There are twelve bedrooms, each with a view of the lake. When we first visited many years ago, their interior was a bit drab, but we are happy to report that they have been redecorated with a simple, old-fashioned charm. My favorite is Camelia, (number 11) a pretty corner room on the third floor with blue floral wall paper, writing desk, armoire, antique iron king-sized bed and shuttered doors leading out to a small balcony. *NOTE:* Take the public scheduled ferry from Stressa, the private water taxis are exorbitantly expensive.

HOTEL VERBANO
Owner: Alberto Zacchera
Via Ugo Ara, 2
28049 Isola dei Pescatori, Stresa
Borromee Isole, Lake Maggiore, (NO) Italy
tel: (0323) 30 408, fax: (0323) 33 129
12 rooms: Double Lire 160,000
Open March to November
Credit cards: all major
Restaurant open daily
80 km NW of Milan, ferry from Stresa

Taking a small road that winds up the hill from the nondescript hamlet of Pievescola, you soon see on your left a big gate leading into a large courtyard faced by a lovely old Castle (in days-gone-by the villa of Pope Julius II). The noble Ricci family live in one part of the castle. The other section is an elegant hotel. Some parts of the castle date from the 14th Century, others from the 16th Century exhibiting a combination of styles, incorporating Renaissance arcades with older, more fortress-like architecture. The public rooms and bedrooms are furnished with dramatic family antiques and an astounding museum-quality art collection. There is not a feeling of this being a slickly run, sophisticated operation: as a result, guests have the sensation of actually living the noble life of a by-gone era. In addition to the guest rooms in the castle, there are simpler rooms in the former horse stables across the road from the castle. Although very pleasant, these rooms are less stately than those in the main house. Also across the road the restaurant, *Oliviera*, located in the former olive pressing building, serves Tuscan cuisine (as well as other specialties), taking advantage of the produce from La Suvera's farm. The wine cellar is extensive, featuring wines produced in vineyards that date back to the 12th Century.

LA SUVERA
Owner: Marchese Giuseppe Ricci
53030 Pievescola di Casole d'Elsa,
Val d'Elsa (SI), Italy
24 rooms: Double Lire 290,000
Suites to Lire 500,000
tel: (0577) 96 03 00, fax: (0577) 96 02 20
Open April 4 to November
Credit cards: all major
Restaurant open daily
25 km W of Siena, 16 km S of Colle Val d'Elsa

It is difficult to find a hotel in Rome with thick enough windows to keep out the ever-present buzz of traffic. Less than an hour's drive from the city, the Borgo Paraelios (a prestigious Relais and Chateaux hotel) offers the perfect solution: a luxurious country villa immersed in the lovely Tuscan-like hills of Sabinia. In this splendid villa, filled to the brim with elegant antiques, rich, warm-colored tapestries and period paintings, it is impossible to find a detail overlooked. It is a masterpiece of harmonizing old and new, as antique terra cotta tile floors, stone fireplaces, beamed ceilings and antique doors from castles and villas were actually brought here and cleverly incorporated into the building. The very inviting bedrooms, each with its own character and color scheme, look out over the lush garden where guests can breakfast among the flower-laden terra cotta pots. Meandering through the gracious living room, two libraries, billiard and bridge rooms, one has the sense of having been invited to the country home of nobility for a weekend of absolute peace and tranquillity. A golf course and a spectacular indoor swimming pool add to the ambiance. For an additional charge, transportation is available to and from Rome. When you return from the bustle of the city, exquisite meals are served in the frescoed formal dining room. *NOTE:* Ask for driving instructions: Borgo Paraelios is tricky to find, but you will discover a true jewel at your journey's end.

HOTEL BORGO PARAELIOS
Owner: Signor Salabe
Località Valle Collicchia
02040 Poggio Mirteto Scalo (RI), Italy
tel: (0765) 26 267, fax: (0765) 26 268
15 rooms: Double from Lire 350,000
Open all year
Credit cards: AX, VS
Restaurant open daily
45 km NE of Rome, 2 km N of Poggio Mirteto
Relais & Chateaux member

Not so far away from the world-famous island of Capri, but definitely out of the limelight, sits the delightful fishing village of Ponza. For reasons unknown—or possibly due to its very short season—the island remains a stranger to foreigners. The hydrofoil (or ferry) makes its one-hour journey from Anzio (one hour south of Rome) to the horseshoe-shaped harbor with its whitewashed and pastel box-like houses covering the hill like building blocks. The pink-walled port, resembling a ship, holds simple shops and sidewalk cafes on the upper deck and a fresh fish market on the lower deck. Crystal clear turquoise waters can be best enjoyed by renting a *gozzo*, the colorful outboard motorboats used by fisherman, for the day to tour the group of islands by the sea. Casa Giulia sits high above the sea on a point opposite Ponza town. The hotel offers a unique accommodation for travelers who want to literally get away from it all. Although a road does exit, the inn is accessed primarily by boat, which picks guests up at the launch and shuttles to and from town at specific times during the day and evening. The whitewashed complex includes twelve rooms, each with balcony or patio, a large terrace overlooking the sea where breakfast is served, and a lovely saltwater pool, all personally overseen by gracious hostesses (and sisters), Daniela and Stefania. The cool, colorfully-tiled rooms with simple bamboo and wicker furniture reflect the true spirit of the island. A nearby beach is reached by foot. A small piece of paradise.

CASA GIULIA MARINE HOTEL
Owners: Daniela and Stefania Vecchiarelli
Località Frontone
04027 Isola di Ponza (LT), Italy
tel: (0771) 80 407, fax: (0771) 80 407
12 rooms: Double Lire 200,000
Open May to September
Credit cards: none accepted
No restaurant, breakfast only
Island of Ponza, ferry from Anzio

Hotel Chiaia di Luna over its thirty-year history has always been considered the best hotel on the island of Ponza. This is due primarily to its enviable position atop a hill, dominating the port of Ponza to one side and overlooking the sea and dramatic crescent-shaped beach to the other side. Cool green and yellow floral handpainted tiles cover the floors of the entrance, followed by a series of sitting rooms where an occasional antique is displayed. A door opens out to a seawater swimming pool, edged by the glassed-in restaurant on two sides and a rather spartan bar/outdoor eating area on the other. Only a few of the recently renovated rooms (Type A) have sea views and a terrace—a must in Ponza—and are tastefully decorated with matching floral spreads and curtains, framed botanical prints, and stenciled borders on walls. The hotel is a five-minute ride from the port and hydrofoil launch where guests are met by the hotel's private mini-van. Depending on whether one wishes to dine poolside or out, there are plenty of very good (mostly seafood) restaurants from which to choose. The Chiaia di Luna certainly stands out among the other rather mediocre accommodations on the island.

GRAND HOTEL CHIAIA DI LUNA
Directors: Flora Visocchi Family
Via Chiaia di Luna
04027 Isola di Ponza (LT), Italy
tel: (0771) 80 113, fax: (0771) 80 98 21
42 rooms: Double Lire 150,000-200,000
Credit cards: all major
Restaurant
Island of Ponza, ferry from Anzio

The Relais El Toulà is a small, super-deluxe inn quietly located in the countryside, less than an hour's drive north of Venice. A lane lined by vineyards leads to tall wrought iron gates. These swing open to a courtyard faced by the Relais El Toulà, an elegant two-story villa with red tiled roof and green shutters. This 18th-century mansion is flanked by two arcaded wings that stretch to the sides, giving the building an elegant, long, low image. Inside there is an abundance of fresh flowers in the superbly furnished lounges. The ambiance in the public rooms and also in the individually decorated bedrooms reflects the skill of a professional decorator. In addition to the secluded, park-like setting and the mood of sophisticated elegance, there is another bonus—the food and wines are outstanding. It is not surprising that the hotel is so exceptional, for its standards were set by former owner Alfredo Beltrame, a real pro in the inn-keeping profession. He was the founder of the very successful Toulà hotel chain. Today the Relais El Toulà caters to the discriminating traveler who is seeking luxurious accommodation, and doesn't mind the cost. The hotel is a member of the prestigious Relais and Chateaux group of hotels and is rated as one of their most deluxe Italian properties.

RELAIS EL TOULÀ
Manager: Giorgio Zamuner
Via Postumia, 63
31050 Ponzano (TV), Italy
tel: (0422) 96 91 91, fax: (0422) 96 99 94
10 rooms: Double Lire 250,000-480,000
Suite Lire 670,000
Open all year
Credit cards: all major
Restaurant open daily
2 km N of Ponzano Veneto toward Paderno
35 km N of Venice, 5 km NW of Treviso
Relais & Chateaux member

The Al Vecchio Convento is a real gem, offering quality accommodation for a moderate price. Its several dining rooms are brimming with rustic country charm and serve delicious meals prepared from local produce. There are nine guest rooms, each with a private bathroom and each tastefully decorated with antiques. The town of Portico di Romagna is, like the inn, inviting yet unpretentious—a very old village surrounded by wooded hills and clear mountain streams. A stroll through medieval pathways that twist down between the weathered stone houses leads you to an ancient stone bridge gracefully arching over a rushing stream. The inn too is very old. At first I thought its origin must have been an old convent because of its name, but the wonderfully gracious owner, Marisa Raggi, told me that the name came from a restaurant, located in a convent, that she and her husband, Giovanni (who is the chef), used to operate. Later, when they moved the restaurant to its present location and added a few guest rooms, they kept the original name, Al Vecchio Convento. The restaurant is still their main focus, featuring fine meals beautifully prepared from local produce. Due to the winding, two-lane mountain highway that leads to the village, it takes about two hours to drive from Florence, but if you enjoy the adventure of exploring Italy's back roads, this small hotel will certainly be one of your favorites as it is mine.

ALBERGO AL VECCHIO CONVENTO
Owners: Marisa Raggi and Giovanni Cameli
Via Roma, 7
47010 Portico di Romagna (FO), Italy
tel: (0543) 96 77 52, fax: (0543) 96 78 77
9 rooms: Double Lire 100,000-120,000
Open all year
Credit cards: all major
Restaurant open daily
75 km NE of Florence, 34 km SW of Forli

The Il Pellicano has been beautifully designed in the traditional villa style and, although not old, looks as though it has snuggled on its prime hillside position overlooking the Mediterranean for many years. The facade is of stucco, painted a typical Italian russet and set off by a heavily tiled roof. Vines enwrap the building, further enhancing its inviting look. One enters into a spacious, attractive lobby where the sun streams through the windows enhancing the white walls, terra cotta floors, and wooden beamed ceilings. The happy ambiance continues with pretty sofas, antique accents, and enormous displays of fresh flowers enlivening every conceivable nook and cranny. The overall impression is one of light and color—and great taste. Beyond the reception area is an outdoor dining terrace, a favorite place to dine when the weather is balmy. Frequently the chef serves elaborate buffets outside—(the food at Il Pellicano is expensive, but excellent). From the terrace, a lawn dotted with trees extends down the hillside to where there is a beautiful pool romantically perched at the cliff's edge. From the pool a staircase leads to a pier at the water's edge. Along this path, small individual terraces with lounge chairs and mats for sunning have been built into the rocks. In front of the hotel is a tennis court, again surrounded by flowers. The Il Pellicano is expensive but superb—a truly idyllic retreat.

IL PELLICANO
Managers: Ennio and Nadia Emili
58018 Porto Ercole (GR), Italy
tel: (0564) 83 38 01, fax: (0564) 83 34 18
30 rooms: Double Lire 580,000-610,000
4 suites in cottages: Lire 476,000-1,150,000
Open March 10 to January 10
Credit cards: all major
Restaurant open daily
South end of peninsula, Hwy 1 exit Orbetello
160 km N of Rome, 4.5 km S of Porto Ercole
Relais & Chateaux member

If money doesn't matter, when in Portofino settle in for a long stay at the incomparable Hotel Splendido. But since not everyone's travel budget can stretch to such luxury, the Hotel Eden is a welcome alternative. Although the price at the Eden might seem high for the accommodation offered, just remember that Portofino is the target of the wealthy from around the world, and rates in restaurants and places to stay reflect this popularity. If you are prepared for simplicity (tempered with the warmth of hospitality offered at family-run hotels), you will be happy to discover the Eden. The hotel is tucked right in the heart of Portofino. Not facing the harbor, but down a little lane, just two-minutes' walk away. Wrought iron gates open to steps that lead to the front garden, a peaceful oasis of flowers and green lawn. A side terrace faces the garden where meals are served outside when the weather is warm. The hotel is a soft mustard-colored villa with green shutters. As you enter, to the right is a porch-like dining room with rather ordinary tables and chairs. Further on, is the registration desk where the personable Signor Osta will probably be waiting to check you in. Don't expect too much in the guest rooms. They are all extremely simple in decor. The best (and the favorite of guests who return each year) is number 7 that has its own small patio. Room 6 (with an antique white iron bed) is another of the better rooms.

HOTEL EDEN
Owner: Ferruccio Osta
Via Dritto 18
16034 Portofino (GE), Italy
tel: (0185) 26 90 91, fax: (0185) 26 90 47
12 rooms: Double Lire 180,000-260,000
Open all year
Credit cards: all major
Restaurant open daily
5 km S of Santa Margherita Ligure
35 km E of Genoa

Located up a winding, wooded road high above the town of Portofino, the super-deluxe Hotel Splendido sits majestically above the beautiful blue Mediterranean, overlooking the boats moored in Portofino's lovely harbor. Stretching across the front of the hotel is a magnificent terrace—a favorite choice of guests who enjoy dining outside with an incredible vista of the sea. There are also romantic little pathways originating from the hotel. You can stroll the wooded grounds and stop along the way at strategically placed benches to enjoy incomparable views. Or, if instead of a stroll you would like more serious exercise, on a terrace below the hotel is an enormous swimming pool. Located in the gardens to the left of the hotel are tennis courts. The public rooms are charming with comfortable chairs covered with floral prints and fresh flowers galore. Every detail is perfect and in excellent taste. The bedrooms too are lovely and decorator perfect. Many have balconies that afford a splendid view of Portofino. The Splendido is expensive, but without a doubt one of the most special resorts in Italy.

HOTEL SPLENDIDO
Manager: Maurizio Saccani
16034 Portofino (GE), Italy
tel: (0185) 26 95 51, fax: (0185) 26 96 14
65 rooms: Double from Lire 850,000-990,000*
*Rate includes breakfast and dinner or lunch
Closed January 3 to March 31
Credit cards: all major
Restaurant open daily
5 km S of Santa Margherita Ligure
35 km E of Genoa
Relais & Chateaux member

The Albergo Casa Albertina is a prime example of what a difference management can make. There is a wide choice of hotels in the picturesque little fishing village of Positano—many, like the Casa Albertina, with spectacular views, pleasant decor, and good meals. However, they don't have Michele Cinque who is an outstanding hotelier: gracious and warmhearted—willing to do whatever is required to make each guest feel very special. It is not surprising that Michele is such a pro—he has been in the hotel business for many years, having been the manager of one of Positano's most deluxe hotels (Le Sirenuse) before deciding to spend full time helping his wife and mother-in-law manage the Casa Albertina. The hotel is really a family operation: Michele is usually at the front desk ready to care for the guests, his mother-in-law is in charge of the kitchen while his wife helps out wherever needed. Two sons are also working at the hotel and Lorenzo Cinque has taken over its official management—and quite ably, I might add. The hotel (which is built into a 12th-century house) clings to the hillside above Positano, a position that affords superlative views, but also means a strenuous walk into town.

ALBERGO CASA ALBERTINA
Owner: Cinque Family
Via della Tavolozza, 4
84017 Positano (SA), Italy
tel: (089) 8 75 143, fax: (089) 81 15 40
20 rooms: Double Lire 250,000-290,000*
*Rate includes breakfast and dinner
Open all year
Credit cards: all major
Restaurant open daily, only for guests
55 km S of Naples, 17 km S of Sorrento

For those who want to be smack in the middle of the colorful fishing village of Positano, the Palazzo Murat might be just your cup of tea. It is superbly located—surrounded by shops and only steps down to the beach. The hotel consists of two parts: the original building (a 200-year-old palace) plus a new wing to the side. The new section is a standard hotel—pleasant but not unusual. However, the palace is quite special, with a faded-pink patina whose charm is accented by wonderful arched alcoves, intricately designed windows and magenta bougainvillea clinging to the walls and cascading from the wrought iron balconies. The entrance to the hotel is through a sun-drenched patio, a favorite gathering spot for guests. Within, the old world feeling is maintained with tiled floors, white walls and formal settings of antique sofas and chairs. My favorite bedrooms are the five located upstairs in the characterful palace section: especially appealing are those with shuttered French doors opening onto small balconies that capture a view of the bay. All the rooms are comfortable and have television, radio, minibar, and air conditioning. In summer a large buffet-style breakfast is served outside on the patio. Breakfast is the only meal served, but this is no problem as there are many enticing restaurants nearby. The hotel has its own boat that three times a week takes guests for excursions along the coast.

HOTEL PALAZZO MURAT
Owner: Mario Attanasio
Manager: Carmine Pallone
Via dei Mulini, 23
84017 Positano (SA), Italy
tel: (089) 87 51 77, fax: (089) 81 14 19
28 rooms: Double Lire 200,000-240,000
Open Easter to mid-October
No restaurant, breakfast only
Near the beach–heart of Positano
55 km S of Naples, 17 km S of Sorrento

The Il San Pietro di Positano is touted as one of the most delightful deluxe hotels in the world. It is. There is no question about it. From the moment you approach the hotel class is evident: no large signs; no gaudy advertising; just an ancient chapel along the road indicates to the knowledgeable that an oasis is below the hill. After parking in the designated area near the road, you take an elevator that whisks you down to the lounge and lobby. You walk out of the elevator to a dream world—an open spacious world of sparkling white walls, tiled floors, colorful lounge chairs, Oriental rugs, antique chests, flowers absolutely everywhere, and arches of glass through which vistas of greenery and sea appear. To the right is a bar and to the left is a marvelous dining room—again with windows of glass opening to the view, but with the outdoors appearing to come in, with the walls and ceilings covered with plants and vines. The bedrooms too seem to be almost a Hollywood creation—more walls of glass, bathrooms with views to the sea, and balconies on which to sit and dream. If you can tear yourself away from your oasis of a bedroom, an elevator will whisk you down the remainder of the cliff to the small terrace at the water's edge. If all this sounds gaudy, it isn't. It is perfect

IL SAN PIETRO DI POSITANO
Owners: Salvatore and Virginia Attanasio
84017 Positano (SA), Italy
tel: (089) 87 54 55, fax: (089) 81 14 49
55 rooms: Double Lire 470,000-650,000*
*Rate includes breakfast and dinner
Closed December to mid-March
Credit cards: all major
Restaurant open daily, only for guests
2 km south of Positano on Amalfi Drive
55 km S of Naples, 17 km S of Sorrento
U.S.A. Rep: E&M: 800-223-9832
Relais & Chateaux member

Le Sirenuse is a superb luxury hotel tucked smack in the middle of the picturesque ancient fishing village of Positano. It is no wonder that so many writers and artists have been attracted to this colorful town of brightly hued houses clinging to the precipitous hillside as it drops down to its own small bay. And it is also no wonder that so many of these famous people have found their way to the oasis of Le Sirenuse. From the moment you enter the hotel lobby the mood is set with fresh white walls, tiled floors, oil paintings on the walls, and accents of antiques. The hotel cascades down the hill and so almost all the rooms capture a wonderful view out over the quaint rooftops and the tiled domed cathedral to the shimmering blue waters of the bay. It is only a short walk through the perpendicular streets until you are on the beach. The dining room has walls of glass that allow the maximum enjoyment of the vista below, but most diners prefer the splendor of eating outdoors where the deck is set with tables for dining. On another level of the hotel there is a small pool for sunning and dipping.

LE SIRENUSE HOTEL
Manager: Antonio Sersale
Via C. Colombo, 30
84017 Positano (SA), Italy
tel: (089) 87 50 66, fax: (089) 81 17 98
60 rooms: Double Lire 480,000-580,000
Open all year
Credit cards: all major
Restaurant open daily
Old fishing village on Amalfi Drive
55 km S of Naples, 17 km S of Sorrento
U.S.A. Rep: LHW 800-223-6800

The Villa Franca, with a commanding position overlooking the sea, is one of Positano's newly renovated classic hotels with an excellent quality/price rapport. There is an immediate warmth and charm as soon as you walk in to the redesigned and redecorated villa. The Russo family wanted to create an attractive full-service hotel without losing the friendliness and service of a small inn. It is just that. The fresh Mediterranean decor is most appealing with royal blue slip-covered armchairs, a profusion of plants, lacquered terra cotta vases, white tiled floors and walls and arched windows everywhere, so that you don't miss a second of the mesmerizing views of the sea. The elegant glassed-in restaurant with floral tapestry chairs and blue tablecloths serves fresh local seafood. The food is exceptional: Mario Russo is himself a talented chef and personally oversees both the food and impeccable service. In the winter, the hotel sponsors a cooking school where Diana Folonari teaches her pupils the art of Italian-Mediterranean specialties. The bedrooms follow the same cheerful theme with colorful ceramic tiled floors, cream bedspreads with green and yellow striped trim and exquisite views. The cherry on top of the cake is the rooftop swimming pool surrounded by yellow chaise lounges and palms with a 360 degree panoramic view over the world's most beautiful coastline.

HOTEL VILLA FRANCA
Owner: Mario Russo
Viale Pasitea, 318
Positano 84017 (SA), Italy
tel: (089) 87 56 55, fax: (089) 87 57 35
28 rooms: Double Lire 220,000-260,000
Open: Easter to October
Credit Cards: all major
Restaurant open daily
55 km S of Naples, 18 km S of Sorrento
U.S.A. Rep: E&M 800-223-9832

The Relais Fattoria Vignale is a very polished, sophisticated small hotel located in the heart of the Chianti wine region in the small town of Radda. The hotel was the manor house of one of the large wine estates where the family's wines are still produced and are readily available in a winery shop across the street. Although located right on the main street near the center of town, there is a country atmosphere because the back of the hotel opens up to lovely views of rolling hills laced with vineyards and dotted with olive trees. Capturing this idyllic vista is a large swimming pool with comfortable lounge chairs along the side. Inside, the rooms are all beautifully decorated with a combination of authentic antiques and excellent reproductions. Care has been taken in the restoration to preserve many of the nice architectural features of the manor such as heavy beams, arched hallways, decorative fireplaces, and painted ceilings. Only 300 meters from the hotel is the *Ristorante Vignale*, which is under the same ownership as the hotel.

RELAIS FATTORIA VIGNALE
Manager: Silvia Kummer
Via Pianigiani, 15
53017 Radda in Chianti (SI), Italy
tel: (0577) 73 83 00, fax: (0577) 73 85 92
26 rooms: Double Lire 230,000–300,000
Open mid-March to mid-November
Credit cards: AX, VS
Restaurant closed Thursdays
In the heart of Chianti wine region
52 km S of Florence, 31 km N of Siena

Vescine, a medieval hamlet in the heart of Chianti, has been restored into a four star hotel, comprised of individual stone cottages accented by red tiled roofs. One of the larger of the old stone buildings is now the reception area, bar, breakfast room, and lounge. Nearby, the guest rooms are in clusters of old houses, romantically connected by stone stairways. The decor is simple, yet extremely appealing and sympathetic to the rustic nature of the village. Tiled floors, beamed ceilings, white-washed walls, wrought iron or wooden headboards, and wooden-shuttered windows lend an authentic country look. All of the bedrooms are similar. A favorite is room 32 with an engaging terrace. Number 18, a corner room with handsome wrought iron bed, is also very attractive. From most of the rooms there is a lovely view. Sixty hectares surround the village, offering vistas of densely wooded hills interspersed by fields of grapes. One of the most magnificent of the views is captured from the swimming pool terrace, which offers a sweeping panorama of the Tuscan hills. Breakfast is the only meal served, but within walking distance is La Cantoniera di Vescine, a restaurant in an ancient farm-house featuring Tuscan cuisine and Chianti wines. *NOTE:* Although the address is Radda, the hotel is not in town, but well signposted—about mid-way on the road that runs between Radda and Castellina.

VESCINE-IL RELAIS DEL CHIANTI
Manager: Birgit Fleig
Località Vescine
53017 Radda in Chianti (SI), Italy
tel: (0577) 74 11 44, fax: (0577) 74 02 63
25 rooms: Double Lire 240,000-300,000
Open March to November
Credit cards: all major
Restaurant open daily
25 km N of Siena, 55 km S of Florence

The Rasun di Sopra, built in 1578 by Count Heufler, is actually a castle, but not one of the large foreboding castles sometimes found high on mountain peaks. This is a friendly, almost chalet-like castle, located in a sunny mountain valley in north-eastern Italy. Although within a short drive of some of the most dramatic vistas in the Dolomites, the Ansitz Heufler's setting is pretty, but does not include dramatic jagged mountain peaks. However, in winter skiing is nearby and in summer walking trails beckon in every direction. The Ansitz Heufler does not seem geared to English speaking guests although we did find one of the staff with whom we could communicate. But even though language might be a problem, the reception is very friendly and everyone seems eager to please. The inn is popular as a restaurant. There is an especially cozy dining room with very old paneled walls and ceiling, planked wooden floors, leaded glass windows, tables set with pretty linens, and appealing chalet-style chairs with carved heart backs. In the summer, guests sit out on the terrace where refreshing drinks and snacks are served. The staircase leads up to a wide hallway off which are the bedrooms. The bedrooms are all different from one another, but are all attractively furnished in a simple, uncluttered style with a liberal use of dark antiques attractively setting off whitewashed walls and freshly scrubbed wooden floors.

ANSITZ HEUFLER HOTEL
Owner: Mediolalium Vita
Manager: Valentin Paul Huber
Valle di Anterselva
39030 Rasun di Sopra (BZ), Italy
tel: (0474) 46 28 8, fax: (0474) 48 19 9
9 rooms: Double Lire 136,000–190,000
Closed May and November
Credit cards: VS
Restaurant closed Wednesdays
90 km NE of Bolzano, 12 km E of Brunico

It is no wonder that the Hotel Caruso Belvedere has such an especially spectacular site in Ravello—it was built as a palace in the 11th Century by a noble family who probably had their pick of real estate. The views of the rugged Amalfi coast from the dining terrace perched high in the clouds is gorgeous. Many of the bedrooms too have vistas. Although the decor is rather drab, the views just can't be surpassed. If you choose the Caruso Belvedere, splurge and ask for one of their most deluxe rooms. These are simply decorated without much style BUT they have enormous balconies that stretch the width of the room to capture again the incredibly romantic coast below. You will wake in the morning to the sound of birds and the scent of flowers intermixed with the fragrance of the vineyards that drifts up from the terraces beneath your balcony. The Hotel Caruso has more to offer than just its marvelous views. The dining room offers excellent food including a divine specialty of the house—a delicious chocolate soufflé that will linger in your memory perhaps as long as the view. The meals are accompanied by wines from the Caruso family vineyards.

HOTEL CARUSO BELVEDERE
Owner: Caruso Family
Manager: Gino Caruso
Via S. Giovanni del Toro, 52
84010 Ravello (SA), Italy
tel: (089) 85 71 11, fax: (089) 85 73 72
24 rooms: Double Lire 210,000–248,000
Open all year
Credit cards: all major
Restaurant open daily
Hilltown above Amalfi coast
66 km S of Naples, 6 km N of Amalfi

The Marmorata Hotel was cleverly converted from the shell of an old paper mill. Only a few of the old paper mills are still in operation, but at one time the Amalfi area was famous for its production of fine paper. The official address of the Marmorata Hotel is Ravello; however, it is not located in the cliff town of Ravello, but rather on the coastal highway. As you are driving north from Salerno to Ravello you will see the sign to the hotel which is snuggled in the rocky cliffs between the road and the sea. As you enter the hotel you notice the nautical theme carried throughout the decor from the chairs in the dining room to the mirrors on the walls. The interior is charming with comfortable leather lounge chairs and small Oriental rugs. There is a lovely terrace plus, on a lower level, snuggled into the rocks, a small swimming pool. The bedrooms are small, but nicely decorated, again with the seafaring motif: the beds seem to be built into captains' sea chests and nautical prints are on the walls. The bathrooms are also small, but modern and attractive. All of the bedrooms have radios, color televisions, telephones, air conditioning and small refrigerators. Many of the rooms have an excellent view of the water and rugged coast.

MARMORATA HOTEL
Owner: Camera d'Afflitto Family
Strada Statale, 163
84010 Ravello (SA), Italy
tel: (089) 87 77 77, fax: (089) 85 11 89
40 rooms: Double Lire 225,000–280,000
Open all year
Credit cards: all major
Restaurant open daily
On the coast below Ravello
62 km S of Naples, 23 km N of Salerno

There is something magical about the Hotel Palumbo, a 12th-century palace, owned since 1875 by the Vuilleumier family. The location is perfect—high in the clouds overlooking terraced vineyards and beyond to the brilliant blue Mediterranean which dances in and out of the jagged rocky coast. The romance begins when you enter the ceramic-tiled lobby with its ancient atrium of arched colonnades, green plants flowing from every nook, masses of fresh flowers, and beautiful antiques. Each small corner is an oasis of tranquillity from the intimate bar to the cozy antique filled tiny lounges. There is a lovely dining room with a crystal chandelier, bentwood chairs and a fireplace, but usually meals are served on the terrace that perches like a bird's nest in the sky. Wherever you dine, the food is expensive, but excellent. There is a delightful garden in the rear featuring a vine-covered terrace overlooking the Amalfi coast. Another tiny patio that captures both the sun and the view is tucked onto the roof of the villa. There are only twenty one bedrooms, each individually decorated and appealing with its own personality. A few guest rooms are located in an annex. The Hotel Palumbo is the most deluxe hotel with charm in Ravello, exuding a romantic ambiance and a wealth of old world character. Although expensive, it has great style.

HOTEL PALUMBO
Owner: Vuilleumier Family
Manager: Marco Vuilleumier
Via S. Giovanni del Toro 28
84010 Ravello (SA), Italy
tel: (089) 85 72 44, fax: (089) 85 81 33
21 rooms: Double Lire 480,000-560,000*
*Rates include breakfast and dinner
Open all year
Credit cards: VS
Restaurant open daily
66 km S of Naples, 6 km N of Amalfi

Hotel Descriptions

The Villa Cimbrone is not only a hotel: its gardens are one of Ravello's most famous attractions. The tourist office proclaims, "The Villa Cimbrone, essence of all the enchantment of Ravello, hangs like a swallow's nest on the cliffs." The villa is reached by a delightful ten-minute walk from the main square of Ravello (the signs are well marked to this favorite sightseeing prize). Once through the gates, the villa and its magnificent gardens open up like magic. The gardens are truly superb—if you have ever received a postcard from Ravello, chances are it showed the view from the terrace of the Cimbrone. Most dramatic of all is the belvedere with its stately Roman statues accenting the dazzling view. Luckily, this outstanding villa is also a small hotel. The rooms are of museum quality with furniture fit for a king. We toured through the marvelous old building that is not open to the public—only to the guests. This fabulous villa was once the prized possession of an English Lord. Later it was sold to the present owner, Marco Vuilleumier, who told us the following romantic tale: toward the end of World War II, the English nobleman (who owned Villa Cimbrone) landed with the Allied troops in Salerno. Somehow he was able to find a jeep, and—you guessed it—wound up the twisting road to see once again his beloved villa.

VILLA CIMBRONE
Owner: Marco Vuilleumier
84010 Ravello (SA), Italy
tel: (089) 85 74 59, fax: (089) 85 77 77
20 rooms: Double Lire 220,000–290,000
Open April to October
Credit cards: none accepted
No restaurant, breakfast only
10 minute walk to parking in town center
66 km S of Naples
6 km N of Amalfi

The Villa Maria is perhaps best known for its absolutely delightful terrace restaurant that has a bird's eye view of the magnificent coast. Whereas most of the hotels in Ravello capture the southern view, the Villa Maria features the equally lovely vista to the north. The Villa Maria is easy to find because it is on the same path which winds its way from the main square to the Villa Cimbrone. After parking your car in the main square of Ravello (or at the Hotel Giordano that is under the same ownership) look for the signposts for Villa Maria. After about a 2-minute walk, you find the hotel perched on the cliffs to your right. The building is a romantic old villa with a garden stretching to the side where tables and chairs are set—a favorite place to dine while enjoying the superb view. Inside, there is a cozy dining room that overlooks the garden. The bedrooms have old-fashioned brass beds and antique furniture. The bathrooms have been freshly remodeled and some even have Jacuzzi tubs. The hotel is owned by Vincenzo Palumbo whose staff speaks excellent English should you call for a reservation. Vincenzo Palumbo also owns the nearby Hotel Giordano that has a heated pool that can be used free by guests at the Villa Maria. Many readers have written to us saying how gracious and warm a welcome they receive at the Villa Maria. How lucky to be able to have the best of all worlds should you be on a budget—a wonderful view and location plus a charming villa.

VILLA MARIA
Owner: Vincenzo Palumbo
Via S. Chiara, 2
84010 Ravello (SA), Italy
tel: (089) 85 72 55, fax: (089) 85 70 71
17 rooms: Double Lire 140,000–390,000
Open all year
Credit cards: all major
Restaurant open daily
66 km S of Naples, 6 km N of Amalfi

Only about a half hour's drive from Florence, easily accessible from the A1 to Rome, is the Villa Rigacci, once a private residence, now an inviting small inn. This 16th-century villa is a picture-perfect example of a Tuscan villa with its faded pink stucco facade, thick walls, heavy weathered red tile roof, green shuttered windows and park like gardens. The owner, Federico Pierazzi, is personally involved with all aspects of running the inn: she is like a hostess overseeing the needs of her house guests. In summer, after a day of sightseeing, guests relax in the back garden where a large pool, surrounded by lounge chairs and umbrellas, stretches out on a terraced lawn. Inside, handsome antiques adorn the sitting rooms and library. The dining room is especially appealing and, according to the guests staying at the inn, the chef is excellent. All of the bedrooms have direct dial telephone, color television, small bar and bathroom. Each is individually decorated with very attractive country-style antiques and lovely fabrics creating rooms that blend beautifully with the old world ambiance of the villa. Although I personally prefer the area of Tuscany that stretches directly south of Florence where the villages seem more secluded, the conveniently located Villa Rigacci offers easy access to the expressway and accommodation with charm, hospitality, and warmth. *NOTE:* Vaggio is a small town southwest of Reggello.

HOTEL VILLA RIGACCI
Owner: Federico Pierazzi
50066 Vaggio-Reggello (FI), Italy
tel: (055) 86 56 718, fax: (055) 86 56 537
20 rooms: Double Lire 180,000–280,000
Open all year
Credit cards: all major
Restaurant closed January
30 km SE of Florence, 5 km S of Reggello

How could one possibly write about hotels in Italy and leave out the historical Albergo del Sole? Dating back to 1467, it is the oldest hotel in Rome—possibly one of the oldest still-operating hotels in the world. In addition to being of great historical interest, the hotel has the blessing of holding a prime location: looking across the ancient Piazza della Rotonda to one of Rome's masterpieces, the Pantheon, which was standing before the birth of Christ. The Albergo del Sole has been meticulously restored, faithfully reflecting its 15th-century heritage. You enter into an attractive long narrow lobby with arched ceiling, red tiled floor, white-washed walls and a very large, ornately framed antique oil painting over the reception desk. From the lobby, doors lead into the various lounges that maintain the same, elegantly simple, uncluttered look with white walls, white upholstered chairs and sofas and antique accent pieces. One floor up is a lovely interior garden-patio that opens onto an intimate breakfast room where the tables are invitingly set with pretty floral print table clothes. The bedrooms are each individual in decor, but similar in mood with color coordinating bedspreads and draperies. The suite is especially attractive with a beautiful antique wooden headboard.

ALBERGO DEL SOLE
Manager: Giancarlo Piraino
Piazza della Rotonda, 63
00186 Rome, Italy
tel: (06) 67 80 441, fax: (06) 69 94 06 89
26 rooms: Double Lire 420,000
Open all year
Credit cards: all major
No restaurant, breakfast only
Located in the center of Old Rome

Hotel rates in the center of Rome are usually very expensive, but the Hotel Carriage, tucked into a tiny side street, is both moderately priced and conveniently situated just a short stroll from the bottom of the Spanish steps. From the outside it is a nondescript, sienna-colored building with green shuttered windows opening directly onto the street. The small entry lobby is flanked by a small breakfast room and a formal parlor with ornate furnishings including brocade chairs, an enormous gilt mirror, a fancy chandelier, and elaborately carved tables. The pretty soft blue walls of this room set the color theme for the hotel; the bedrooms I saw that had been redecorated were also done in varying shades of blue. Some of the guest rooms are very small so it is best to pay a bit more and request one of the best twin-bedded rooms. However, no matter what the size, all the rooms have air conditioning, telephone, radio, small refrigerator, and an old world flavor. One of the nicest features of the hotel is a rooftop terrace where on summer evenings guests may sit at tables and enjoy the view over a jumble of tiled roofs to the twin spires of the 16th-century church, Trinita dei Monti. The Hotel Carriage is not luxurious, but offers a less expensive alternative for lodging in Rome.

HOTEL CARRIAGE
Manager: Giampiero Cau
Via delle Carrozze, 36
00187 Rome, Italy
tel: (06) 69 90 124, fax: (06) 67 88 279
30 rooms: Double Lire 270,000–285,000
Suites Lire 300,000–350,000
Open all year
Credit cards: all major
No restaurant, breakfast only
Located near the bottom of the Spanish steps

For location, the Gregoriana is superb: it is situated on Gregoriana Street that runs into the Piazza Trinita dei Monti at the top of the Spanish Steps. In spite of the perfect location, when I first saw the Gregoriana I just did not see how I could include it in our book because it has no antique ambiance: in fact, the decor motif might be classified as Chinese with a mish-mash of art deco. If you are looking for a hotel with a refined taste, this is not it. However, after staying at this hotel, I just did not see how I could not include it—it is such a well-run small hotel and has such a sparkle of personality that it brightens the otherwise often impersonal city of Rome. You will not be just one of the thousands of tourists in Rome—upon arrival, the concierge will probably already know you by name and will continue to greet you personally as you come and go. Instead of feeling like a face that goes with a key hanging on the wall, you will experience a warmth and intimacy—as if you were a guest in a private home. The bedrooms are simple and spotlessly clean. Those at the rear are especially quiet and some enjoy a balcony with a view over the rooftops of Rome. Only breakfast is served. However, there is a concierge on duty twenty-four hours a day to cater to your special needs.

HOTEL GREGORIANA
Owner: Ernesto Panier-Bagat
Manager: Aldo Basso Bondini
Via Gregoriana, 18
00187 Rome, Italy
tel: (06) 67 94 26 9, fax: (06) 67 84 25 8
19 rooms: Double Lire 260,000 to 300,000
Open all year
Credit cards: none accepted
No restaurant, breakfast only
Located near the top of the Spanish Steps

The Hotel Hassler is a landmark in Rome. Located in the heart of the elegant shopping area, on the Piazza Trinita dei Monti at the top of the Spanish Steps, this small, elite hotel was once a palatial private home. Its entrance is sedate and elegant. The reception rooms are a little somber, but this mood is quickly relieved by an inner courtyard—a superb oasis with stone walls covered with vines, statues, flowers, cozy little tables, and a bar. You can linger in the garden, take a refreshment in the afternoon or perhaps meet a friend for an aperitif in the evening. The dining room at the Hassler is also spectacular, boasting one of the finest views in Rome: the entire panorama of the city surrounds you as you dine. As the evening deepens and the city lights begin to flicker, the scene will become one of romance. If money is no object, the Hotel Hassler offers some magnificent suites, some with enormous terraces and a view so beautiful that you will be sorely tempted never to set foot from this gorgeous hotel.

HOTEL HASSLER
Manager: Oscar Wirth
Trinita Dei Monti, 6
00187 Rome, Italy
tel: (06) 67 82 65 1, fax: (06) 67 89 99 1
100 rooms: Double Lire 590,000–650,000
Open all year
Credit cards: all major
Restaurant open daily
Located at the top of the Spanish Steps
U.S.A. Rep: LHW 800-223-6800

The deluxe Hotel d'Inghilterra, definitely one of the finest small hotels in Rome, exudes an ambiance of warmth and dignified charm. The interior is enhanced by strategically placed antiques, lovely paintings, pretty Oriental carpets, antique mirrors and fresh flowers. Down the hallway from the reception lounge is a charming bar that seems to be the rendezvous spot for everyone staying at the hotel. This appealing bar has beautiful dark wood paneling adorned with colorful prints, intimate little tables, fine antique carpets, and comfortable leather sofas. There is also a very popular English-style restaurant where the chef specializes in light, innovative preparation of food. The bedrooms are well-decorated in traditional decor. A few deluxe rooms have small terraces—a romantic spot for breakfast overlooking the rooftops of Rome. The location of the d'Inghilterra is excellent. A short walk in one direction will lead you through lovely shopping avenues to the bottom of the Spanish Steps. A short walk in the other direction will lead you to the Trevi Fountain with its hubbub of activity. Originally, the Hotel d'Inghilterra was built as a guest house for the famous Torlonia Palace and you will certainly see and appreciate traces of grandeur that are still apparent throughout this once-regal residence.

HOTEL D'INGHILTERRA
Manager: Luigi Richard
Via Bocca di Leone, 14
00187 Rome, Italy
tel: (06) 69 981, fax: (06) 69 92 22 43
105 rooms: Double: 455,000-530,000
Open all year
Credit cards: all major
Restaurant open daily
Located near the bottom of the Spanish Steps
U.S.A. Rep: Utell International 800-448-8355

The Hotel Lord Byron is owned by a fascinating man and superb hotelier, Amedeo Ottaviani, who believes that "Hospitality is like an exquisite flower, it must be surrounded by a thousand delicate attentions"—a concept which transforms each of his hotels into far more than just a place to spend the night. Each is designed to be a home away from home—a quiet sanctuary, well-run and full of character. Ottaviani's chain of small, unique hotels includes the Lord Byron—tucked on a tiny lane surrounded by glamorous homes, it is much more like a private townhouse than a commercial establishment. The reception desk is discreetly located in the foyer which opens onto an elegant lounge. An elevator takes guests to the bedrooms, each individually decorated: fabrics, carpets, and the materials used on the custom-built pieces of furniture are carefully chosen to suit the personality and exposure of the room. Most of the furniture is new—modern yet traditional in feel. The colors used in fabrics, wall coverings, and carpets are mostly strong, bold colors—frequently with large, bright floral prints, but consistently of excellent quality. On the lower level is an intimate drawing room-bar where guests can relax before or after dining—adjacent is an elegant restaurant, the *Relais Le Jardin*, serving without a doubt some of the finest cuisine in Rome.

HOTEL LORD BYRON
Owner: Amedeo Ottaviani
Via G. de Notaris, 5
00197 Rome, Italy
tel: (06) 32 20 404, fax: (06) 32 20 405
37 rooms: Double Lire 350,000–540,000
Open all year
Credit cards: all major
Restaurant closed Sundays
Located on the edge of Villa Borghese Park
U.S.A. Rep: LHW 800-223-6800
Relais & Chateaux member

The Hotel Majestic Roma, located on the famous Via Veneto, has emerged from her recent renovation as one of Rome's newest jewels. Like other luxury hotels in Italy, the rates are very high, but so is the quality. From the moment you enter through the circular revolving doorway into the spacious, high-ceilinged lobby with a few well-chosen antiques and bouquets of fresh flowers, the mood of quiet elegance is established. Instead of one large lounge, there are a series of intimate parlors where guests can gather. In each room there are beautifully upholstered chairs, and opulent fabrics on the walls and richly draped windows. Be sure to peek in and see the fabulous frescoed ceiling of the 19th-century *Salone Verdi* which is used for special banquets. A wonderful old-fashioned wrought-iron elevator with polished brass trim takes guest to the bedrooms. As in a private home, each has its own personality, all are elegant in decor and traditionally furnished in an old world style, opulent style. On warm days, an outdoor terrace with a view of the city is a perfect place to pause for a cool drink. There is also a beautifully decorated, formal dining room specializing in typical Mediterranean dishes, as well as continental cuisine.

HOTEL MAJESTIC ROMA
Manager: Silvano Pinchetti
Via Veneto, 50
00187 Rome, Italy
tel: (06) 48 68 41, fax: (06) 62.22.62
98 rooms, Double: Lire 500,000–580,000
Open all year
Credit cards: all major
Restaurant open daily
In the heart of Rome on Via Veneto

La Residenza was recommended to us by several readers who claimed it to be their favorite place to stay in Rome, and after a personal visit, we are happy to be able to include it in our guide. This former villa really is quite different from most of the large, commercial places to stay in the center of Rome, appearing to be more like a private residence. Its facade looks very Italian with typical brown shuttered windows, greenery and flowers behind a small paved courtyard where guests may park their cars. The front hall has been converted into a reception area flanked by several guest lounges. The decor of these public rooms is not outstanding: some have contemporary, grass-cloth wallpaper, but others are more traditional in feeling and have a smattering of antique furniture. The breakfast room is spacious, although a bit dark, but the red bentwood chairs add a bit a sparkle. Because the hotel was fully occupied at the time of my visit, I was only able to see a few guest rooms, but those I did see were modern and seemed to be quiet adequate. The location just off the Via Veneto is glamorous, so even though the interior of La Residenza does not abound with charm, it is a good choice for travelers who want a small hotel in a good location without paying a fortune.

LA RESIDENZA
Manager: Signor. M. Petruccelli
Via Emilia, 22
00187 Rome, Italy
tel: (06) 48 80 789, fax: (06) 48 57 21
27 rooms: Double Lire 235,000, Suite Lire 265,000
Open all year
Credit cards: all major
No restaurant, breakfast only
Located between Via Veneto and the Spanish Steps

Finding the appealing Romantik Golf Hotel brought us an unexpected bonus: we discovered a niche of Italy that hugs the border north of Trieste: an absolutely gorgeous region of wooded hills, rolling fields, and vineyards. The Castello Formentini, superbly positioned on a hillock overlooking the countryside, has belonged to the Counts of Formentini since the 16th Century. For many years there has been a restaurant within the castle called *Castello Formentini* which still serves excellent meals and a medieval banquet on Saturdays. Just outside the castle walls, one of the historic buildings of the castle complex has been converted into a small, charming luxury inn. The attractive, gracious owner, Isabella Formentini, says that all of the magnificent antique furnishings in the hotel are family heirlooms. Everything is authentic, even the wonderful prints and paintings. In fact, Isabella says the furniture is more valuable than the castle. From the intimate lobby to each of the spacious guest rooms, everything is decorator perfect and exudes a delightful country manor ambiance. Only four of the rooms are within the castle, but all guests can stroll through the gate and into the castle grounds where the swimming pool lies invitingly on the shaded lawn. There is also a tennis court plus a nine hole pitch and putt golf course. *NOTE:* The closest town on the Hallwag map is Gorizia.

ROMANTIK GOLF HOTEL
Owner: Isabella Formentini
San Floriano del Collio
34070 Gorizia (GO), Italy
tel: (0481) 88 40 51, fax: (0481) 88 40 52
16 rooms: Double Lire 240,000
Open March to December
Credit cards: AX, VS
Restaurant closed Mondays
30 km N of Trieste, 7 km N of Gorizia
U.S.A. Rep: Euro-Connection 800-645-3876

Without a doubt, San Gimignano is one of the most picturesque places in Tuscany: a postcard perfect hilltop village punctuated by 14 tall towers. During the day, the town bustles with activity, but after the bus loads of tourists depart, the romantic ambiance of yester-year fills the cobbled streets. For the lucky few who spend the night, there is a jewel of small inn, the Hotel L'Antico Pozzo. What a pleasure to see a renovation done with such excellent taste and meticulous attention to maintaining the authentic character of the original building. The name of the hotel derives from the an antique stone well (pozzo) which is softly illuminated just off the lobby. The fact that only the most affluent families could afford the luxury of a private well, indicates that this 15th-century town house was at one time a wealthy residence. A worn-with-time stone staircase leads up to the air-conditioned bedrooms, tucked at various levels along a maze of hallways. Each one of the quietly elegant rooms has its own personality: frescoed walls, thick stone walls, terra cotta floors, and beautifully framed antique prints-plus satellite television. One of my favorites, number 20, is a large room with the palest of pastel peach-colored walls, windows opening onto the terrace, and, a fabulous domed ceiling, painted with ancient Roman designs. Another that won my heart was 34—a small, romantic room with a large arched window capturing a fabulous view. Breakfast is the only meal served, but restaurants abound, including the superb *La Mangiataoia*.

HOTEL L'ANTICO POZZO
Manager: Emanuele Marro
Via San Matteo, 87
53037 San Gimignano (SI), Italy
tel: (0577) 94 20 14, fax: (0577) 94 21 17
18 rooms: Double Lire 130,000-170,000
Open all year
Credit cards: all major
No restaurant, breakfast only
55 km S W of Florence, 38 km N of Siena

San Gimignano is one of the most fascinating of the medieval Tuscany hill towns. Most tourists come just for the day to visit this small town. As you approach, this looks like a city of skyscrapers: come even closer and the skyscrapers emerge as 14 soaring towers—dramatic reminders of what San Gimignano must have looked like in all her glory when this wealthy town sported 72 giant towers. If you are lucky enough to be able to spend the night, San Gimignano has a simple but very charming hotel, La Cisterna. The hotel is located on the town's main square, and fits right into the ancient character of the surrounding buildings with its somber stone walls softened by ivy, arched shuttered doors, and red tile roof. Once inside La Cisterna the medieval feeling continues with lots of stone, vaulted ceilings, leather chairs, and dark woods. The bedrooms are not fancy, but pleasant, and some have balconies with lovely views of the valley. Renovations in 1991 added air conditioning in the restaurant and satellite TV (for European channels). La Cisterna is probably more famous as a restaurant than as a hotel. People come from miles around because not only is the food delicious, but the dining rooms are delightful. Especially charming is the dining room with the brick wall, sloping ceiling supported by giant beams, and picture windows framing the gorgeous Tuscany hills.

LA CISTERNA
Owner: S. Salvestrimi
Piazza della Cisterna, 24
53037 San Gimignano (SI), Italy
tel: (0577) 94 03 28, fax: (0577) 94 20 80
50 rooms: Double Lire 110,000-160,000
Suites to Lire 174,000
Open March 10 to November 10
Credit cards: all major
Restaurant closed Tuesdays and lunch on Wednesdays
54 km SW of Florence, 38 km NW of Siena

The Castel San Gregorio is a sensational, small 12th-century stone castle just a short drive from Assisi, reached after following a winding road through a forest that emerges at the top of a hill to a truly romantic, secluded hideaway. There is a terrace to the side where tables and chairs are strategically placed to capture a splendid view of the valley far below. The castle, dating from 1140, has been meticulously reconstructed preserving its original appearance without, and maintaining a castle-like ambiance within. The interior of the hotel is quite dark due both to the character of the building and the wall coverings. The old world ambiance is further enhanced by the bountiful use of excellent antiques. The reception desk is in the front lobby: to the left as you enter is an ornate living room; to the right is a dining room where one large table is set each night for the guests to eat together family style. A restaurant is located on a lower level, open to the general public, where elegant dining is offered in a beautifully decorated room. The bedrooms I saw, although somewhat dark, were all quite outstandingly decorated with a collection of fine antiques. Surrounding the hotel are many walking paths leading through the quiet wooded hills. The Castel San Gregorio is an outstanding value for a hotel with so much character. *NOTE:* The closest town on the Hallwag map is Pianello, the Castel San Gregorio is on a small road that goes south from town.

CASTEL SAN GREGORIO
Owner: Claudio Bianchi
Via San Gregorio, 16 (Near Pianello)
06081 San Gregorio, Assisi (PG), Italy
tel: (075) 80 38 009, fax: (075) 80 38 904
12 rooms: Double Lire 195,000*
*Rate includes breakfast and dinner
Closed January
Credit cards: all major
Restaurant open daily, only for guests
16 km NW of Assisi, 2 km S of Pianello

Staying at Villa Arceno is truly like staying with friends in a sumptuous Italian villa. If you enjoy luxury, exquisite decor, breathtaking vistas, impeccable service, and warmth of welcome, this will definitely be your cup of tea. The mood of grandeur is set as you approach by a seemingly-endless private road that winds through lovingly-tended vineyards to a classic, three-story, ochre colored villa. At one time the summer home of royalty, this 17th-century Palladian villa has been masterfully restored, both outside and within. The public rooms are more like lounges in a private home with a sophisticated, yet comfortable, elegance. The sixteen individually decorated guest rooms in the main villa are gorgeous. Even the standard rooms are enormous and splendidly decorated. All the rooms are so outstanding it is difficult to choose, but I think my favorites are 104 and 204, both with sweeping vistas of vine-covered fields. By the time you arrive, sixteen more guest rooms should be available in the characterful winery overlooking the garden. In addition to just enjoying the utter peace and quiet or sightseeing in nearby-Siena or exploring the wonders of Tuscany, there are bicycles available, a swimming pool, tennis court, and best of all a park. Here you can stroll for hours along romantic lanes shaded by imposing rows of centuries-old Cypress trees or meander on paths through the forest, passing almost-hidden statues and small temples, down to an idyllic, secluded lake.

HOTEL VILLA ARCENO
Manager: Gualtiero Mancini
53010 San Gusmè (SI), Italy
tel:(0577) 35 92 92, fax: (0577) 35 92 76
32 rooms: Double Lire 350,000-450,000
Open March to October
Credit cards: all major
Restaurant open daily
22 km NE of Siena, 9 km NW of Castelnuovo

If you are looking for a place to stay in the heart of Tuscany that is moderately-priced, yet does not sacrifice one ounce of charm or quality of accommodation, the family-run, Hotel Belvedere di San Leonino is unsurpassable. Ceramic pots of geraniums, trellised grape vines, and climbing roses soften and add color to the weathered stone buildings that were originally a cluster of 15th-century farmers' cottages. Off the central patio area is a small reception area, a living room that is blandly decorated with contemporary furniture, and an attractive dining room with tiled floors, rustic beamed ceiling, and appropriately simple wooden tables and chairs. When the weather is warm, meals are served outside in the garden. Because the rooms are tucked into various parts of the old farm houses, they vary in size and shape. They also differ in decor, but all have an antique ambiance with wrought iron headboards, beautiful old armoires, and pretty white curtains. Number 46, a large room overlooking the swimming pool, is especially attractive. What adds the icing to the cake for the Hotel Belvedere is its setting. Nestled in the very heart of the Chianti wine region, the scenery is absolute perfection—every direction you look there are idyllic, sweeping vistas of rolling hills dotted with vineyards, olive groves and pine forests. Another plus, Hotel Belvedere is conveniently located, only a short drive to the freeway

HOTEL BELVEDERE DI SAN LEONINO
Manager: M. Orlandi
Località San Leonino
53011 Castellina in Chianti (SI), Italy
tel: (0577) 74.08.87, fax: (0577) 74.09.24
28 rooms: Double Lire 120,000
Open mid-March to mid-November
Credit cards: all major
Restaurant open daily
16 km N of Siena, 65 km S of Florence

The Residence San Sano is a small hotel in San Sano—a hamlet in the center of the Chianti wine-growing region. We were charmed by the hotel that is incorporated into a 16th-century stone building. The gracious young owners, Giancarlo Matarazzo and his German wife, Heidi, were both school teachers in Germany prior to returning to Italy to open a small hotel. They have done a beautiful job in the renovation and in the decor. A cozy dining room serves guests excellent meals—featuring typically Tuscan-style cooking. Each of the bedrooms is delightfully furnished in antiques and each has a name incorporating some unique feature of the hotel—the name evolving from the time during reconstruction when Heidi and Giancarlo remembered each room by its special feature. My favorite room was the Bird Room: here birds had claimed the room for many years and had nested in holes that went completely through the wall. With great imagination, the holes were left open to the outside, but on the inside were covered with glass. Now the birds can still nest and guests have the fun of watching the babies. One room is named for a beautiful, long-hidden Romanesque window that was discovered and incorporated into the decor, another room for its very special view, and another for an antique urn uncovered during renovation. On our latest visit, the inn looked even lovelier than ever and a new pool now nestles in the vineyards. *NOTE:* The closest town on the Hallwag map is Radda.

HOTEL RESIDENCE SAN SANO
Owners: Heidi and Giancarlo Matarazzo
Località San Sano
53010 Lecchi in Chianti (SI), Italy
tel: (0577) 74 61 30, fax: (0577) 74 61 56
14 rooms: Double Lire 160,000
Closed November to mid-March
Credit cards: all major
Restaurant closed Sunday, only for guests
60 km S of Florence, 9 km S of Radda

The Locanda San Vigilio is truly special: our favorite among the tiny luxury inns in the beautiful lake district of northern Italy. And, although it is expensive, it costs less to stay here than at some of the famous well known queens along the lake. Not only is it a superb small hotel, but the location is unsurpassed. The Locanda San Vigilio is a 16th-century building romantically positioned fronting the water on an exquisite, park-like peninsula that juts out into Lake Garda. There is not much action here. If you want to see and be seen by the rich and famous, the glamorous Villa d'Este should be your hub, but if you desire tranquillity, accented by lovely accommodations, then try the San Vigilio. Here you will find understated luxury, nothing commercial at all. Hardly a sign marks the tree-lined entrance just a few kilometers north of the town of Garda. After parking your car in the designated area, you walk past a gorgeous Italian villa and then down a path to the hotel, a 16th-century sturdy stone building so close to the water that waves gently lap the walls. The dining room is lovely and if you are lucky, you can eat at one of the cozy tables overlooking the lake. The food is sensational and the decor is faultless. Upstairs the prize guest rooms overlook the lake. If you long for tranquillity, this is it. Churchill came here to paint, and after visiting the San Vigilio you may also be inspired to take up painting.

LOCANDA SAN VIGILIO
Owner: Conte Agostino Guarienti di Brenzone
37016 San Vigilio, Lake Garda (VR), Italy
tel: (045) 72 56 68 8, fax: (045) 72 56 55 1
7 rooms: Double Lire 340,000-390,000
Open March to November
Credit cards: all major
Restaurant open daily, only for guests
154 km W of Venice, 3 km N of Garda

The Pitrizza is a tiny jewel of a hotel located on the Emerald Coast of the Island of Sardinia—the playground of the Aga Khan and the jet set of the world. From the moment you enter through the front gate, marked only with a discreet sign, you are in a world of tranquillity and beauty. There is a central clubhouse that has a beautiful lounge, a delightful dining room with hand-hewn wooden chairs, a card room, and a bar. A small protected patio extends from the dining room where meals are served when the weather is warm. French doors from the lounge open onto the terrace that leads down to a most unusual swimming pool, cleverly designed into the natural rock. Once in this wonderful pool, you have the impression that you are swimming in the sea, not a pool, because the water level matches that of the bay. The bedrooms are tucked away in small cottages that blend into the landscape. The rooms are not especially large, but beautiful, with every detail of the finest quality. If your idea of a vacation is a frenzy of activity and things to do then the Pitrizza is definitely not for you. There are no planned activities, no sports director, no loud music. Only lovely quiet, gourmet food, a beautiful pool, and a delightful small white sand beach.

HOTEL PITRIZZA
Manager: Pier Angelo Tondina
07020 Porto Cervo, Sardinia, Italy
tel: (0789) 91 500, fax: (0789) 91 629
51 rooms: Double Lire 1,322,100-1,898,400*
*Rate includes breakfast and dinner
Open mid-May to September
Credit cards: all major
Restaurant open daily
NE tip of Sardinia, airport Olbia
Island of Sardinia
Relais & Chateaux member

Having heard about a lovely little chalet tucked amidst the pines high in the Italian Alps near the French border, I was beginning to wonder what awaited me as the road wound through the ski town of Sauze d'Oulx with its unattractive jumble of modern concrete ski hotels. However, the road soon left the resort town and continued up, twisting higher and higher into the mountains until suddenly Il Capricorno came into view nestled in the forest to the left of the road. Just as you enter there is a tiny bar, and, beyond, a cozy dining room enhanced by dark wooden chalet-style chairs, rustic wooden tables, and a stone fireplace with logs stacked neatly by its side. There is not a hint of elaborate elegance—just a simple cozy country charm: the perfect kind of inn to come home to after a day of skiing or walking the beautiful mountain trails. The bedrooms, too, are simple but most pleasant with dark pine handmade furniture, neat little bathrooms, and, for a lucky few, balconies with splendid mountain views. However, the greatest assets of this tiny inn are the owners, Mariarosa and Carlo Sacchi. Carlo personally made most of the furniture and will frequently join the guests for skiing. Mariarosa is the chef, a fabulous gourmet cook. This is a very special little hideaway for very special people.

IL CAPRICORNO
Owners: Mariarosa and Carlo Sacchi
Les Clotes
10050 Sauze d'Oulx (TO), Italy
tel: (0122) 85 02 73, fax: (0122) 85 04 97
8 rooms: Double Lire 220,000
Open July to mid-September
and Christmas to May
Credit cards: VS
Restaurant open daily, only for guests
2 km E of Sauze d'Oulx via small lane
60 km W of Turin, 28 km W of Susa

The Maremma, a beautiful area in the coastal foothills of southern Tuscany, quite undiscovered by tourists, offers a wealth of sightseeing possibilities: walled villages, Etruscan ruins, archaeological sites and lovely landscapes. Until recently there were few places to stay with charm. Happily this problem was solved when the Pellegrini family recently converted a 200-year-old stone farmhouse into a small hotel. Here you will find true Tuscany hospitality from the moment you enter. Although the Pellegrinis do not speak English, they have made sure to employ front desk personnel who do. The dining room is the heart of the inn and has tables set in a beamed-ceilinged room that is filled with sunlight from large French doors that open onto a terrace where meals are served on warm days. The guest rooms are small, but comfortable, immaculately clean and each with a private bathroom. The warmth and gracious country-style hospitality of this simple small hotel make a stay here special. Another real bonus is the food. It is wonderful. Everything is homemade, including marvelous pastas prepared by the talented chef, Tullio Sassi, and the hotel even produces its own wines that are served with the meals. A specialty of the inn is trekking (or, as we say, horseback riding). In the corral below the hotel, horses are groomed each day for guests' use; in fact, special room rates are offered which include riding in the Maremma countryside.

ANTICO CASALE DI SCANSANO
Owner: Massimo Pellegrini and Family
58054 Castagneta-Scansano (GR), Italy
tel: (0564) 50 72 19, fax: (0564) 50 78 05
16 rooms: Double Lire 140,000-180,000
Closed mid-January to March
Credit cards: all major
Restaurant open daily
30 km S of Grosseto
2 km W of Scansano

Although the Berghotel Tirol is a new hotel, it happily copies the typical chalet style of the Dolomites. Inside too, the tasteful decor follows the delightful Alpine motif with light pine furniture, baskets of flowers, and a few antiques for accent pieces. However, what is so very special about the Berghotel Tirol is its marvelous location on a hillside looking over the lovely village of Sexten and to the fabulous mountains beyond. Many of the rooms have large balconies that capture the view and the warmth of the mountain sun. The Berghotel Tirol is not actually in the town of Sexten (*Sesto*), but in a suburb called Moos (*Moso*). This is one of the most scenic areas of the Dolomites and the town of Sexten one of the most attractive of the mountain towns. In addition to the natural beauty, there is a wonderful network of trails leading in every direction to tempt all into the crisp mountain air. When you return at night to the hotel it is rather like a house party. Most of the guests come for at least a week and table hopping is prevalent as the knicker-clad guests share their day's adventures. Acting as hosts to the house party are the extremely gracious, cordial owners, the Holzer family, who seem to be dedicated to seeing that everyone has a good time.

BERGHOTEL TIROL
Owner: Kurt Holzer and Family
39030 Sexten (Sesto) (BZ), Italy
tel: (0474) 70 386, fax: (0474) 70 455
46 rooms: Double Lire 170,000-280,000*
*Rate includes breakfast and dinner
Open Christmas to Easter
and mid-May to October
Credit cards: none accepted
Restaurant open daily
Dolomites–near Austria
2 km SE of Sexton toward Moos
44 km E of Cortina, 116 km W of Bolzano

Agrigento is home to Valle dei Templi, justifiably the most visited archeological site in Sicily. To savor these Greek temples to their fullest, be sure to plan ahead so that you can secure a room at the Villa Athena. Its location is absolute perfection. Behind the hotel, the gardens (where a large swimming pool is nestled) extend to the very edge of the archeological site. If you enjoy walking, there is no need for a car—just steps from the hotel, a path leads in one direction to the temples and in the other to the museum where many of the fabulous artifacts from the site are beautifully displayed. In front of the hotel, in a separate building opposite the parking area, is the hotel's restaurant—a popular luncheon stop for tour groups. In the summer, guests of the hotel enjoy dinner served outside on a pretty terrace. As you enter the hotel, there is a reception area that opens onto a contemporary-style bar and lounge with black leather sofas and chairs. The modern bedrooms are all similar in style with comfortable, simple furnishings. What is special about the Villa Athena is not the decor, but the ambiance of the 18th-century villa, and above all—the awesome views. This is one place you should splurge. Request one of the rooms overlooking the ruins. And, if you really want to go all out, ask for a balcony! To wake up in the morning and watch the first rays of the sun cast their glow on the marvelous temple of Concordia is magical.

VILLA ATHENA
Owner: Francesco d'Alessandro
Via dei Templi, 33
92100 Agrigento, Sicily, Italy
tel: (0922) 59 62 88, fax: (0922) 40 21 80
40 rooms: Double Lire 220,000-275,000
Open all year
Credit cards: all major
Restaurant open daily
128 km SE of Palermo, 212 km SW of Taormina

Hotel Descriptions   231

Hugging the crest of a rocky coastal mountain rising 750 meters above Trapani, Erice's authentic testimony to yesteryear is broken only by several tall communication towers just outside the ancient walls. This appealing town of twisting cobbled streets makes a convenient overnight stop when visiting the Greek temple and theater at Segesta. As you wind up the hill toward Erice watch for the parking area near Porta Trapani. Park here and walk through the arched stone entrance and up the Via Vittorio Emanuele to the Hotel Moderno. The intimate reception area is fresh and inviting with fresh flowers and attractive prints on the walls. A hallway leads to a lounge accented by chairs grouped around small round tables where guests can just relax or enjoy a cold drink from the adjacent bar. A stone staircase leads up the guest rooms, all of which are immaculately clean and fresh with white-washed walls and white tiled floors. Some bedrooms are decorated with light knotty-pine furniture; others have an antique motif. One of my favorites, room 35, has a handsome king-sized iron bed with brass trim and an antique armoire. About half of the rooms are located just across the street in another very old building that has been renovated. These rooms are similar and equally pleasant. My favorite in the annex is number 71, an especially spacious room with a king-sized bed with a handsome French-style headboard.

HOTEL MODERNO
Owner: Giuseppe Catalano
Via Vittorio Emanuele, 63
91016 Erice (TP), Italy
tel: (0923) 86 93 00, fax: (0923) 86 91 39
41 rooms: Double Lire 180,000-190,000
Open all year
Credit cards: all major
Restaurant open daily
15 km NE of Trapani, 96 km SW of Palermo

Tenuta Gangivecchio is far off the beaten path, but oh-so-worth a detour. Not only will you discover a jewel of a small inn, but the adventure of finding Gangivecchio leads you through Sicily's beautiful Madonie region. The Tornabene family began by converting a room in their home (a characterful 13th-century Benedettino monastery) into a restaurant serving a set menu lunch based upon fresh produce from the farm. Although a two-hour-drive, the excellence of the simple, yet delicious meals soon brought guests from as far away as Palermo. Happily for the traveler who loves to stay in the countryside, the enterprising Tornabene family have now renovated the stables of the monastery into nine, tastefully decorated guest rooms—appealing in their simplicity with rustic red-tile floors, fresh white-washed walls, hand-loomed scatter rugs, dark wood accents, rough-hewn beamed ceilings, attractively framed old prints on the walls, and pretty cotton floral bed spreads. Delicious, home-cooked meals are served to guests in a pretty dining room on the ground floor of the inn. Plan to arrive on a weekend for a lunch prepared by Signora Wanda and her daughter Giovanna, served in the dining room of the monastery. *NOTE:* Drive east through Gangi on SS120. Just outside town, turn right at a small signpost for Gangivecchio. Go for about a kilometer and turn left at a tiny yellow sign. Continue up the hill for about 5 kilometers. Tenuta Gangivecchio is on your right

TENUTA GANGIVECCHIO
Owners: Betty and Paolo Tornabene
C. da Gangivecchio
90024 Gangi, (PA), Sicily, Italy
tel: (0921) 89 191
9 rooms: Double Lire 170,000*
*Rate includes breakfast and lunch or dinner
Closed 1 or 2 weeks end of June
Credit cards: DC
Restaurant open daily
125 km SE of Palermo, 130 km NW of Catania

The Villa Igiea Grand Hotel is an oasis of blissful tranquility in the midst of the large and rather unattractive city of Palermo. With all the fabulous archaeological sites and marvelous cathedrals in the area it is wonderful to have such a splendid hotel to come home to at night. The approach to the Villa is not scenic, but from the moment you enter the gates you are in another world: a world of spacious lobbies, sweeping verandas, formal dining rooms, and generously sized, well furnished bedrooms with large modern bathrooms. Many of the bedrooms have private balconies overlooking the gardens to the sea. The hotel is called a villa, but it is much more like a small deluxe castle built right at the edge of the sea. A lovely freeform swimming pool fits itself onto a ledge that overhangs the water. Next to the pool the hotel has its very own ancient Greek temple—now how many hotels can top that? The most outstanding attributes of the hotel are the gardens that envelop the building in a nest of beautiful pines and masses of gorgeous flower beds intertwined with twisting pathways. Altogether, a most delightful spot.

VILLA IGIEA GRAND HOTEL
Manager: Franco Arabia
Via Belmonte, 43 (Acquasanta)
90142 Palermo, Sicily, Italy
tel: (091) 54 37 44, fax: (091) 54 76 54
117 rooms: Double Lire 330,000
Open all year
Credit cards: all major
Restaurant open daily
On the northern coast of Sicily
U.S.A. Rep: Utell International 800-223-9868

With a glorious, unobstructed view to the sea, the Hotel Belvedere can definitely lay claim to one of the prime positions in the picturesque town of Taormina. Of course this location is not just luck because undoubtedly when the Belvedere (one of the first hotels in town) was constructed at the turn of the century, the site was carefully chosen. The gentleman who originally built the hotel is the grandfather of the present owners—a continuity that adds greatly to the care and warmth of welcome given to the guests. From first glance, the hotel is immediately appealing—a pale ochre-colored villa laced with ivy and accented by wrought iron balconies. Flowers abound on the walkways and a romantic garden terraces down below the hotel, providing quiet shady nooks for guests to enjoy the view. On one of the lower terraces, a large pool swimming pool is practically hidden by a lush blanket of shrubs, shade trees, and towering palms. This cool oasis is a favorite gathering spot for guests, and although there is no formal restaurant, light refreshments including pasta, sandwiches, and cold drinks are available by the pool. The lounges of the hotel are pleasantly decorated in contemporary furniture accented by some family antiques. The guest rooms are modern with built in beds. But it is not the decor that captures the hearts of guests who return each year, but rather the friendliness of the staff and the superb setting.

HOTEL BELVEDERE
Owner: Pecaut-Castorina Family
79 Via Bagnoli Croci
98039 Taormina, Sicily, Italy
tel: (0942) 23 791, fax: (0942) 62 58 30
47 rooms: Double Lire 177,000-187,000
Closed October to mid-March
Credit cards: EC, MC, VS
Snack bar open daily for lunch
On the eastern coast of Sicily

The San Domenico Palace is a super deluxe hotel cleverly incorporated into what was formerly a Dominican monastery. Don't let the monastery bit deter you: absolutely no trace of a life of denial remains. In fact, this is one of the most super deluxe hotels in Italy, catering to your every whim. As you enter the building the lobby opens onto the core of the hotel, the beautiful arcaded Renaissance cloister. Around this inner courtyard the vaulted walkway is now glassed in, but filled with light. Leading off the courtyard are various lounges, writing rooms and game rooms. The dining room is a masterpiece: it has high backed wooden chairs, enormous arched windows and a paneled ceiling. The chapel has been converted into a bar. Throughout the hotel there are priceless antiques of a quality that would make a museum blush with pride. Many of the bedrooms look out to the beautiful bay of Taormina. In the rear of the hotel there is a lovely garden filled with gorgeous flowers and laced by pathways with small nooks where you can stop to soak in the splendid sea view. A swimming pool is squeezed into the property just as it drops down to the road below. There is no doubt that this is a MOST dramatic hotel.

SAN DOMENICO PALACE
Manager: Luigi Menta
Piazza San Domenico, 5
98039 Taormina, Sicily, Italy
tel: (0942) 23 701, fax: (0942) 62 55 06
100 rooms: Double Lire 550,000-682,000
Open all year
Credit cards: all major
Restaurant open daily
On the eastern coast of Sicily
U.S.A. Rep: E&M 800-223-9832

For those who want to visit the beautiful, yet expensive, resort town of Taormina, and yet do not want to pay to pay deluxe hotel rates, the well-managed, friendly, home-like Villa Fiorita is an excellent choice. It is easy to find since the hotel is located on the main access into town, just across from the funicular that whisks guests down to the beach. Although facing directly onto a busy street, the hotel is carved into the rocks of the steep hillside so that the rooms are staggered up many levels, a situation that provides intriguing nooks and crannies for small terraces, intimate little gardens laced with fragrant blossoms, and even a swimming pool. The decor has an old-fashioned, somewhat tired look, that is fortunately relieved by a few pieces of antique furniture that add a bit of interest. The bedrooms vary in personality. Some are much more attractive than others. However, all are air-conditioned, have direct-dial telephone, radio, television, mini bar, and either a terrace or balcony. And, you will certainly not be disappointed if you are lucky enough to snare a room such as number 12—a real gem with a colorful tiled floor, antique brass bed, an attractive writing desk, and most wonderful of all, French doors that open to a secluded terrace with a romantic view of the sea. When the weather is warm, breakfast is served outside in the garden with a memorable, sweeping vista of the dramatic coastline.

VILLA FIORITA
Manager: Vincenzo Manganaro
Via Luigi Pirandello, 39
98039 Taormina, Sicily, Italy
tel: (0942) 24 122, fax: (0942) 62 59 67
24 rooms: Double Lire 150,000
Open all year
Credit cards: all major
No restaurant, breakfast only
On the eastern coast of Sicily

Although only a few kilometers down a twisting road from the colorful, medieval hilltop town of Erice, Valderice cannot compete in old world charm with its neighbor. But don't be discouraged as you drive through the congested town, because as you take the road S187 east toward Castellammare, you are once again in the countryside and will see on your right the Baglio Santacroce—an appealing small, family-run hotel built into a rustic stone farm house, dating back to 1636. The thick exposed stone walls, tiled floors accented by hand-woven rugs, and simple furnishings of the guest rooms are in harmony with the original structure. No two bedrooms are alike, yet all are attractive and have antique headboards and chairs fashioned from olive wood. Nestled on the terrace to the side of the hotel is a small, pretty swimming pool—a welcome retreat after a day of sightseeing. While relaxing by the pool, the view to west is interrupted a bit by modern buildings, but the vista straight ahead to the sea is outstanding. The hotel portion of the Baglio Santacroce has a charming antique ambiance. However, the style changes completely in the newly built restaurant that wraps around the front of the hotel. Here the mood is jarred by the starkly modern decor, but the sweeping view over the olive and lemon trees out to the sea is beautiful. Mediterranean-style cooking is featured, specializing in freshly caught fish.

BAGLIO SANTACROCE
Owner: Cusenza Family
1 km E of Valderice on S187
91019 Valderice (TP), Sicily, Italy
tel: (0923) 89 11 11, fax: (0923) 89 11 92
25 rooms: Double Lire 130,000
Open all year
Credit cards: all major
Restaurant open daily
1 km E of Valderice 80 km SW of Palermo

If you would like to combine your sightseeing of Siena with a luxury resort, then the Certosa di Maggiano might be just your cup of tea. This is an expensive hotel, but delightful and unique. Outside, the hotel looks quite ordinary—just a wall facing the road—but when you step inside it is a fairyland. It doesn't resemble a hotel in the slightest. And it is no wonder: the hotel is built into the restored ruins of a 700-year-old Carthusian monastery. As you enter the arcaded courtyard you can almost see the ghosts of priests, their dark robes flowing, silently walking beneath the vaulted roof of the cloisters. On three sides of the courtyard are arranged the guest rooms, the lounges, the game rooms, the library, the bar and the exquisite dining room. The fourth side of the courtyard is formed by a small church. The guest rooms are spacious and pleasant but not outstanding in decor. However, the public rooms are smashing, with antiques galore, and all of the finest quality. Another bonus: there is a beautiful pool in the gardens that is never crowded since this is such a tiny hotel. There are so few people around, that it truly is like being a guest in a private estate.

CERTOSA DI MAGGIANO
Manager: Anna Recordati
Via Certosa, 82/86
53100 Siena, Italy
tel: (577) 28 81 80, fax: (0577) 28 81 89
5 rooms: Double Lire 495,000
12 suites: Lire 670,000-790,000
Open all year
Credit cards: all major
Restaurant
2 km E of Siena, near the Porta Romana gate
Relais & Chateaux member

The Locanda dell'Amorosa makes a wonderful base for exploring the hill towns south of Florence. It is very accessible since it is located in Sinalunga which is just a few minutes from the expressway between Rome and Florence. From the Locanda dell'Amorosa it is an easy drive to such sightseeing delights as Siena, Pienza, Orvieto, Todi and Assisi. However, it is not location alone which makes this hotel so perfect: there is far more. Truly, the Locanda dell'Amorosa would be marvelous if there were nothing nearby—in fact, the hotel is a tiny town a few miles south of Sinalunga. The approach to *town* is a road lined by a majestic row of cypress trees. Park your car and enter the walls of the 14th-century medieval town where you are greeted by an enormous plaza with its own little church—exquisite inside with its soft pastels and its lovely fresco of the Madonna holding the Christ child. To the right of the main entrance to the courtyard are the stables that have been converted to a beautiful restaurant whose massive beams, and natural stone and brick walls are original and tastefully enhanced by arched windows, thick wrought iron fixtures and wooden tables. The guest rooms, located in a separate building to the left of the main entrance, are tastefully appointed with a few antiques and matching bedspreads and draperies. The rest of this tiny village spreads out behind the main square and the buildings are used for other purposes—including the production of wine. The hotel is hoping to add a swimming pool.

LOCANDA DELL'AMOROSA
Manager: Carlo Citterio
53048 Sinalunga (SI), Italy
tel: (0577) 67 94 97, fax: (0577) 67 82 16
15 rooms: Double Lire 336,000-515,000
Closed January 20 to February 28
Credit cards: all major
Restaurant closed Mondays
80 km S of Florence, 45 km E of Siena

What a sense of impending grandeur you experience as you wait for the giant metal gates of the Villa Cortine Palace to swing open. Once inside the road winds and curves impressively past fountains and statues, flower gardens and mighty trees until you reach the summit where the Villa Cortine Palace reigns. This beautifully situated villa has been expanded so that the original wing now boasts a new section which appears to have more than doubled the size of the original castle. Some of the remodeling has a too modern feel: one rather wishes that perhaps more of an old world ambiance could have been preserved. However, in the old section of the villa, which is to the left as you enter the lobby, the rooms still maintain their grandeur with incredibly ornate furniture, soaring ceilings and stunning paintings. Upstairs the guest rooms are large and are decorated with color coordinated drapes, chairs and bedspreads. What leaves absolutely nothing to be improved upon are the gardens—what a gorgeous sight. They are absolutely awe-inspiring. The villa is surrounded by graveled walkways that wind in and out amongst the fountains, ponds, statues, and glorious rose gardens, all overlooking the lovely Lake Garda.

VILLA CORTINE PALACE HOTEL
Manager: Roberto Cappelletto
25019 Sirmione (BS), Italy
tel: (030) 99 05 890, fax: (030) 91 63 90
*55 rooms: Double Lire 429,000-528,000**
*2 suites: Lire 825,000-990,000**
**3 night minimum*
Open April to November
Credit cards: all major
Restaurant open daily
Park setting–overlooks Lake Garda
127 km E of Milan, 35 km W of Verona

Located about an hour's drive south of Milan's Linate airport, the Locanda del Lupo makes a convenient stop if you plan to drive directly south toward Florence. Soragna is a sleepy little town in the countryside whose main point of interest is a walled, medieval fortress. Around the central plaza buildings of great character are interspersed with modern construction. The Locanda del Lupo, built in the 18th Century by the noble Meli Lupi family, is easy to find—just a block off the plaza. The inn is best known as a gourmet restaurant: there are a series of beautiful dining rooms with gleaming copper hanging from white-washed walls, terra cotta floors, dark beamed ceilings, antique clocks, and 17th-century oil paintings. To the left of the reception is a cozy bar and beyond a formal living room furnished in antiques. A flight of stairs leads to the guest rooms whose old world ambiance is enhanced by beamed ceilings, tiled floors and thick walls. Each guest room is individually decorated and exudes a refined, country-house ambiance. Authentic antique furnishings (including fine wooden chests and wrought iron bedsteads) exude a feeling of quality. *NOTE:* From the Milan-Bologna expressway, take the Fidenza exit and follow signs to Soragna.

LOCANDA DEL LUPO
Manager: Alessandro Pezzani
Via Garibaldi 64
43019 Soragna (PR), Italy
tel: (0524) 69 04 44, fax: (0524) 69 350
46 rooms: Double Lire 215,000
Suite Lire 325,000
Closed August
Credit cards: all major
Restaurant open daily
100 km S of Milan, 118 km N of Bologna

The Grand Hotel Excelsior Vittoria has a superb location high on the cliff overlooking the port and bay of Sorrento and surrounded by an orange grove and park of about four acres with a swimming pool. The hotel is a grand old villa with a real old world atmosphere, entered through a formal gate which is just a short stroll from the center of town. The furnishings, for the most part, continue the antique mood. The Excelsior Vittoria is a good place to splurge and reserve one of the superior rooms with a view of the sea. The ceilings in some of the reception rooms and in the marvelous airy dining room have gorgeous frescoed designs. The terraces and gardens surrounding the hotel offer wonderful views, as do the bedrooms which face the bay. When we first saw the Grand Hotel Excelsior Vittoria there was a gracious, though faded, elegance to the hotel giving it a slightly worn look. However, this magnificent villa has since been lovingly restored under the guidance of Lidia Fiorentino, the owner's wife, carefully retaining the unique turn-of-the-century mood. Staying here will certainly delight anyone who loves the feeling of reliving the grandeur of days gone by in a villa by the sea.

GRAND HOTEL EXCELSIOR VITTORIA
Owner: Fiorentino Family
Manager: Mario Damiano
Piazza Torquato Tasso, 34
80067 Sorrento (NA), Italy
tel: (081) 80 71 044, fax: (081) 87 71 206
125 rooms: Double Lire 320,000-450,000
Suite Lire 580,000-1,000,000
Open all year
Restaurant open daily
Credit cards: all major
48 km S of Naples, 250 km S of Rome
U.S.A. Rep: JDB Associates (703) 684-3834

It was love at first sight as I drove up the long graveled road through forest and vineyard and suddenly caught my first glimpse of the Borgo Pretale, a tiny cluster of weathered stone buildings nestled next to their 12th-century watch tower. My first impression was more than justified. This small inn is truly paradise. There is absolute serenity and beauty here with nothing to mar its perfection. Civilization seems miles away as the eye stretches over a glorious vista of rolling hills forested with oaks, juniper and laurel, interspersed with square patches of vineyards. But although this small village is seemingly remote, it is only a short drive south of Siena, thus a perfect hideaway from which to enjoy the magic of Tuscany. And although the buildings seem rustic, this tiny hotel, tucked into a 12th-century hamlet, offers some of the finest accommodations in all of Italy. Each room is a showplace of fine country antiques and splendid designer fabrics, blended together with the artful eye of a skilled decorator. Every piece is selected to create a sophisticated yet rustic elegance. The lounge beckons guests to linger after dinner by the roaring fire. A path leads to a groomed tennis court and further on to a swimming pool on a hillside terrace. *NOTE:* Pretale-Sovicille is not on any map we could find. The closest town on the Hallwag map is Rosia, which is about 5 km SE of Borgo Pretale.

BORGO PRETALE
Manager: Daniele Rizzardini
53018 Località Pretale-Sovicille (SI), Italy
tel: (0577) 34 54 01, fax: (0577) 34 56 25
33 rooms: Double Lire 350,000-450,000
Open mid-March to mid-November
Credit cards: all major
Restaurant open daily
18 km SW of Siena on Rte 73

The walled hill-town of Spoleto is a must for any trip to Umbria. What Spoleto has that is so outstanding is its Bridge of Towers (*Ponte delle Torri*), an absolutely awesome feat of engineering. Built in the 13th Century on the foundations of an old Roman aqueduct, this bridge, spanning a vast crevasse, is supported by ten Gothic arches that soar into the sky. Built into the hillside, the Hotel Gattapone (a mustard yellow building with dark green shutters) provides a box seat location to admire this architectural masterpiece. As you enter, there is a cozy reception area. To the left, is a bright, sunny lounge with modern black leather sofas, a long black leather bar, very pretty deep blue walls, large pots of green plants, an antique grandfather clock, and, best of all, an entire wall of glass that offers a bird's eye view of the bridge. To the right of the reception, steps sweep down to another bar and lounge where breakfast is served. This room is even more starkly modern with deep red wall coverings. The newer wing of the hotel houses the superior category bedrooms, each with a sitting area and large, view windows. In the original section of the hotel, the bedrooms are smaller, but also very attractive and every one with a view. Tucked below the hotel is a sunny terrace. Although most of the hotels in this guide have more of an antique ambiance, the Gattapone is highly recommended—a special hotel offering great warmth of welcome and superb vistas.

HOTEL GATTAPONE
Owner: Hanke Giulio
Via del Ponte, 6
06049 Spoleto (PG), Italy
tel: (0743) 22 34 47, fax: (0473) 22 34 48
13 rooms: Double Lire 190,000-270,000
Open all year
Credit cards: all major
No restaurant, breakfast only
Located 130 km N of Rome, 48 km S Assisi

As you twist up the steep narrow road from Spoleto toward Monteluco, you will see on your left an appealing, ochre-colored villa just peaking out from a dense cloak of trees. The setting looks so fabulous that you will hope this is your hotel. It is, and you won't be disappointed. The Eremo delle Grazie is an astounding property—truly a living museum. History simply oozes from every nook and cranny. The property has been the home of the Lalli family for many years, but its roots date to the 5th Century to a small religious grotto (where pious men lived) that is now behind the bar. From its humble beginnings, the religious importance of this little cave grew. In the 15th and 16th Centuries one of Italy's important Cardinals called Eremo delle Grazie home. His bedroom is now one of the guest rooms. The cardinal knew how to live in comfort—his cave was not carved in the rocks, but painted onto his bedroom walls. One of my favorite places in Eremo delle Grazie is the tiny, incredibly beautiful, vaulted chapel with beautifully preserved, 15th-century paintings of the life of Mary. Another favorite is the splendid terrace with a sweeping view of the glorious Umbrian landscape. Just below the hotel, a swimming pool is tucked onto a terrace. According to Signor Lalli, Michelangelo was once a guest at Eremo delle Grazie. In his letter to Vasari, Michelangelo wrote that he left part of his heart at Eremo delle Grazie. You will too.

EREMO DELLE GRAZIE
Owner: Professor Pio Lalli
06049 Monteluco, Spoleto (PG), Italy
tel: (0743) 49 624, fax: (0743) 49 650:
11 rooms: Double Lire 350,000-450,000
Open all year
Credit cards: none accepted
Restaurant open daily during high season
3.5 km E of Spoleto, 124 km N of Rome

The road to the Pensione Stefaner winds up a tiny mountain valley in the heart of the Dolomites. The road is spectacular. As we rounded the last curve before St Zyprian (*San Cipriano*) the valley opened up and there spread before us was a sweeping vista of majestically soaring mountains. Across soft green meadows painted with wildflowers and dotted with tiny farm chalets, soared an incredible saw-toothed range of gigantic peaks. A tiny church with a pretty steeple added the final touch of perfection to the already idyllic scene. There are many places to stay in this region. None are glamorous resorts, but rather small family run pensions. One of our favorites is the Pensione Stefaner, an attractive, chalet-style hotel with flower-laden balconies. There is a smattering of antiques, but most of the furniture is new. The hotel is efficiently, and warmly managed by the young, attractive Villgrattner family. Signora Villgrattner is a genuinely gracious hostess and her husband (the chef) provides wonder home-cooked meals for the guests. The simple bedrooms are all impeccably tidy. Some have balconies with mountain views. *NOTE:* Tiers is called Tires on some maps. The town of St Zyprian (*San Cipriano*) rarely shows up on any maps, but it is just 3 km east of Tiers (*Tires*).

PENSIONE STEFANER
Owner: Villgrattner Family
39050 Tiers-St. Zyprian (BZ), Italy
tel: (0471) 64 21 75
fax c/o tourist office (0471) 64 21 75
15 rooms: Double Lire 130,000-140,000*
*Rate includes breakfast and dinner
Closed mid-November to mid-December
Credit cards: none accepted
Restaurant open daily, only for guests
NE Italy in Dolomites
17 km E of Bolzano, 3 km E of Tiers

Le Tre Vaselle is a very sophisticated inn located in the small wine town of Torgiano which is very near Assisi. The decor of the hotel is one of a lovely country manor. The owners are the Lungarotti family, famous for their production of superb wines: Signor Lungarotti owns all of the vineyards around Torgiano for as far as the eye can see. The hotel probably evolved to fill the need for a place for business associates and friends to stay when visiting the vineyards. The accommodations are extremely comfortable and have all the amenities of a large city hotel. The most amazing aspect of Le Tre Vaselle is that it has stunning conference rooms furnished in antiques with intimate adjacent dining rooms. The Lungarotti family has thought of everything: to keep the wives happy while their husbands are in meetings, the hotel schedules cooking classes in one of the most professional kitchens I have ever seen. The Lungarottis also have a private wine museum that would be a masterpiece anywhere in the world. Not only do they have an incredible and comprehensive collection of anything pertaining to wine throughout the ages, but the display is a work of art. The museum alone would be worth a detour to Le Tre Vaselle.

LE TRE VASELLE
Owner: Lungarotti Family
Manager Charles E. Merchie
Via Garibaldi, 48
06089 Torgiano (PG), Italy
tel: (075) 98 80 447, fax: (075) 98 80 214
61 rooms: Lire 280,000–390,000
Open all year
Credit cards: all major
Restaurant open daily
17 km SW of Assisi, 158 km N of Rome

The Baia Paraelios is an absolutely delightful hotel tucked onto the spur of land that juts from the toe of Italy near the ancient port of Tropea. The hotel is actually a resort that follows the contours of the hillside from the highway down to the beach. The reception office is located at the top of the hill and the mood is set from the moment you register. The small office is tastefully decorated with plants and charming old prints on the walls and the personnel in the office are gracious and warm in their welcome. The rooms are all bungalows that are artfully terraced down the hill to capture the best view possible from each. Midway down is a lovely pool. At beach level is a beautiful dining room and a comfortable, inviting lounge. The bungalows each have one or more bedrooms, a sitting room and a deck or patio. The decor is simple but in excellent taste with tiled floors and earth tones used throughout. One of the most beautiful white sand beaches I saw in Italy stretches invitingly in front of the complex. The Baia Paraelios makes a nice stop along your route south. Not only will you have the benefit of a lovely break in your travels, but also the nearby ancient town of Tropea, which hangs on the cliffs above a beautiful bay, is fun to explore.

BAIA PARAELIOS
Owner: Adolfo Salabe
88035 Parghelia, Tropea (CZ), Italy
tel: (0963) 60 03 00, fax: (0963) 60 00 74
70 bungalows: Double Lire 530,000*
*Rate includes all meals
Open May 10 to September 25
Restaurant open daily
Southern Italy–near tip of toe
420 km S of Naples, 5 km N of Tropea

The Stella d'Italia is located in San Mamete, a tiny, picturesque village nestled along the northern shore of Lake Lugano, just a few minutes' drive from the Swiss border. The hotel (which has been in the Ortelli family for three generations) makes an excellent choice for a moderately priced lakefront hotel. Mario Ortelli, an extremely cordial host, showed us throughout the hotel that has two adjoining wings, one quite old and the other a new addition. My choice for accommodation would be in the original part that has more old world ambiance—the rooms I saw here were very pleasant with large French windows opening onto miniature balconies capturing views of the lake. The lounges and dining room have a few antique accents, but basically have a modern ambiance. The nicest feature of the hotel is the superb little lakefront garden—in summer this is where all the guests live. Green lawn, fragrant flowers, lacy trees, and a romantic vine-covered trellised dining area make this an ideal spot for whiling away the hours. Steps lead down to a small pier from which guests can swim. The ferry dock for picking up and dropping off passengers is adjacent to the hotel. Another interesting feature for golf enthusiasts is that there are several golf courses within an easy drive from the hotel—one of these (near the town of Grandola) is one of the oldest in Italy.

STELLA D'ITALIA
Owner: Mario Ortelli
San Mamete
Lake Lugano 22010 Valsolda (CO), Italy
tel: (0344) 68 139, fax: (0344) 68 729
36 rooms: Double Lire 130,000–150,000
Open April to September
Credit cards: all major
Restaurant open daily
Lakefront hotel
8 km E of Lugano, 100 km N of Milan

The Pensione Accademia is enchanting—a fairytale villa with delightful gardens, and a romantic canal-side location. The hotel has a fabulous setting on an oasis of land almost looped by canals. In front is a beautiful, completely enclosed, secret garden whose walls are so heavily draped with vines that it is not until you discover black iron gates that you see steps leading down to the villa's own gondola landing. As you leave the garden and enter the wisteria-covered palazzo, you come into a spacious old-fashioned parlor with reception desk on the left. A staircase leads upstairs where some of the guest rooms are located in the original villa and others, connected by a hallway, in a portion of the hotel borrowed from an adjacent building. No two of the guest rooms are alike. None are decorator perfect—they are like guest rooms in a private home. There is an on-going program of renovations. Some of the guest rooms in the front have canal views, but are noisier than those looking over the garden. The only hitch to this picture of perfection is that your chances are slim of snaring a room in this romantic hideaway—the hotel is so special that loyal guests reserve their own favorite room for the following year as they leave. Spring and fall are most heavily booked—your chances are better in July and August and the prices are even a little lower.

PENSIONE ACCADEMIA
Owner: Giovnna Salmaso
Dorsoduro 1058
3123 Venice, Italy
tel: (041) 52 37 84 6, fax: (041) 52 39 15 2
26 rooms: Double Lire 160,000–210,000
Double without private bath Lire 110,000–130,000,
Open all year
Credit cards: all major
No restaurant, breakfast only
Near the Accademia boat stop

The Agli Alboretti Hotel is conveniently located just steps from the Accademia boat landing. Although only a two star hotel, it has more charm than many others charging much higher prices. But it is not price alone that makes the hotel appealing: there is a cozy ambiance from the moment you step into the intimate lobby, paneled with dark mellowed wood and decorated with some attractive prints on the walls and a perky ship model in the window. At the front desk will be either Dina Linguerri or her daughter Anna. I did not meet Anna, but her mother is most gracious and speaks excellent English. Beyond the reception area is a small lounge and then one of the very nicest features of the hotel—a tranquil garden sheltered by an overhanging trellis which in summer is completely covered by vines—a welcome, cool oasis after a day of sightseeing. White wrought iron tables and chairs are set for morning breakfast, afternoon tea, or summer evening dinner. The guest rooms vary in size, but all have a private bath or shower. Be sure to request a guest room with a bathtub because the showers are the type without a separate enclosure. Whichever room you have, however, it should be quiet since the hotel is tucked onto a peaceful square. The restaurant serves dinner every night except Wednesday.

AGLI ALBORETTI HOTEL
Owners: Dina and Anna Linguerri
Dorsoduro 882-884
30123 Venice, Italy
tel: (041) 52 30 05 8, fax: (041) 52 10 15 8
20 rooms: Double Lire 160,000–180,000
Open all year
Credit cards: all major
Restaurant closed Wednesdays
Near the Accademia boat stop

The Hotel Flora is reached down a tiny lane, just off one of the main walkways to St Mark's Square: a secluded hideaway, protected from the bustle of the city yet conveniently close to all the action. At the end of the tiny alley the doors open into a small lobby, beyond which is an enchanting small garden, an oasis of serenity with white wrought iron tables and chairs surrounding a gently tinkling fountain. Potted plants, small trees and lacy vines complete the idyllic scene. The hotel encloses the garden on three sides: doors open to the right to a dear little bar and the breakfast room. The lounges are Victorian in mood with dark furniture. The bedrooms vary greatly in their size and decor, but all have antique furnishings. Victorian-style wallpaper covers many of the walls. The ambiance has a definite old world atmosphere. There is no restaurant at the hotel, which is absolutely no problem since Venice abounds with wonderful places to dine. Breakfast, of course, is served to guests. Signor Romanelli, who owns this small hotel, personally sees that his guests are well taken care of. The Hotel Flora is a favorite of many travelers to Venice. Although it is a relatively simple hotel and would not appeal to those looking for deluxe accommodations, the Hotel Flora is a rare find for those who want a relatively inexpensive place to stay in the heart of Venice that combines a superb location, warmth of welcome and charm.

HOTEL FLORA
Owner: Roger Romanelli
Calle larga 22 Marzo, 2283/a
30124 Venice, Italy
tel: (041) 52 05 844, fax: (041) 52 28 217
44 rooms: Double Lire 255,000
Open all year
Credit cards: all major
No restaurant, breakfast only
3-minute walk from St Mark's Square

If you love opulent elegance, and if cost is of no consequence to you, the Gritti Palace is an excellent choice for your hotel in Venice. The location is marvelous—just a short walk from St Mark's Square yet far enough removed to miss the city's noise and summer mob of tourists. With careful planning, you can be entirely insulated in a private and very special world from the moment you arrive until you reluctantly depart. If you take a private motor launch from the airport or the Piazza Roma, you can descend stylishly at the deluxe little private pier in front of the hotel where porters will be waiting to whisk you to your room to be pampered and spoiled. All at a price, of course. The Gritti Palace is expensive, very expensive. But then what would you expect when staying in the 15th-century palace of the immensely wealthy Venetian Doge, Andrea Gritti. The Gritti Palace has a charming terrace on the bank of the Grand Canal where you dine in splendor and watch the constant stream of boat traffic. The lobby and lounge areas open off the terrace and are grandly decorated with antiques. The bedrooms are large and very fancy in decor, and those that face the canal are presented with a 24-hour show.

HOTEL GRITTI PALACE
Manager: Paolo Danieli
Campo Santa Maria del Giglio, 2467
30124 Venice Italy
tel: (041) 79 46 11, fax: (041) 52 00 942
99 rooms: Double Lire 669,000–732,000
Open all year
Credit cards: all major
Restaurant open daily
Near St Mark's Square
U.S.A. Rep: CIGA Hotels 800-221-2340

The Hotel La Fenice et Des Artistes, although not inexpensive, costs less than many other hotels that do not offer nearly its charm. The lobby is small, but seems spacious since there are two small garden patios that open from it. Here guests sit in the late afternoon for a cup of tea or an aperitif before dinner. Doors to the right lead to a club-like lounge and an intimate bar. The reception area is a triangle that connects the original building on the right with a newer wing on the left. Both sections are nice, and both are completely air-conditioned—a welcome relief on a hot day. The bedrooms are not large, but adequate, and color coordinated with a different wallpaper in each room setting the theme. Within a few blocks there is a fabulous choice of appealing places to dine. *Taverna La Fenice*, one of the oldest and most elegant restaurants in Venice, is incorporated into the old Wing of the hotel. The fascinating La Fenice Theater, one of the oldest and most beautiful theaters in Europe, is just around the corner—most conveniently located for music lovers.

HOTEL LA FENICE ET DES ARTISTES
Manager: Dante Appollonio
Campiello de la Fenice, S. Marco 1936
30124 Venice, Italy
tel: (041) 52 32 333, fax: (041) 52 03 721
75 rooms: Double Lire 200,000-280,000
Open all year
Credit cards: EC, MC, VS
Restaurant open daily
Near La Fenice Theatre

A fellow travel writer first recommended the Locanda Sturion to us as an intimate hotel where, with only 11 rooms, each guest is known by name and given personal attention. We quite agree that for a reasonably priced hotel, just a 3-minute walk from the Rialto Bridge, the Locanda Sturion has a definite appeal. If you have a problem climbing stairs, be aware that the hotel is not at street level. You ring a bell and the receptionist unlocks the front door that leads to a very long flight of white marble steps. At the top is another door and then a small reception area. Just beyond is one of the nicest features of this small hotel, an intimate parlor-like breakfast room with red brocaded walls, cozy tables with pretty carved chairs, a Venetian glass chandelier, and on the end wall, a series of three large windows overlooking the Grand Canal. What a wonderful place to eat breakfast and start your day! The guest rooms are all similar in decor with an old fashioned look. I don't think they are original antiques, but good copies of antique wooden headboards are used throughout. One of the most attractive rooms is number 1—a spacious room with windows overlooking the Grand Canal. Although not on the canal, room 8 is also very large and attractive. If you choose the Locanda Sturion, you will not be the first to enjoy its ambiance. The hotel dates back to the 13th Century when it was built as an inn by the Doge of Venice to house itinerant merchants.

LOCANDA STURION
Manager: Sergio Fragiacomo
San Palo, 673, Calle del Sturion
30125 Venice, Italy
tel: (041) 52 36 243, fax: (041) 52 28 378
11 rooms, Double Lire 180,000-240,000
Open all year
Credit cards: AX, VS
No restaurant, breakfast only
3-minute walk to the Rialto Bridge

At first glance the exterior of the Pensione Seguso appears quite bland: a rather boxy affair without much of the elaborate architectural enhancements so frequently evident in Venice. However, the inside of the pensione radiates warmth and charm with Oriental rugs setting off antique furniture and heirloom silver service. The hotel is located on the left bank of Venice—across the Grand Canal from the heart of the tourist area, about a 15-minute walk to St Mark's Square (or only a few minutes by ferry from the Accademia boat stop). For several generations the hotel has been in the Seguso family who provide a homelike ambiance for the guest who does not demand luxury. In front there is a miniature terrace harboring a few tables set under umbrellas. Several of the bedrooms have views of the canal (although these rooms are the noisiest due to the canal traffic). Remember this is a simple pension, most of the rooms share a bathroom: if you are looking for the amenities offered by a hotel, the Pensione Seguso would not be for you. But, the most pleasant surprise is that the value-conscious tourist can stay at the Pensione Seguso with breakfast and dinner included for what the price of a room alone would cost for most hotels in Venice. The Seguso has an elevator—handy if you have a problem with stairs.

PENSIONE SEGUSO
Owner: Seguso Family
Grand Canal Zattere, 779
30123 Venice, Italy
tel: (041) 52 86 858, fax: (041) 5222340
36 rooms: Double Lire 200,000-250,000*
* includes breakfast and dinner
Open all year
Credit cards: all major
Restaurant open daily, only for guests
10-minute walk from the Accademia boat stop

The Hotel Cipriani was founded by the late Giuseppe Cipriani, who during his lifetime became almost a legend in Venice. This beloved man, who founded the internationally famous Harry's Bar in Venice, had a dream of building a fabulous hotel within easy reach of St Mark's Square and yet far enough away to guarantee seclusion and peace. He bought three acres on the island of Giudecca and with the financial assistance of some of his prestigious friends, such as Princess Briget of Prussia and the Earl of Iveagh (head of the Guinness brewing company in Dublin), he accomplished his dream—an elegant Venetian palace-style hotel. The Cipriani is the perfect hotel for those of you who must have a pool, for it is the only hotel with a pool in Venice. And what a pool—it is Olympic size and surrounded by beautiful gardens. The splendor continues inside where the lounges are tastefully decorated in whites and beiges and the bedrooms are large and elegant. Since our last visit, 7 super deluxe apartments, some overlooking St Mark's Square, have opened in the renovated Palazzo Vendramin, adjacent to the hotel. We have not yet been able to inspect this new addition, but from the pictures, it looks beautiful. You truly have the best of all worlds at the Cipriani—you are at a superior resort yet only minutes from the heart of Venice in the private launch that waits to whisk you, any time of the day or night, to St Mark's Square.

HOTEL CIPRIANI
Manager: Dr. Natale Rusconi
Isola della Giudecca, 10
30123 Venice, Italy
tel: (041) 52 07 74 4, fax: (041) 52 03 93 0
105 rooms: Double Lire 792,000–1,090,000
Palazzo Vendramin: Lire 1,350,000–2,640,000
Open all year
Credit cards: all major
Restaurant open daily
On Giudecca Island

If the idea of being close to Venice and yet near a beach and casino appeals to you, then perhaps you should consider a hotel located on the Lido, a small island opposite St Mark's Square. A fifteen-minute boat ride and a short taxi trip brings you to the Albergo Quattro Fontane, a charming inn which reminds me more of a French country home than an Italian villa. It has a white stuccoed exterior with gabled roof, green shutters, and vines creeping both over the door and around some of the small balconies. To the left of the main building is a lovely courtyard whose privacy is established by another wing of the hotel giving the garden a cozy, walled in effect. Inside the hotel there is an ambiance of a country home with antiques cleverly used throughout the lounges. The beach is only a short distance away and the Albergo Quattro Fontane can make arrangements for you to reserve a private beach cabana when you arrive at the inn. The cost per day will vary, depending both upon the location and the comparative luxury of the cabana you choose. The beach is wide and the water inviting and clear, although the sand is not as fine and white as we have seen on some of the beaches in southern Italy. It is quite an experience to sample the interesting hierarchy of the Italian beach system.

ALBERGO QUATTRO FONTANE
Manager: Bente Bevilacqua
Via 4 Fontane
30126 Lido of Venice
Venice, Italy
tel: (041) 52 60 22 7, fax: (041) 52 60 72 6
68 rooms: Double Lire 280,000–320,000
Open end of April to October 20
Credit cards: all major
Restaurant open daily
On the Lido, across from Venice

The tiny island of Torcello is located about fifty minutes from Venice by boat. This lovely, sleepy little island is usually considered a short stop for the tour boats as they ply their way among the maze of little islands surrounding Venice. But, for those who want to linger on Torcello, where they can be close to Venice yet feel out in the country, there is a deluxe inn that is owned by the Cipriani family. This small inn, the Locanda Cipriani, is well known to knowledgeable gourmets as a fantastic restaurant. Many arrive every day from Venice just to dine, and depart never knowing that upstairs this restaurant also has guest rooms. The inn is very simple, much more like a small farmhouse than a deluxe hotel. Inside there is a rustic, cozy dining room and outside a beautiful dining terrace surrounded by gardens brilliant in summer with all varieties of flowers. There are only a few bedrooms—all are suites. Breakfast and dinner are included in the room rate. This is an expensive inn, but an elegant hideaway for relaxing and dining royally in a beautiful country setting. Many famous guests have already discovered this oasis—including Hemingway, who came here to write. I think you will share his belief that the Locanda Cipriani Torcello is a very special place.

LOCANDA CIPRIANI TORCELLO
Owner: Carla Cipriani
Manager: Bonifacio Brass
30012 Isola Torcello
Venice, Italy
tel: (041) 73 01 50, fax: (041) 73 54 33
5 suites: Lire 520,000
Rate includes breakfast and dinner
Closed November 4 to March 15
Credit cards: all major
Restaurant closed Tuesdays
Island location
Reached by boat from Venice

The Hotel Gabbia d'Oro, superbly positioned in the heart of romantic Verona, is truly a gem. From the moment you step inside you are surrounded by an understated elegance. Although a very deluxe hotel, there is no feeling of stiff formality—your welcome is genuinely warm and friendly. Just off the spacious reception area, is a cozy lounge with massive beamed ceilings, ancient stone walls, fine antiques, and handsome old prints in gold frames. Beyond the lobby is an intimate bar with rich wood paneling set off to perfection by chairs upholstered in cheerful cherry red fabric. There is also a lovely, quiet, inner garden courtyard where on occasion intimate concerts are held. The guest rooms are individually decorated, reflecting exquisite taste: antiques abound and rich, color coordinating fabrics are used throughout. Nothing has been spared to make each room beautiful. The standard bedrooms are very pretty, but if you can afford to splurge, the junior suites are much more spacious. It is such a pleasure to see a new hotel emerge after renovation that reflects so beautifully the authentic rich heritage of the original building. The Hotel Gabbia d'Oro truly captures the romance of Verona. Although excellent restaurants abound in Verona, the hotel offers a buffet and pre-theater restaurant, exclusively for guests. Also, in summer, private, elegant dinners can be arranged with advance notice.

HOTEL GABBIA D'ORO
Manager: Camilla Balzarro
Corso Porta Borsari 4/A
37121 Verona, Italy
tel: (045) 80 03 060, fax: (045) 59 02 93
27 rooms, Double: Lire 280,000-455,000
Suites Lire 380,000-610,000
Open all year
Credit cards: all major
Restaurant open on request, only for guests
Located in the heart of Verona

The entrance to the Hotel Victoria is starkly modern—almost with a museum-like quality. The white walls, white ceiling, white floors, and an enormous skylight are softened by green plants. At first glance I was disappointed since I had heard so many glowing reports of the merits of this small hotel. However, the mood begins to change as you enter the reception area with its Oriental carpets. By the time you arrive in the lounge area, the feeling is definitely moving toward an antique ambiance. Here you find original heavy ancient wooden beams and one of the original stone walls exposed, leather chairs, and some lovely antique tables. The bedrooms are extremely modern and beautifully functional with good reading lights, comfortable chairs, and excellent bathrooms. The Victoria actually dates back centuries and the new hotel is built within the shell of an ancient building. The architect even incorporated some of the archaeologically interesting finds of the site into a museum in the basement level. When the hotel is not full and all of the tables are not needed, special "windows" open up on the floor of the bar and the museum below is lit so that you can study the artifacts as you enjoy an aperitif.

HOTEL VICTORIA
Manager: Andrea Tamburini
Via Adua, 8
37121 Verona, Italy
tel: (045) 59 05 66, fax: (045) 59 01 55
46 rooms: Double Lire 186,000-284,000
Open all year
Credit cards: all major
No Restaurant, breakfast only
In the heart of Verona
U.S.A. Rep. Harry Jarvinen 800-876-5278

The Hotel Turm belongs to the Romantik hotel chain. Just being a member of this exclusive club indicates the hotel is pretty special because to belong the inn must have the owner personally involved in the management and the interior must have an antique ambiance. The Hotel Turm is no exception. There is an especially attractive little dining room with vaulted whitewashed ceilings and chalet-style rustic wooden furniture. There are a few antiques in the hallways and lounges. The bedrooms are simple, but very pleasant, with light pine furniture and fluffy down comforters on the beds. There is a swimming pool on the terrace where one can swim or lounge while gazing out to the little town and the mountains beyond. There is even a small indoor pool. The Hotel Turm dates back to the 13th Century and Signor Pramstrahler takes great care to maintain touches of the old world charm by interspersing antique chests, cradles, chairs and ancient artifacts. *NOTE:* Völs is called Fié on some maps.

ROMANTIK HOTEL TURM
Owner: Pramstrahler Family
Fié Allo Schiliar
1-39050 Völs am Schlern
Sudtirol (BZ), Italy
tel: (0471) 72 50 14, fax: (0471) 72 54 74
24 rooms: Double Lire 230,000-258,000
Closed November 6 to December 20
Credit cards: EC, MC, VS
Restaurant closed Thursdays
16 km E of Bolzano, 7 km S of Siusi (Seis)
U.S.A. Rep: Euro-Connection 800-645-3876

HOTEL RESERVATION REQUEST LETTER IN ITALIAN

HOTEL NAME AND ADDRESS—clearly printed or typed

Vi prego di voler riservare:
I would like to request:

_____ Numero delle camere con bagno o doccia privata
Number of rooms with private bath or shower

_____ Numero delle camere senza bagno o doccia
Number of rooms without private bath or shower

_____ Data di arrivo _____ Data di Partenza
Date of arrival *Date of departure*

Vi prego inoltre de fornirmi le seguenti informazioni:
Please let me know as soon as possible the following:

		SI	NO
Potete riservare le camere richieste?		SI	NO
Can you reserve the space requested?		*Yes*	*No*
I pasti sono compresi nel prezzo?		SI	NO
Are meals included in your rate?		*Yes*	*No*
E necessario un deposito?		SI	NO
Do you need a deposit?		*Yes*	*No*

Prezzo giornaliero _____
Price per night

Quanto e necessario come deposito? _____
How much deposit do you need?

Ringraziando anticipatamente, porgo distinti saluti,
Thanking you in advance, I send my best regards,

YOUR NAME AND ADDRESS—clearly printed or typed

MAP SECTION

Regions of Italy

Valle d'Aosta

Trentino-Alto-Adige

Friuli-Venezia-Giulia

Milan

Piedmont

Lombardy

Veneto

Venice

Liguria

Genoa

Emila-Romagna

Florence

Marches

Tuscany

Umbria

CORSICA
(France)

Abruzzo

ROME

Lazio

Molise

Bari

Campania

Naples

Basilicata

Puglia

Sardinia

Cagliari

Calabria

Palermo

Sicily

266

KEY MAP

267

Map 1

BELLUNO

Follina

Vittorio Veneto

A23

UDINE

13

San Floriano

A23

SLOVENIA

VENETO

Asolo

Ponzano

A27

247

248

348

53

A4

Castel Franco

53

Cavasagra

13

TREVISO

A4

TRIESTE

VICENZA

47

Padua

Dolo

Mira

Torcello

VENICE

Lido

Rome

● *Places to Stay*

○ *Orientation/*
 Sightseeing

Map 2

AUSTRIA

AUSTRIA

● Rasun di Sopra

49

49

38 ● MERANO

Lana ●

A22

● Bressanone
(Brixen)

51

● Sexten
(Sesto)

BOLZANO
(Bolzen)

38

● Castelrotto
● Völs (Fiè)

● Corvara

48

● CORTINA

○

● Tiers
(Tires)

42

42

48

51

42

● Obereggen

○ 48

Cavalese

ALTO ADIGE

51

A22

BELLUNO ○

● Places to Stay
○ Orientation/
  Sightseeing

Rome ●

TRENTO ○
● Pergine

47

50

Feltre ○

269

Map 3

Austria

München

Brenner Pass

Map 4

Valsoda - San Mamete

LUGANO

VERBANIA

STRESA

Isola dei Pescatori

Orta San Giulio

Lake Maggiore

Lake Lugano

Argegno

Bellagio

Lake Como

LECCO

Cernobbio

COMO

BERGAMO

A9

A8

Vizzola Ticino

Malpensa Airport

A26

A4

Novara

MILAN

Linate Airport

LOMBARD

A7

A1

Rome

Maleo

Cremona

PIACENZA

A21

• Places to Stay

○ Orientation/ Sightseeing

271

Map 5

Martigny

SWITZERLAND

Chamonix

Champoluc

Courmayeur

A4

AOSTA

● *Places to Stay*

○ *Orientation/*
  Sightseeing

Rome

A26

TO MILAN

FRANCE

A5

A4

Vercelli ○

A26

25

Casale ○

TURIN
(Torino)

590

457

Sauze d'Oulx

Moncalvo ○

457

● *Cioccaro di*
  Penango

A21

ASTI

A21

ALESSANDRIA

Map 6

PIEDMONT

590

Casale

Montcalvo

457

ASTI

A26

A21

Cioccaro di
Penango

A21

ALESSANDRIA

to MILAN

A7

A21

PIACENZA

A1

Maleo

Cremona

A1

Soragna

PARMA

to BOLOGNA

A26

A7

A7

LIGURIA

A15

• Places to Stay
○ Orientation/
  Sightseeing

A10

GENOA

A12

Camogli

Portofino

Chiavari a Leivi

Sestri
Levante

A12

to FRANCE

Finale Ligure

Levanto

Cinque Terre

La Spezia

Porto Venere

Rome

273

Map 7

Map 8

Fiesole

FLORENCE

Candeli

Empoli

67

2

Nord San Casciano

Sud San Casciano

Bargino

Tavernelle

429

San Donato

Barberino
Val d'Elsa

Poggibonsi

2

SAN GIMIGNANO

Colle d'Val d'Elsa

San Leonino

68

Monteriggioni

Badesse-Nord

Badesse-Sud

Pievescola

541

Souvicille-
Pretale

SIENA

Rosia

73

Reggello

Incisa

Vaggio

T U S C A N Y

Greve
in Chianti

Panzano

222

Radda
in Chianti

Castellina

Valdarno

408

429

Gaiole
in Chianti

San
Sano

San Gusmé

408

Castelnuovo
Berardenga

73

Arezzo

A1

Monte
San Savino

A1

Val d'Chiana

73

Serre di Rapolano

Sinalunga

222

A1

- ● *Places to Stay*
- ○ *Orientation/*
  Sightseeing
- ◎ *Exit from*
  Expressway

Rome

275

Map 9

Places to Stay

Orientation/ Sightseeing

Exit from Expressway

Map 10

ANCONA

ADRIATIC SEA

Porto S. Giorgio

SIENA

Sovicille
Pretale

Sinalunga

Montefellonico

GROSSETO

Cetona

Scansano

Orvieto

Bashi

ORBETELLO

Porto
Ercole

74

313

3

PERUGIA

Pianello

San Gregorio

ASSISI

Montefalco

Trevi

Spoleto

Monteluco

Terni

Rieti

Poggio Mirteto

Rome

CIVITAVECCHIA

LADISPOLI

La Posta Vecchia

Rome Airport

FIUMICINO

Ostia

ROME

A24

A25

E1/A2

148

MEDITARRANEAN SEA

Anzio

● Places to Stay
○ Orientation/
   Sightseeing

Map 11

Map 12

Isole Tremiti

GARGANO

Barletta

BARI

Monopoli

E58

Alberobello

Potenza

Matera

407

A3

Acquafredda

Maratea

TARANTO

BRINDISI

LECCE

CROTONE

Parghelia

A3

TROPEA

A3

Sicily

REGGIO

Rome

● Places to Stay

○ Orientation/
Sightseeing

Map 13

Sicily

Stromboli

Filicudi
Salina
Lipari
Alicudi
Vulcano

MESSINA

MILAZZO

Valderice
Erice
TRAPANI

PALERMO

CEFALÙ

A20

Villa San
Giovanni

Egadi Isles

A19

113

A3/E1

MARSALA

A29

A19

Gangi
Gangivecchio

TAORMINA

A18

189

640

A19

ENNA

"Toe"
of Italy

Rome

AGRIGENTO

417

CATANIA

114

SYRACUSE

115

115

● *Places to Stay*
○ *Orientation/*
Sightseeing

Map 14

Sardinia

PORTO CERVO

OLBIA

SASSARI

597

ALGHERO

131

131

NUORO

537

ORISTANO

SARDINIA

131

Rome

● Places to Stay
○ Orientation/
   Sightseeing

CARBONIA

CAGLIAR

INDEX

M

Karen Brown's Country Inn Guides
The Most Reliable & Informative Series on Country Inns

Detailed itineraries guide you through the countryside. Every recommendation, from the most deluxe hotel to a simple B&B, is personally inspected, approved and chosen for its romantic ambiance and warmth of welcome. Our charming accommodations reflect every price range, from budget hideaways to the most luxurious palaces.

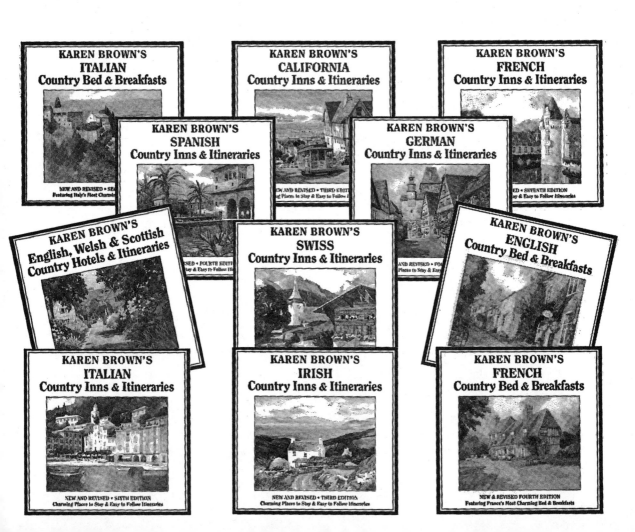

U.S.A. Order Form

Please ask in your local bookstore for KAREN BROWN'S GUIDES. If the books you want are unavailable, you may order directly from the publisher.

California Country Inns & Itineraries $14.95

English Country Bed & Breakfasts $15.95

English, Welsh & Scottish Country Hotels & Itineraries $14.95

French Country Bed & Breakfasts $15.95

French Country Inns & Itineraries $14.95

German Country Inns & Itineraries $14.95

Irish Country Inns & Itineraries $16.95

Italian Country Bed & Breakfasts $14.95

Italian Country Inns & Itineraries $16.95

Portuguese Country Inns & Pousadas (1990 edition) $6.00

Spanish Country Inns & Paradors $14.95

Swiss Country Inns & Itineraries $16.95

Name _____ Street _____

City _____ State ____ Zip _____ tel. _____

Credit Card (MasterCard or Visa) _____ Exp: _____

Add $4.00 for the first book and 50 cents for each additional book for postage & packing. California residents add 8.25% sales tax. Order form only for shipments within the U.S.A. Indicate number of copies of each title; send form with check or credit card information to:

KAREN BROWN'S GUIDES
Post Office Box 70, San Mateo, California, 94401, U.S.A.
Tel: (415) 342-9117   Fax: (415) 342-9153

We Love to Hear from Karen Brown's Readers

ACCOLADES: We'd love to hear which accommodations you have especially enjoyed—even the shortest of notes is greatly appreciated. It is reassuring to know that places we recommend meet with your approval.

COMPLAINTS: Please let us know when a place we recommend fails to live up to the standards you have come to expect from Karen Brown. Constructive criticism is greatly appreciated. We sometimes make a mistake, places change, or go downhill. Your letters influence us to re-evaluate a listing.

RECOMMENDATIONS: If you have a favorite hideaway that you would like to recommend, please write to us. Give us a feel for the place, if possible send us a brochure and photographs (which we regret we cannot return). Convince us that on our next research trip, your discovery deserves a visit. All accommodations included in our guides are ones we have seen and enjoyed. Many of our finest selections are those that readers have discovered—wonderful places we would never have found on our own.

Please send information to:

KAREN BROWN'S GUIDES
Post Office Box 70
San Mateo, California 94401, U.S.A.
Telephone (415) 342-9117   Fax (415) 342-9153

Be a Karen Brown's Preferred Reader

If you would like to be the first to know when new editions of Karen Brown's Guides go to press, and also to be included in any special promotions, simply send us your name and address. We encourage you to buy new editions and throw away the old ones. You'll be glad you did. Don't miss a wealth of wonderful new discoveries—or run the risk of staying in places that no longer meet our standards. We cover the miles searching for special places so that you don't have to spend your valuable vacation time doing so.

Name _____

Street _____

Town _____ State _____ Zip _____

Telephone: _____ Fax: _____

Please send information to:

KAREN BROWN'S GUIDES
Post Office Box 70
San Mateo, California 94401, U.S.A.
telephone (415) 342-9117   fax (415) 342-9153

HIDDEN TREASURES OF ITALY
Reservation Request Form

Name(s) of traveler(s):_____

Total number in party: _____ Number of children: _____ Ages: _____

Address: _____

_____

Tel: _____

Fax: _____

Hotel name and location: _____

Second choice: _____

Type of accommodation: single _____ double _____ triple _____ apt._____

Dates desired: (Arrival) _____ (Departure) _____

Number of nights: _____

Meal plan: B&B _____ half board _____ full board _____ does not apply _____

Special Requests:

Hidden Treasures of Italy, 934 Elmwood Avenue, Wilmette IL 60091, U.S.A.
Tel: (708) 853-1312, Fax: (708) 853-1340

HIDDEN TREASURES OF ITALY

Hotel/Bed & Breakfast Booking Service

You may conveniently reserve any of the hotels in this guide through Hidden Treasures of Italy's booking service. Car rentals and special interest tours (cooking classes, garden tours, or horseback riding excursions) for small groups can also be arranged. Simply fill out the reservation-request form opposite this page and fax or mail it along with a $35 booking fee per hotel to:

HIDDEN TREASURES OF ITALY
934 Elmwood Avenue
Wilmette, IL 60091
Tel: (708) 853-1312, Fax: (708) 853-1340
From Europe
Tel: (Italy) (06) 4424.3882, Fax: (Italy) (06) 855.7753

There will be no booking charge made for multiple requests (i.e., more than 3 hotel reservations or more than 3 nights in the same hotel). Upon confirmation of your request(s), exact rates with current exchange rate will be quoted and full prepayment or one-night deposit by check or VISA credit card will be required within 15 days from the date of notification. After receipt of payment, a written voucher will be issued to you to present to the hotel upon arrival.

CANCELLATION AND CHANGE POLICY

We will do our best to accommodate changes in dates or hotel choice, however this can never be guaranteed. Each additional request will require a supplementary $35 booking fee. Full refund of prepayment (excluding the booking fee) will be given up to 30 days prior to arrival date. No refund will be made within 30 days of your arrival. Booking fee is refundable ONLY in the case where neither first nor second choices are available.

Cancellation insurance is strongly recommended

Karen Brown's
Italian Country Bed & Breakfasts
Bed & Breakfast Travel in Italy

The Latest and Delightfully Inexpensive Way to Experience
True Italian Hospitality and the Beautiful Italian Countryside

Italian Country Bed & Breakfasts is the exciting new companion guide to *Karen Brown's Italian Country Inns & Itineraries*. Bed & Breakfast travel is a recent trend in Italy, and this is the first book ever written describing places to stay. The author personally visited hundreds of Bed & Breakfasts throughout Italy, selecting only the very best. All the pertinent information you need to plan your trip is given—in depth description of the B&B, sketch, prices, precise driving directions, level of English spoken, meals offered, owner's name, telephone and fax numbers, dates open, region, and types of rooms available.

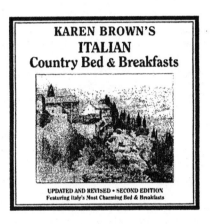

KAREN BROWN'S
ITALIAN
Country Bed & Breakfasts

UPDATED AND REVISED • SECOND EDITION
Featuring Italy's Most Charming Bed & Breakfasts

Karen Brown's *Italian Country Bed & Breakfast* does not replace *Italian Country Inns & Itineraries*—together they make the perfect pair for the traveler wanting to explore the countryside of Italy. Both books describe places to stay with charm, warmth of welcome and romantic ambiance. The difference is *Italian Country Inns & Itineraries* features lovely small hotels and inns, whereas *Italian Country Bed & Breakfasts* features accommodations in private homes. The selections (located throughout Italy) offer an appealing choice of accommodations from rustic Tuscan farmhouses and enchanting stone cottages to country villas. Traveling the *bed & breakfast way* provides a unique opportunity to meet Italians in their homes and be welcomed like a friend of the family.

KAREN BROWN published *French Country Inns & Chateaux* in 1979. This original book is now in its 7th edition and ten more titles books have been added to the series. The Karen Brown guides have become known as the most personalized, reliable reference library for the discriminating traveler. Although Karen's staff has expanded, she is still personally involved in the publication of her guide books. Karen, her husband, Rick, their daughter, Alexandra, and their son, Richard, live on the coast south of San Francisco at their own country inn, Seal Cove Inn, in Moss Beach, California.

CLARE BROWN has many years of experience in the field of travel where she earned the designation of Certified Travel Consultant. Since 1969 she has specialized in planning itineraries to Europe for her clients, recommending charming small hotels in the countryside. Clare now spends full time in travel research and writing. The focus of her job remains unchanged, but her expertise is now available to a larger audience—the readers of her daughter Karen's Country Inn guides. Clare lives in the San Francisco Bay area with her husband, Bill.

BARBARA TAPP, the talented artist responsible for all of the hotel sketches and delightful illustrations in this guide, was raised in Australia where she studied in Sydney at the School of Interior Design. Although Barbara continues with freelance projects, she devotes much of her time to illustrating Karen's Country Inn guides. Barbara lives in the San Francisco Bay area with her husband, Richard, their sons, Jonothan and Alexander, and young daughter, Georgia.

JANN POLLARD, the talented artist responsible for the beautiful painting on the cover of this guide (and the others in the Karen Brown series), has studied art since childhood. She is well-known for her outstanding impressionistic-style water colors which she has exhibited in numerous juried shows, winning many awards. Jann travels frequently to Europe (using Karen Brown's guides) where she loves to paint old world architecture. Jann lives in the San Francisco Bay area with her husband, Gene, and their two daughters.

SEAL COVE INN—LOCATED IN THE SAN FRANCISCO AREA

Karen Brown Herbert (best known as author of the Karen Brown's Guides) and her husband, Rick, have put seventeen years of experience into reality and opened their own superb hideaway, Seal Cove Inn. Spectacularly set amongst wild flowers and bordered by towering cypress trees, Seal Cove Inn looks out to the ocean over acres of county park: an oasis where you can enjoy secluded beaches, explore tide-pools, watch frolicking seals, and follow the tree-lined path that traces the windswept ocean bluffs. Country antiques, original-watercolors, flower-laden cradles, rich fabrics, and the gentle ticking of grandfather clocks create the perfect ambiance for a foggy day in front of a crackling log fire. Each bedroom is its own haven with a cozy sitting area before a wood-burning fireplace and doors opening onto a private balcony or patio with views to the distant ocean. Moss Beach is a 35-minute drive south of San Francisco, 6 miles north of the picturesque town of Half Moon Bay, and a few minutes from Princeton harbor with its colorful fishing boats and restaurants. Seal Cove Inn makes a perfect base for whale-watching, salmon-fishing excursions, day trips to San Francisco, exploring the coast, or best of all, just a romantic interlude by the sea, time to relax and be pampered. Karen and Rick look forward to the pleasure of welcoming you to their hideaway by the sea.

Seal Cove Inn, 221 Cypress Avenue, Moss Beach, California, 94038, U.S.A.
telephone: (415) 728-7325   fax: (415) 728-4116